The Swedish Drug Control System

Tim Boekhout van Solinge

The Swedish Drug Control System

An in-depth review and analysis

UITGEVERIJ JAN METS
CEDRO
AMSTERDAM

This study was financed by the Dutch Ministry of Health, Welfare and Sport and was made possible with the help of the Swedish National Institute of Public Health

Contents

FOREWORD

National drug control systems are complicated constructions. They develop in culturally – and historically – specific ways over years of experience and within boundaries shaped by other public concerns, social policies, and legal systems. In our series of studies on France, Germany, the United States of America, Belgium, and Sweden, we have tried to understand drug control systems from within. It is easy enough to read and summarise laws and policy documents, but this approach yields only a formal and superficial understanding of how drug control systems originate and operate. A much deeper understanding is possible when the many players within a drug control field are interviewed in person and in depth and when drug control is observed in action at the local level. This is the approach we have taken.

To understand a drug control system from within is to recognise that it is inextricably linked to a nation's policies and ways of making policy in other fields. Drug control is only in part about laws; it is more importantly about the application of laws. Further, health policy, social security, methods of managing deviance, and the judicial system are all more or less intimately connected to drug control. That is why a system of drug control can not be understood as autonomous from the institutional, socio-cultural, and political contexts that give it shape.

The study of drug control systems is also complicated by the fact that drug policies serve functions far beyond drug control. In France, for example, public discourse about drug issues and drug control laws themselves are symbols that help to continuously re-establish ideas about 'civility'.[1] And, as in France, the Swedish drug control system is related to how the Swedish State in general has been defined. The specific form of the Swedish drug control system also may have been shaped by the development of the European Union. Closer economic relationships with the rest of Europe have led some Swedes to fear that the cultural influence of Europe will also increase; and some see the 'urban' or 'cosmopolitan' cultures of Europe as incompatible with Swedish norms and morals. Such concerns sometimes make it appear that the strict Swedish drug control system is rooted more in myth and orthodoxy than in scientific evidence and reasoning. But if that system is considered in the light of the symbolic and other functions it serves, then we are in a better position to understand why Sweden has the drug policies it has and why many Swedes feel these policies are effective. In short, to begin to understand the Swedish drug control system from within, one has to take these and many other factors into account.

Yet we do not believe one can fully understand a drug control system only from within. A full analysis cannot accept at face value local or culturally-specific notions of, for example, the 'causes' of drug use. In this report, therefore, we also attempt a critical analysis – not to 'criticise' the Swedes, but to stand far enough outside their assumptions and world views to see the modes of reasoning that inform their drug policies. To do any less would teach us very little, for a true understanding of any one society's drug control system requires a comparative view of how drug policy 'happens' in other countries.

Peter D.A. Cohen, Ph.D.
CEDRO – Centre for Drug Research, University of Amsterdam

Introduction

The Swedish drug policy is one of the most debated drug policies in recent years, a development that has accelerated since Sweden became member of the European Union in 1995. Whereas formerly in the European Union a tendency towards more a liberal approach to the drug question could be observed, Sweden's joining of the EU meant there now was a member that advocated a restrictive line and stated too that they were successful with it. Since Sweden has been promoting its drug policy on the European scene, repeated references are made to the 'Swedish model'.

The Swedish drug policy is restrictive, which means that drug use is not tolerated. In 1977 the authorities formulated the drug-free society as society's objective. For the implementation of this goal, substantial sums of money have been allocated for prevention and information, control policy, and treatment; the three pillars of the Swedish model. The fact that other countries refer to the Swedish model, does no mean that this is done with any accuracy. References to the Swedish case in international drug policy discussions are rarely based on facts. Both prohibitionists and anti-prohibitionists often perpetrate inaccurate messages about the Swedish example, which obscures the issue. If you believe the prohibitionists, a drug addict in Sweden is taken from the street by the police, then directed to a social worker who decides what kind of treatment programme is most appropriate. Then, after a long and intensive period of treatment and rehabilitation the person is brought back into society and becomes a 'normal citizen' again. On the other hand, if you give credence to the stories sometimes told by anti-prohibitionists, cannabis smokers in Sweden are arrested by the police and put into compulsory treatment.

The more widely-accepted image that exists of the Swedish drug policy is that it is only by a rare example of a principled, non-pragmatic policy of not wanting to accept drugs by any means, that the drug problem is effectively reduced, without developing the negative consequences for drug users that are usually associated with restrictive zero-tolerance policies. On the contrary, Sweden would have encountered negative consequences of its drug policy in the period when it had a more liberal approach. An experiment of legal prescription of drugs from 1965-1967 would have proved to be a disaster. Learning from this experiment, the policy was drastically shifted towards a more restrictive approach that would have proved to be more effective. Hence, after having tried several models, the restrictive option would have turned out to be the best: a low prevalence of experimental drug use, and the number of drug addicts would be relatively limited and have a low incidence rate.

In this study it will be shown that the practice of the Swedish drug policy is much more complex than it is often perceived and presented. To begin with, the 'drug situation' in Sweden differs substantially from other European countries. For example, the most widely used illicit drug among Swedish drug addicts is not heroin, but amphetamine which in most cases is administered intravenously. Furthermore, few other countries go as far as Sweden in taking measures to reduce the extent of the drug problem. This has both a financial side, since this policy is very expensive, and an ethical side, in the sense that in the name of a drug-free society the authorities can intervene profoundly in a person's private life. As a matter of fact, the goal of the drug-free society seems to justify all kinds of means, which are difficult to imagine in many other countries.

The available indicators show that both prevalence of drug use and the number of drug addicts are relatively low in Sweden as compared to most European countries. But, as always, the underlying question is whether this has been the result of the drug policy that has been applied, or that other reasons are responsible for this situation. For example, it is often forgotten that Sweden has, for a long time, been a rich welfare State with not only the financial resources at its disposal to implement an extensive drug policy, but also the means to invest heavily in its people's well-being in general.

However, in the 1990s this picture has changed since Sweden was hit by an economic crisis which also had its effect on the drug policy. In recent years there have been substantial cuts in the drug policy budget, which has particularly hit the expensive treatment sector. The changes have been drastic and one could even wonder if the so-called Swedish drug policy model still exists today. These changes are occurring in a period when the use of drugs in Sweden is on the increase. Not only has experimental drug use among teenagers been rising recently, a more striking development is the increase in the use of brown (smoked) heroin.

The aim of this book is to give an outline of the Swedish drug policy and its background, thereby discussing what is true and what is not true about the Swedish drug control model.

1 Relevance and Methodology

1.1 Background and Relevance

This study of the Swedish drug policy is part of a series of studies on drug policies in Europe that are being carried out by the *Centre for Drug Research* (CEDRO) of the University of Amsterdam. The ultimate goal of this series is to obtain a deeper insight and better understanding of the different drug policies in Europe. Too often different drug policies are judged only on the basis of some figures, like prevalence figures, seizure data, and the number of arrests for drug law violations. A serious analysis should also take into account the wider societal context in which this policy has developed. Drug policies cannot be understood without considering closely related issues, such as the policy towards other licit drugs like alcohol, the general social policy, the public health and the criminal policy and their place within society, the way a society deals with deviant behaviour, and the symbolic or functional role drugs and the fight against drugs can have. The ultimate goal is to be able to make a more serious and thorough comparison of different drug control systems.

Another reason for this study is that the Netherlands and Sweden have decided to work together in the field of drug policy. Both the Netherlands and Sweden consider their drug policy as a relative success. Of course, it is not surprising that governments and government officials present their policy as successful, but the Swedish and Dutch cases are exceptional in the sense that there is, at least at first sight, a quite broad consensus that the applied policy has had positive results. The reason for this success is that both countries are reporting that they have a relatively low number of drug addicts which they attribute to the drug policy that has been undertaken. The Netherlands and Sweden have therefore decided to begin a collaboration to see what and how they can learn from each other's experience. This decision has certainly facilitated this study.

A collaboration between the Netherlands and Sweden in the field of drugs is interesting for several reasons. Both countries are rich Protestant welfare states that, in the international arena, have the reputation of being moralistic and conceited. Both think they are 'right' in the way they have organised their societies and think they are international forerunners, which means they can disseminate their views in an almost missionary-like fashion. With regard to the drug policy, both think they are on the right track and they see themselves as being 'ahead' of the other countries; and it is only a matter of time before other countries will adopt their policy. This probably explains why they are so determined to stick to their policy. In this position, a foreign perspective on one's drug policy can be refreshing. With respect to this study about Swedish drug policy this certainly is the case, since one cannot escape the impression that Swedes are seemingly too convinced of the rightness of their drug policy. For example, the State Secretary of Social Affairs, Anna Hedborg stated herself to be absolutely convinced a comparison between Sweden and the Netherlands on drug policies would turn out to be to Sweden's advantage. She also stated that in accordance with Swedish customs they would not even contemplate changing their drug policy.[1]

It is interesting to note that the two countries give two completely different reasons for their 'success', reasons that are actually contradicting. Sweden considers the basis of its success to be the restrictive drug policy it has been implementing, whilst on the other hand the Netherlands considers that its liberal policy regarding cannabis explains their positive results. Looking at the available statistics there is little doubt the two countries do indeed seem to have a relatively low number of drug addicts. Whatever the explanation may be, it is interesting to see that both countries, although having very different approaches to the drug question, attribute this success to the drug policy that has been applied.

Notwithstanding the differences, the drug policies of the Netherlands and Sweden also have their similarities. The first relevant aspect at which one should look is that both countries have a (real) drug policy; which cannot be said of all countries. The second similarity is that both invest heavily in prevention measures such as drug education. The third similarity the two countries have in common is that they both have quite extensive treatment facilities for drug addicts. Finally, there is a similarity that may not be overlooked in this respect, namely that both countries are rich welfare states. Not everyone will immediately see the relationship with the drug policy or the number of drug addicts, but this study will try to show the relevance of this point.

Notwithstanding the similarities that exist between the Swedish and Dutch drug policy, they are nothing compared to the differences. The principles of the two drug policies are actually almost completely opposite. In the Swedish drug policy model all drug use is unacceptable and considered deviant. The aim of policy is to isolate and remove this deviant behaviour. Moreover, the Swedish model considers that the more drugs become available, the more people will try drugs and the larger the number of problematic drug users or drug addicts there will be. As a result, the policy focuses on limiting the availability of drugs. The policy also tries to break the 'drug chain', of which the drug user is seen as the weakest link. Hence, in practice the policy focuses on making it difficult for drug users to take drugs. The Dutch drug policy model on the other hand, tries to make drug use less deviant. "It has been conceptualised within a 'normalising' model of social control, aiming at depolarisation and integration of deviance [...]".[2] The Dutch 'normalising model' also implies that one does not contest the availability of drugs too much, since it is considered that these attempts will tend to increase their damaging (social) effects as well as their psychological and economic attractions.[3]

Besides the more general differences in approach, the differences between Swedish and Dutch drug policies become most apparent when it comes to cannabis. In Sweden cannabis is regarded as a (very) dangerous drug and its use is regarded as the beginning of a career in drugs. Hence it is thought that the best way to prevent new recruits, is to limit the number of people experimenting with cannabis. As a result, in Swedish drug prevention, most attention is put on cannabis. In the Netherlands cannabis is regarded as an illicit drug with a relatively low, acceptable health risk, which is why the sale of cannabis is allowed in the so-called coffee-shops. It is argued that the wider availability of cannabis in non-deviant outlets leads to a separation of the markets for soft drugs (cannabis products) and hard drugs (other illicit drugs).

The differences in approach between the two countries is indicated in the terms used concerning illicit drugs. Since all drug use in Sweden is unacceptable, the general term used to designate any drug use is 'abuse' or 'misuse'. Unlike alcohol consumption, no distinction is made between use and abuse; the only 'permitted' expression to designate consumption is abuse. In the Netherlands on the other hand, one usually speaks of drug use.

It is beyond dispute that both use and abuse exist when it comes to the consumption of the substances concerned in this study. The problem is to define the exact dividing line between the two, which is influenced by the moral standards that are being attributed to the intake of (illicit) substances. To avoid any moral judgement and with the aim of giving a description in the most neutral way, the most common term in this study is 'drug use'.

1.2 Methodology

To write this study a lot of information has been collected. First of all, a lot of relevant literature was studied, like government reports, scientific books and articles, newspaper articles, and information material from government institutions, popular movements, treatment centres, etc. Fortunately, a lot of literature on Swedish drug policy was available in English. At the same time the references are limited in the sense that few Swedish texts have been studied. However, some articles and (parts of) texts that seemed very relevant were translated into Dutch or English.

Besides consulting written sources, a large number of people directly or indirectly concerned with this question were interviewed in Sweden. Since the purpose of this study was to get a general overview of the drug situation in Sweden and to obtain a thorough understanding of the applied policy, people were interviewed from every corner of the Swedish drug field. During two three-week' stays in Sweden (Gothenburg, Malmö, Stockholm, and their surroundings) meetings were held with several dozens of people, for example government officials at several ministries and government institutions, police officers (from both the 'street level' and high ranks), prosecutors, physicians, social workers, staff members of treatment centres, researchers, representatives of popular movements, etc. To get an impression of the Swedish 'drug scene' several places that were known as places where drugs are used and/or sold were extensively visited. Due to the marginal and deviant character that drug use has in Sweden, it was not possible to really observe drug use in an 'open setting' which would have enabled a comprehension of the Swedish drug use culture and its consumption patterns. Although several locations such as bars and clubs were visited which had a reputation as places where drugs were being used, it appeared that drugs are rarely openly used in Sweden. At these and other locations many drug users and some (former) drug dealers were interviewed to gain an idea of the Swedish drug market.

Since it is difficult to understand a drug policy without its broader context, many people have been interviewed with the purpose of achieving a better understanding of Swedish society. For example, in the Netherlands, several Dutch people who are familiar with Sweden and Swedes living in the Netherlands were consulted. In Sweden journalists, sociologists, and foreigners (non-Swedes) were interviewed to discuss various aspects of Swedish society and culture. In this respect the conversations with Finns were particularly interesting. Not only are Finns the largest immigrant group in Sweden with a long and extensive history of immigration to Sweden, the fact that they originate from another Nordic country made them very suitable to discuss Swedish matters with.

2 Understanding Sweden

2.1 Introduction

To understand a country's drug policy, it is important to grasp the wider context in which this policy has developed. The point is that non-Swedes generally know very little about Sweden, except for some very general ideas and stereotypes. Sweden probably has a reputation of being a modern, egalitarian country with high standards of living for most of its population. Another characteristic of Sweden in the eyes of many may be that it has for a long time acted as a pioneer for many other (Western) countries. Indeed, Sweden has, compared to most Western countries, been a pioneer in the fields of welfare policy, women's emancipation, child psychology, and more.

All these positive virtues of welfare could not have been possible without the economic success Sweden has enjoyed during the twentieth century. There are several reasons for this achievement, but what may be more important is that Swedish welfare does not have a long history, but is actually a relatively recent phenomenon. As will be described in the following section, Sweden's economic history has been very remarkable: the country developed from one of Europe's poorest countries in the nineteenth century to one of the richest a century later. In the course of the twentieth century Sweden also developed the often praised Swedish welfare system. This system offered the people a high degree of 'security', best described by the Swedish expression *trygghet*. The feeling of security is strengthened by Sweden's long history of neutrality in international conflicts, the last war they experienced being in 1814.

The rapid economic growth Sweden experienced during this century, has created a country with a dual identity. One the one hand Sweden is a modern and progressive country, not only regarding the virtues that have already been mentioned, but also with respect to the widespread use of modern technology, as indicated by the large number of people who have for example mobile phones, internet connections and other kinds of consumer electronics. On the other hand however, Sweden is still a traditional country, with a strong rural tradition and, in some respects, a corresponding attitude.

In the 1990s Swedish society has undergone profound changes. Most importantly, the country was hit by the most severe economic crisis since the 1930s which meant a fragmentation of the Swedish welfare State known as the 'Swedish Model'. After decades of an expanding welfare system, financial constraints forced the Swedish State to cut down on it. The economic crisis created an entirely new situation, as it meant that for the first time in their lives many people experienced unemployment. Generally speaking this new situation ended the *trygghet* (security) most Swedes had grown up with.[1]

This chapter does not intend to give a full description of Sweden's history, economy and political system, but aims to address some questions that are important for an understanding of the Swedish drug policy. A part of this description is largely based on one source, *Swedish Mentality* by Åke Daun, and may therefore be somewhat limited. Moreover, in this brief presentation of Sweden it is difficult not to slip back into stereotypes. It is inevitable that in a description like this, the 'typical' Swedes are being portrayed, without doing justice to the more diverse aspects of Sweden that (also) exist. However, the features that have been discussed in this chapter, even if they may have been overstated in the eyes of some, are all relevant in serving as the background against which the drug policy has to be placed.

2.2 Geography and the People

Sweden is one of Europe's largest countries, covering 450,000 km². The Nordic location of Sweden, similar to Alaska and Greenland, means that there is an important contrast between summer and winter. Given the long distance between the North and South (1,600 km) this difference largely depends on one's geographical position, but generally the days are long in summer and short in winter. In the northern part Sweden has summers in which the sun only sets for a very short time, whilst the winters on the other hand only have a few hours of sunlight. Needless to say, besides being dark, the winters are cold as well.

Compared to the country's size, the number of inhabitants is small, 8.8 million. Despite this relatively low number of residents, the population has increased considerably over the last century. Despite this growth Sweden still is one of the European Union countries with the lowest population density. About one third of the total population lives in the country's three urban areas, Stockholm with 1.6 million, Gothenburg with 760,000 and Malmö with 500,000 inhabitants. A significant part of the population is still living in the countryside, which means Sweden continues to be a predominantly rural country. More important than the actual size of the rural population, is the fact that most Swedes have their traditions and roots in the countryside. Even today, many Swedes living in urban areas, like to spend their weekends and holidays in a cottage in the country. Generally, Swedes show a lot of respect for the natural environment.

Combining the several elements that define Sweden, the latitude, the climate and the low population density, leads some people to believe that these conditions have shaped, or have at least influenced the Swedish mentality. A long history of cold, dark, and long-lasting winters, people living in isolation with one house situated a few kilometres from the next, would have created the typically closed personalities of the Swedes as they exist today. Indeed, as Daun has pointed out in his comprehensive *Swedish Mentality*, Swedes are rather solitary people and few feel inclined to talk in the company of strangers.[2] Daun also describes how Swedes see themselves: "the national stereotype is: a peaceful person who dislikes unruliness and disorder and who prefers calm, and who may be described as clean, quiet, industrious, and modern."[3]

Another aspect of Sweden is that the population is relatively homogeneous. The large majority of the population, almost 90%, is Lutheran. Although only a minority of 10% goes to church regularly, many of the church traditions are still present: most children are baptised, most make a confession of faith at the age of 15, and marriages and funerals usually take place in church.[4] Also from an ethnic-sociological perspective, Sweden can be labelled a homogenous society. Notwithstanding the fact that more than one million of the population (13%) is defined as immigrant – one of the reasons Swedes speak of a multicultural society – this figure gives a slightly misrepresentational picture of the situation as most immigrants in Sweden originate from other Nordic countries. Actually a very large proportion of the immigrant population is comprised of Finns. In reality this means that the multicultural society in Sweden is not the same as what many other Western societies would understand by 'multicultural'. Another reason for this difference is of course the fact that Sweden has not had important colonies outside Europe. For a rich European country, Sweden did not have many immigrants coming from cultures very different from its own. It is only since the 1960s that immigrants to Sweden started to include groups from further afield, like workers from the Mediterranean countries of Yugoslavia, Greece and Turkey, and political refugees from the Middle East (Lebanese, Syrians) and Latin America (especially Chileans). Compared to many other European countries however, these numbers are relatively small.

In the late 1980s and early 1990s Sweden no longer received immigrant workers. The only immigrants coming to Sweden since then are the family members of earlier immigrants and political refugees. The latter group has increased greatly over recent years, especially from former Yugoslavia, the Middle East (Iranians, Iraqis, Curds) and East Africa (Eritreans, Ethiopians and Somalis). The large size of these recently arrived groups, has meant that the composition of the immigrant population has changed considerably.

Besides the fact that the population is homogeneous, the social values in Sweden are also oriented towards conformity. In the capital Stockholm, with more than one million inhabitants, one does not observe many signs of a strongly evident counterculture, like eccentrics or people wearing alternative clothing. Conformity seems to be the norm, which could be confirmed by the fact that many Swedes consider their own views as normal.[5] Eccentricity is not positively regarded and all deviance from group norms and common group patterns is regarded as a potential threat to the individual.[6] Daun has summarised it as follows: the more alike the better. The somewhat conformist views of the Swedes and the emphasis they put on similarities instead of differences between people, also helps to understand the attitude towards deviant behaviour in general. Swedes do not easily accept deviant or 'strange' (unfamiliar) behaviour and habits like homosexuality, prostitution, and drug use.

Homosexuality has been officially accepted and integrated. Since 1979 it is no longer classified as an illness, and in 1995 the law was changed to allow same sex couples to register and have the same legal rights as heterosexual couples (except the right to adopt children). On the other hand one could say this acceptance and integration of homosexuality has also had its 'price'. For example, it is difficult to display homosexuality (too) overtly. Furthermore, homosexual behaviour has been 'restricted' with the passing of the Sauna Clubs Act in 1987 and the Contagious Disease Act in 1989.

Another aspect closely related to the attitude towards 'strange' behaviour and habits is the fact that Swedes are not really familiar with people from other cultures, as immigrants from outside Europe can acknowledge. In fact, many of them feel totally isolated from what seems an unfriendly, cold culture.[7] For most Swedes this is not a question of a racism, but just a question of unfamiliarity. The strong emphasis on group norms and group pressure for sameness, to which foreigners have difficulty in adjusting, also helps to understand why immigrants and foreign students have difficulties finding a job.[8] In recent years the attitude towards immigrants seems to have deteriorated. In smaller towns more young Swedes have joined extreme-right movements and incidents have occurred with local youths throwing molotov cocktails at refugee camps.

In discussing Swedish people and culture, it is relevant to stress that Sweden's geographical position, on the periphery of Europe, also may have had influence on the way in which international cultural developments penetrate the country. Needless to say, these international, cultural developments are strongly related to metropolitan cultures and lifestyles. Hence, one could expect that these phenomena do not develop to the same extent in Sweden as elsewhere. The 1960s, the decade of big social-cultural changes, did not seem to have the same impact in Sweden as in many other Western European countries.

2.3 *History and Economy*

The history of Sweden over the last century is remarkable. In the mid nineteenth century Sweden was one of the poorest countries in Europe. A very large part of the population, 70%, worked in agriculture, many of them under very difficult circumstances.[9] In the second half of the nineteenth century the Swedish economy underwent many profound changes. Industry developed, facilitated by new inventions and more advanced technology. International demand for goods such as timber, wood products, and steel arose, and the infrastructure improved. In other words, Sweden became part of the international economy.

In the beginning of the twentieth century Sweden became an industrial country. However, the big economic shifts that have occurred since the mid-nineteenth century, did not mean that the standards of living went up. In fact, the consequences of the agricultural and industrial revolutions were so severe that, around the turn of the century, Sweden still was a country with widespread poverty, which explains the emigration 'exodus' of people hoping to find a better future abroad. The destination was, in many cases, North America, the United States in particular. The total number of Swedes that emigrated between the mid-nineteenth century and the 1930s was 1.5 million, which was roughly a third of the total population, which totalled 3.5 million in 1850 and 6 million in the 1930s. As was stated earlier, the reasons for the mass emigration were mainly economic: "poverty was becoming rampant in underdeveloped Sweden which could not provide jobs for its burgeoning population".[10]

The general trend in the Swedish economy from the beginning of the twentieth century onwards was one of relative prosperity with a further expanding industry, although the economy has also known some short downturns. Generally however, Sweden did succeed in suffering less from the international economic recessions than most other countries did, as was the case in the years immediately following the First World War (a war in which Sweden was neutral), and during the recession of the 1930s which hit the Swedish economy relatively slightly.[11]

During the Second World War, Sweden was once more neutral, or as its position was officially called 'non-belligerent'. The attitude of Sweden in the period 1939-1945 can best be described as pragmatic. Being neutral, Sweden traded with both Allied and Nazi Germany. Because of the money Sweden earned on its exports during the war (e.g. iron to Germany), Sweden was a relatively rich country in the aftermath of the war. It would seem the war has helped to provide the basis for the impressive economic developments that occurred after 1945.[12] Whereas most European countries were occupied with post-war reconstruction during the late 1940s and 1950s, Sweden's economic structure was still intact, which enabled it to develop further, and the country's social and political climates were stable. This situation, very different from most other European countries, might explain why Sweden in the 1940s and 1950s was already confronted with what we nowadays would describe as modern Western civilisation problems, like people wanting to slim and taking medicines for this purpose, for example amphetamines.

The 1960s was Sweden's golden decade, the economy grew steadily and the labour shortage led to the immigrant workers coming from several countries, like from Mediterranean countries, but more especially from Finland. With regard to its immigrant labour force, Sweden is a somewhat exceptional case in this respect, as it was in the situation of having a relatively poor neighbouring country, Finland, from where it could recruit the required work-force. Many other European countries had to go outside Europe to find this work-force (e.g. in Turkey and North Africa).

During the seventies the Swedish economy experienced some difficulties, partly due to the international oil crisis. Moreover, Swedish industry experienced increasing international competition, from which some economic sectors like shipbuilding suffered severely. The growth figures of the Swedish economy slowed down, but this was never translated into negative growth. Hence, one could not speak of an economic crisis. During the 1980s the economy recovered and developed further until the early 1990s. Although the Swedish economy has had its ups and downs in the 1970s and 1980s, the general trend was steady economic growth. The history of the Swedish economy from the late nineteenth century to the 1990s shows a steady development from an agricultural society and one of Europe's poorest countries to one of Europe's richest and most industrialised countries. In the words of Hans-Ingvar Johnsson, "it was a dramatic change".[13]

In the same period the Swedish welfare state developed. The origin of the welfare state dates back to the 1930s when the Social Democratic government, in close collaboration with the trade unions, laid the foundation for what was soon to be called 'the Swedish model', a combination of advanced industrial capitalism directed towards export and a State controlled egalitarian social policy. After the Second World War the Swedish economy would develop further, and until the 1990s Sweden managed to keep its economy in enviably sound shape, offering a high general standard of living for the large majority of the population. This situation offered a high degree of security to most people. The Swedish welfare state took care of the people by offering jobs, housing, and a secure future. The long history of the Swedish welfare state helps to explain why most Swedes have always had a high degree of confidence in the society or 'the system'.

In the early 1990s this extraordinarily favourable economic picture came to an end; the Swedish wonder was over. Sweden was faced by the deepest and longest economic crisis since the 1930s: in a period of three years the GDP declined by 7.5 %.[14] Sweden encountered several economic difficulties, the national debt as a percentage of GDP climbed from 45% in 1991 to 80% in 1994, an exceptionally high figure among the OECD countries.[15] Unemployment rose from 1% in 1990 to 8.9% in 1993. This may be a not very surprising figure for a European country, but between 1970 and 1990 the unemployment rate in Sweden had always been very low (between 1.2% and 3.5%) and had never exceeded 4%. Notwithstanding expectations that the trend would be reversed, the situation actually turned out be chronic. The unemployment rate in the 1990s stayed around 8-9% and, if government-financed or subsidised training programmes are included, the unemployment rate was 12%-13%.

For a non-Swede it might be difficult to imagine, but all this has meant that in the 1990s many Swedes were, for the first time in their lives, confronted with a high unemployment rate, a phenomenon previously unknown and by which some were themselves touched. This also meant an end to the high degree of security the system had offered most people and that they had become accustomed to.

2.4 Social Democratic Tradition

Sweden has a history of feudalism and a poor working class struggling against poverty. In the (early) nineteenth century the feudal and hierarchical past ended and a foundation was laid for the more equal and egalitarian society that still exists today. One of the explanations for its endurance is probably Sweden's history of widespread poverty. The mass exodus around the turn of the century – between 1880 and 1910 one million people emigrated – is said to have alerted even the most conservative to see the need for improving social conditions, with the objective that the remaining population would stay. The new Sweden that took shape offered security to the people.

The Social Democratic Party, founded in 1889, has played a central role in this development. In 1932 the Social Democratic party came to power. Except for a three-month interregnum in 1936, the party would stay in government till 1976. By that time, the Social Democrats had been governing for 44 years, a period that has not been matched by any other social democratic party. The Social Democrats came to power again from 1982 to 1991 and since the 1994 elections they are governing again. This makes Sweden probably the democratic country with the longest history of social democratic rule. From the moment the Social Democratic Party came into office, they started developing a programme for the social welfare state, or as it was called, the 'people's home' (*folkhemmet*). The Swedish model that developed came to be symbolised by Social Democrat Per Albin Hansson who was Prime Minister from 1932 to 1946. The society, attributing an important role to the State, would protect all individuals and no-one would have to suffer anymore from any distress or poverty. If someone might 'fall out' for one reason or the other, society's 'safety net' would come to rescue.

In shaping the welfare state the Social Democrat Party did not stand alone. Since its inception the party had close ties with the trade unions and throughout the development of the Swedish model the trade unions have always played their part. It is often forgotten that the expression 'the Swedish model' was initially used to describe the labour market. Through the organised efforts of the unions, in close interaction with the employers and the social democrats, a situation developed in which labour disputes were kept to a minimum and employment was offered to most of the work-force, in some periods leading to a full employment situation. It is for this reason is it often said in Sweden that the trade unions changed the country. In the polls the Social Democrats have depended heavily on the support of trade unions: the blue-collar trade union federation LO representing over two million workers, which corresponds to 90% of the blue-collar work-force and 50% of the entire labour-force, and a part of the white-collar trade union federation TCO that represents 75% of the white-collar labour-force.[16]

The Swedish model, the welfare state that developed in the 1930s, consisted basically of the combination of economic growth (based on a Keynesian economic policy) and the distribution of the welfare among the people (by conducting a social welfare policy). Especially after the Second World War the welfare model matured, with a progressive tax system, a pension system, universal health insurance, an active labour market policy, and housing subsidies. This package was supplemented by lesser measures, which all together led to, in the words of Tilton, "the Swedish welfare state's distinctive character – provision of largely universal services of high quality affording *trygghet*, (a Swedish word more evocative and warm than its translation 'security')".[17]

The exceptionally long period that the Social Democratic Party has been in power in Sweden, means that a social democratic tradition has gradually arisen. Even the other major political parties like the Moderate Party and the Liberal Party never seem to have really disputed the basic elements of the Social Democratic model. The fact that social democratic virtues have become so deeply rooted in society has led some commentators to believe that all Swedish parties are somehow social democratic. In any case, there seems to be an underlying current in Swedish society whereby some of the traditional socialist ideas have become generalised which can easily create a situation where one gets the impression that 'almost everyone' in Sweden is a social democrat.

Social democracy in Sweden has connotations of pride and solidarity. The people are proud of what they have achieved; the country has developed from a poor to a rich country, where poverty no longer exists. Perhaps this is where one comes to the most important virtue of the Swedish

Social Democracy, the *trygghet*. Older people especially, who have experienced the gradual changes, are proud of the Swedish accomplishments. The pride of the achievements of the Swedish social democratic welfare state probably explains the traits that are sometimes attributed to Swedes; arrogant and moralistic. Swedes have a reputation of thinking they are right, or otherwise of knowing what is right. This attitude could also be the result of the international belief that Sweden is a social pioneer, which can lead to a situation in which one persuades oneself this is true. The achievements of the 'people's home' might also explain the Swedes' positive attitude to the 'State' and the 'system' and their, in the eyes of some foreigners, honesty, trustworthiness and, in a manner of speaking, naivety. Since most people have experienced the virtues of the State and thus the 'social engineering capacities' of 'the system', bringing well-being, welfare and security, their attitude towards the State can generally be described as (very) positive, and rarely suspicious or distrustful as is the case in many other countries. It should be noted though that in recent years the positive attitude towards the State and the politicians is declining.

On the 1st of January 1995 Sweden joined the European Union. This decision was taken after a long debate in the country, a debate that centred on a question that had been for so long central in Swedish foreign policy: the independent, non-aligned position of the country. The debate about joining the EU was taking place during a very difficult period for Sweden – the deep economic crisis which heralded an end to the 'protected' society in which most people grew up.

2.5 The Role of Popular Mass Movements

Sweden is a very organised country. This does not only apply to the organisation of the state, but to the way the people are organised as well. This section will deal with popular mass movements (*folkrörelse*), since they play a vital role in Swedish society, especially an incentive to bring changes about. This section does not intend to give a complete overview of popular mass movements in Sweden, but tries to present some of the essential elements of the role these organisations play. This section is meant as a basis to section 4.3 where the role some of these popular mass movements have played in the field of drugs will be discussed.

Many Swedes are members of a club or association, such as sport clubs, study circles and popular mass movements. Compared to international standards, a large proportion of Swedes belong to associations. Swedish associations have approximately 32 million members which means, considering the population is 8.8 million, that on the average every Swede is member of four associations. Less than one out of ten Swedes is not a member of any association.[18]

The background of study circles is socialistic and revolutionary; study circles were closely linked to the labour movement, as was already the case when the first study group was formed in the 1860s. The emergence of study groups has to be placed in the societal context of the 19th century: the existence of a poor working class. Learning or people's education (*folkbildning*) was seen as a means to change society. Today thousands of study groups still exist. Since the 1930s the socialistic aspect is not very evident, but many study groups are still connected to political parties. There still exists a notion among people that it is important to have knowledge and to get organised if you want something done in society. Obviously, the influence of the organised efforts of the trade unions throughout the economic success period has also played its part in this respect.

More important and influential than study groups are the popular mass movements (*folkrörelsen*). An 'official' definition of the term *folkrörelsen* does not exist, but the term is very commonly and widely used in Sweden, without needing to specify its exact meaning. The first attempts to interpret it were made in the 1940s by Thörnberg, who defined the movements as "organised efforts in relation to certain values".[19] An important aspect of these movements is that they are based upon a general idea or theme, the conviction something has to change, sometimes with a touch of rebelliousness, and the belief that is possible to satisfy these desires. Furthermore, Wijkström has pointed out that popular mass movements have a strong positive connotation. The term *folkrörelsen* implies goodwill, a positive link to the general public, and it could even be viewed as a term of honour with an almost ceremonial significance: "The word appears still today to have a tremendously positive ring. There is a smell of participation, active and engaged people, protest and democracy – people on the move towards a goal."[20] The way popular movements function and the importance they have in Swedish society, probably explains the notion of the 'collective' that is so strongly present in Sweden.

To be called a Popular Movement, an organisation must be nationally established, having several regional or local branches, which allows them to receive State subsidy. Some of the popular mass movements are politically active and they sometimes have formal links to a political party. Popular mass movements are deeply rooted in Swedish society. The Swedish non-profit sector of today cannot be understood without paying attention to the role the earlier popular mass movements have played in this respect. It is sometimes stated that the role these movements and their members play in Swedish society in the public debate, is of fundamental importance to its democracy and welfare.[21]

The history of popular mass movements goes back to the nineteenth century. Strong traditional popular mass movements are the labour movement, the free church movement, and the temperance movement. The free church movement consisted of the formation of new Protestant churches alongside the traditional and established Lutheran State church. This development has to be put into the perspective of the major social changes that were occurring in Sweden in the 19th century like agrarian reforms, the increased mobility of people and urbanisation, factors that led to a decline in the role of the rural parish churches.[22] The popular movements at the time were, in their context, progressive and reformist, and sometimes revolutionary. "In a historical sense, the traditional Swedish and Scandinavian popular mass movements were also part of an anti-authoritarian – although comparatively peaceful – struggle against oppressive state and capitalist structures during the formative years."[23]

The rise of the temperance movement has to be understood by the high alcohol consumption that occurred at the time. In 1820 alcohol consumption, especially Vodka-like strong liquors, was about five times higher than it is today. People were allowed to distil their own spirits (*brännvin*) until 1860, when Parliament took away this right under pressure from the temperance movement.[24]

In 1902 the temperance movements founded CAN, the Swedish Council for Information on Alcohol and other Drugs.[25] Originally CAN only dealt with alcohol. In the 1950s, when young people started experimenting with solvents such as glue, thinner and gasoline, CAN's sphere of activity was expanded to alcohol and solvents. Amphetamine use was seen as a medical problem at the time, for which reason drugs were outside the scope of the organisation. However, illicit drugs were added at a later stage to its remit. Today, CAN deals with alcohol, solvents and drugs, both pharmaceutical and illicit. Tobacco is not part of its field of activity.

CAN is a neutral organisation that aims to disseminate information. In 1906 the CAN library was founded which has today an extensive collection. CAN can be viewed as an umbrella organisation of 43 different non-governmental organisations and popular movements that are active in the field of alcohol and drugs. Organisations have the opportunity to join CAN on the condition that they are national, meaning they must be established nationwide with several local branches. The 43 members include specialised organisations working in the field of alcohol and drugs, study organisations and several temperance movements. Although the latter have been present since the origin of CAN, they are gradually losing their influence. Actually, temperance movements are slowly dying out in Sweden; they are mainly composed of elderly people and the number of members is declining fast.

The traditional popular mass movements have fewer members today and, therefore, no longer have the influence they once had. On the other hand, because they have had a significant presence for a long period of time, "many of the earlier popular mass movements have come to be highly integrated with established society and are now part and parcel of that".[26] In the footsteps of the traditional popular mass movements new popular movements have arisen that are working in other fields, such as the environment, human rights issues, culture and recreation, and, last but not least drugs. Not only have these relatively new social movements become more important than the traditional ones, the system seems to have developed to an extent that one sometimes speaks of a 'social movement industry'. According to Wijkström, "the Swedish popular mass movement of today [...] seem to be large *systems* of organisations. Most of the popular mass movements found nowadays are actually giant complex of organisations [...]".[27] Another existing concept is that the Social Movement Industry, "comprises all social movements pursuing similar goals".[28] As shall be discussed later in section 4.3, it seems that this situation is applicable to the popular mass movements active in the field of drug policy.

2.6 Conclusion

Without meaning to generalise and typecast, this chapter has tried to draw a picture of Swedish society, thereby discussing its geography, history, economy, politics, and mentality. This description also discussed two important particular aspects of Sweden, the Social Democratic tradition, characteristic of the Swedish political scene throughout the twentieth century, and the importance of popular movements in Swedish society. In a short overview like this chapter, not every Swedish reader will (completely) identify with 'the Swedes' as they are portrayed. In a text like this one it is inevitable that some reductions of complexity may look like stereotypes or generalisations. It is however, not the intention to simplify complexity in ways that are misrepresentative of the actual situation.

Sweden is generally known to be one of the richest countries in the world. What makes the Swedish case so special is that it combined this prosperity with a social welfare policy. Few people know that Sweden's economic prosperity is actually relatively recent. In the past Sweden was a feudal society with an economic distribution system from which the poor peasantry suffered. Notwithstanding the great economic shifts that took place in the second half of the nineteenth century, large parts of the population were still living in poverty at the beginning of the twentieth century, making Sweden one of the poorest countries in Europe. Many sought a solution in emigration; between 1850 and 1930 a mass exodus occurred with roughly one third of the population leaving the country, mostly to North America.

Social democracy has played a central role in Sweden's development from a poor, rural country to a modern, industrialised nation. The *folk-hemmet*, the people's home, that the Social Democrats started building in the 1930s, thereby attributing an important role to the State, was to offer the people prosperity and, most of all, *trygghet*, security. The virtues the welfare state has brought can explain why people generally have a firm belief that Social Democratic 'social engineering' can solve all problems, resulting in a general positive attitude towards the State and 'the system'. However naive and short-sighted this may look to other nationals, this attitude is not surprising since the people, especially the older genera- tions, have experienced that 'the system' brought nothing but good.

The great economic and societal developments Swedes have encoun- tered during the twentieth century, hence, in a relatively short period of time, makes Sweden quite an unusual combination of both a traditional and a modern country. Despite all the modern virtues of Sweden, many Swedes still come across as having a basically non-metropolitan, some- what provincial mentality. Of course, this can partly be explained by the fact that many Swedes still live in relatively rural areas or otherwise have their roots there. In this respect Sweden's geographical position, on the outskirts of Europe and far from the cultural centres like Berlin, London, and Paris, should not be underestimated. It is relevant to note that social values in Sweden are strongly oriented towards conformity, not leaving much room for deviance.

Another important aspect here is that Sweden is a very homogeneous society. Although it had received immigrants in the past, they mostly orig- inated from other Nordic countries, especially Finland. This neighbour- ing country not only served as a 'colony' in history, which explains why there was less need for Sweden to look for overseas colonies compared to many other European countries, in the twentieth century Finland provid- ed Sweden with the labour force it needed. Once again the location of Sweden explains why they did not have to get a labour force from south- ern Europe or outside Europe. This all results in the situation that, gener- ally speaking, Sweden did not have much experience of different or 'exot- ic' cultures. It is more recently, in the late 1980s, that non-European immigrants have come to Sweden on a comparable scale to many other EU countries.

In the 1990s the Swedish 'wonder' came to an end as the country was hit by the biggest economic crisis since the 1930s. Many people now en- countered for the first time in their life unemployment, which amounted to 12% to 13% if state-run training programmes are included in the calculations. More important than a rise in unemployment is that the economic crisis meant the *trygghet* (security) partly lost its meaning.

What have all these topics to do with drugs? The point is that a drug policy is always deeply rooted in a society. One of the ways to understand a drug policy is by looking at how a society reacts to deviance. For various reasons Sweden was a relatively solid, homogeneous and in a sense protected society where most problems were recognised. Drugs were something strange and unknown to most people; one reason being that in its history Sweden had not encountered other mind altering substances other than alcohol, unlike some other European countries who had experiences of for example cannabis and opium. Sweden's position on the outskirts of Europe, combined with the absence of a strong metropolitan culture and mentality, led to the assumption that a deviant social phenomenon like drug use, generally very much connected to urban, metropolitan cultures, will not be easily accepted or understood, and may be interpreted as a 'threat'. These sentiments can become even stronger in the light of the economic crisis of the 1990s that caused the secure welfare system to disintegrate. In such a situation many of the changes that are occurring, the European Union membership, an increasing number of foreigners (mainly political refugees), and a rise in drug use, might all be perceived as external dangers.

3 The Swedish Drug Experience

3.1 Introduction

Like most Western countries, Sweden was faced with an increasing drug use in the 1960s. The year 1965 is usually referred to as a turning point in the extent of drug use. Unlike some other European countries, in particular those with a colonial past, Sweden did not have a long record of non-medical drug use. In the period before 1965 drugs like cannabis and opiates were only being used for medical purposes. Cannabis preparations were used as tranquillising agents in medications until 1950, opiates were being prescribed to relieve people from pain. The extent of the non-medical use of cannabis and opiates was very limited though. The number of people using opiates for non-medical purposes was estimated to be around 200.[1] Cannabis was smoked to a very limited extent, in particular among jazz musicians and other entertainers.[2] Generally speaking, until 1965 drug use was very limited and it was hardly being regarded as a serious social problem, which was why there was no specific research being done on this subject.[3] Around 1965 there were clear signs drug use was on the increase for which reason *the Committee of Treatment for Drug Abuse* was created in the same year.

The drugs people used around 1965 were amphetamines, cannabis, LSD and opiates. Young people especially started experimenting with drugs. There was some increase in the use of LSD and opiates, but this was limited. Opiate use primarily comprised of opium smoking and some use of morphine. Heroin was used on a very limited scale.[4] Cannabis, in the form of hash, was the drug most widely used. The second most used drugs were central nervous system stimulants (CNS), mostly amphetamines.

When it comes to problematic drug use in the 1960s and 1970s, Sweden is a special case. Whereas in other Western countries heroin became the main drug that was posing problems, use of this drug was still quite rare in Sweden. Instead, in Sweden it was the use of amphetamines that was causing harm. The population of compulsive drug users or drug addicts basically consisted of people injecting amphetamines, many of whom originated from a criminal subculture. Several reasons can be given for this exceptional Swedish case of problematic amphetamines use. As shall be shown in this chapter, one of the reasons being that Sweden already had a long history of use of amphetamine-type drugs.

Sweden is said to have had the experience of both a repressive and a more liberal approach to the drug question. The present drug policy should be the result of the lessons learned in the past. These arguments can be read in several official publications.[5] However, it remains to be seen whether this has really been the case. As shall be demonstrated in this chapter, Sweden has had a limited two-year experiment of legally prescribed drugs, but one can wonder if this practice alone, and especially the way the experiment was conducted, is sufficient to be labelled as a liberal approach.

This chapter will give an account of what is known about Sweden's experiences with drugs. After a description of the period in which central stimulants were legally obtainable, the 1965-67 experiment of legally prescribed drugs will be discussed. Repeated references are made to it in international drug policy debates, in most cases without a thorough knowledge of the facts. This chapter will also enlarge upon the conclusions drawn from the experiment, and its consequences, as it seems to have created the basis for a more restrictive approach to the drug question.

3.2 Traditional Use of Central Nervous System Stimulants

This section will describe the use of amphetamines in the period prior to the late 1960s. As has been mentioned in the introduction to this chapter, there is something special about drug use in Sweden. As stated previously, Sweden is the only country in Europe where the most widely used 'hard drug' is not heroin, but amphetamine. There is a longer history of widespread amphetamine use than one would expect. The only two countries that are said to have a comparable amphetamine history are Japan and Korea.[6]

The possible reasons for the Swedish amphetamine history are as follows. First, as has been described in the previous chapter, Sweden had been neutral during the Second World War. Therefore, in the after war period, Sweden was not in a state of reconstruction as most other European countries were. Instead of having become poorer during the war years, Sweden, as a neutral state, had become richer. During the war years, it had seen its exports increasing, especially iron to Germany. This explains why in the 1940s and 1950s Sweden was already confronted with 'welfare problems', like growing obesity, and considering this to be a problem. Amphetamine in these cases could be the cure; and it was being prescribed to people wanting to lose weight. Another explanation of the relatively widespread amphetamine use has to do with the stimulant properties of amphetamine and the Swedish character. Since Swedes have the reputation to be a hard working people, the stimulating effects of amphetamine could thus be useful.

Amphetamines were introduced in Sweden by the pharmaceutical industry in 1938. These central stimulants were being sold over the counter under the brand names Benzedrine and Phenedrine. At the time, the media launched them as slimming pills and stimulants. Newspapers, magazines and radio broadcasts recommended the 'pep pills' for all kinds of people, from students to tired housewives: "Two pills are better than a month's vacation".[7] In the following years, the substance became increasingly popular; large segments of the population had tried amphetamine. Surveys at the time showed that 70% to 80% of the interviewed students had tried amphetamine. To curb increased use, amphetamine was put on prescription in 1939. The immediate effect was that the sales figures were constant for one year, but increased again in the 1940s.

The number of amphetamine users (1-4 times a year) in 1942-1943 was estimated at 200,000, i.e. 3% of the Swedish population. The majority of the users were occasional users: 140,000. This group was composed of two groups, one half taking the drug only once, the other half two to four times a year. 60,000 people were consuming from several times a year to twice a month. The number of regular users (taking two or three tablets once a week) was 4,000, whilst 3,000 people were taking higher doses, ranging from several tablets a week to a daily intake of 5 to 10 tablets. A small number of approximately 200 people were considered excessive users, taking up to 100 tablets a day on a more or less continuous basis, and showing somatic and psychic symptoms.[8] Börje Olsson has stated that most amphetamine users were 'normal' citizens, who did not have any particular problems, but were taking the substance to stimulate and increase their mental and physical capacities or to lose weight.[9]

During the early 1940s, the total number of tablets dispensed increased gradually, up to six million in 1942. Within a period of five years, from 1938 to 1943, the total sales had increased twenty-fold.[10] Because of the negative effects and the risks of uncontrolled use, a warning was issued by the National Medical Board in 1943, which led to a sharp decline in amphetamine use. A year later, in 1944, the Medical Board submitted stricter regulations for the prescription of amphetamine, which in practice meant the substances were treated in (almost) the same way as narcotics. However, these stricter rules did not apply when it came to imports, exports, production, and possession.

The increasing difficulty in procuring amphetamine opened the way for other central stimulants to be used, like phenmetrazine (brand name: Preludin), and methylphenidate (brand name: Ritalina). These drugs were introduced for the same reasons as amphetamine two decades earlier, because of their weight-reducing properties. These drugs were thought to be not habit-forming.[11] Leonard Goldberg summarises it as follows: "this period lasting up to the early 1950s is thus characterised by a vast and widespread use of stimulant drugs, but relatively few cases of abuse, a tenth of one percent of the total number of users".[12]

The use of central stimulants gradually increased; in 1959 the total registered sale of central stimulants amounted to 33.2 million doses.[13] Use increased particularly among younger people, often with a criminal background.[14] In other words, as has also been the case in other countries, use of these stimulant drugs became fashionable in a criminal subculture, and thus, became an integral part of the lifestyle of this section of society. The increase in use of stimulant drugs led to the inclusion of central stimulants in the National Narcotic Drug Act. Amphetamines were put on the list in 1958, phenmetrazine (Preludin) in 1959, and hylphenidate (Ritalina) in 1960.

Despite stricter regulations it was still relatively easy to get the stimulants, mainly because of the liberal prescription procedures. What it boils down to is the diversion of legally obtained supplies. They also could be purchased on the illegal market, after having been obtained by theft from pharmacies, falsification of prescriptions, theft of prescription forms, and through import from other European countries where they could be bought legally in pharmacies without prescription.

Olsson has pointed out that in the period from the end of the war until 1965 the partition of different types of amphetamine use underwent important changes. In the beginning, consumption was characterised by a widespread (occasional and regular) use, but a very limited number of addicts. In later periods one could observe a decreasing number of occasional and regular users on the one hand, but a growing number of dependant users on the other hand. Table 3.1 shows the number of users of central stimulants, specified into different categories.

Table 3.1 Number of Users of Central Stimulants (Amphetamines).

Type of users	1943	1959	1961	1965
Occasional	133,000	175,000 - 225,000	75,000 - 125,000	40,000 - 60,000
Experimental	60,000	75,000 - 125,000	40,000 - 60,000	20,000 - 30,000
Regular	4,000	7,500 - 12,500	7,500 - 12,500	12,500 - 17,500
(Ab)user	3,000	2,000 - 3,000	2,000 - 3,000	2,225 - 3,225
Severe Abuser	200	500 - 1,000	750 - 1,250	1,000 - 1,500

Source: Börje Olsson (1994)

The table clearly shows that with the increased restrictions on the availability of amphetamine, the number of 'normal' users (incidental and experimental) has gone down considerably. The registered sales of central stimulants showed a dramatic decrease after 1959, when phenmetrazine and methylphenidate were put in the National Narcotic Drug Act, meaning they could only be procured on prescription. The registered sales dropped from 33.2 doses in 1959 to 7.2 million in 1966, a decline of 78%. On the other hand, the number of regular and addicted users increased after 1959. Needless to say, more severe restrictions on the supply side, opened the way for the black market, facilitated by the fact that central stimulants could be bought legally and without prescription in several European countries. This was especially true of Spain which was becoming a popular holiday destination. Besides that, illegal production also started in Sweden.

Considering that the registered sales of stimulants like phenmetrazine and methylphenidate dropped dramatically after 1959 when they became prohibited, and taking into account the number of users and the large amounts taken by a small group of users (up to 100-300 tablets a day), it is likely that the black market was very substantial. Leonard Goldberg estimated the black market to be around 20-40 million tablets a year.[15] Table 3.2 shows the registered legal sales of some stimulant drugs. The fact that the legal sales gradually decreased, implied that the share of the black market was getting bigger. As a matter of fact, a black market had always existed since the substances were regulated by legislation, but when the legislation became more severe and the use got an increasingly subcultural character, the black market became bigger.

Table 3.2 Legal Sales of Some Stimulant Drugs (in Millions of Doses)

	1959	1960	1961	1962	1963	1964	1965	1966
Methamphetamine +								
Amphetamine (5 mg)	2.8	9.5	4.2	1.7	2.5	1.6	2.1	5.9
Dexamphetamine								
(5 mg)	22.0	9.5	9.0	5.8	3.1	1.1	1.8	0.5
Phenmetrazine								
(Preludin) (25 mg)	8.4	7.9	3.5	1.4	0.6	0.5	0.5	-
Methylphenidate								
(Ritalina) (25 mg)	-	-	2.2	1.2	0.7	0.6	0.6	0.8
Total	33.2	26.9	18.9	10.1	6.9	3.8	5.0	7.2

Source: Leonard Goldberg (1968b), p. 21.

Summarising the developments, one can observe the transformation of central stimulants from a socially accepted medicine to an illicit drug.

Olsson has explained this evolution by the fact that the individual, non-deviant use of amphetamine was very sensitive to control measures and by the fact that users were increasingly aware of the possible risks. However, these measures were relatively moderate, and amphetamine were still easily accessible to the general public. But, since amphetamine abuse was strongly related to a criminal subculture, this pattern of use was hardly influenced by the control measures that were put in place.[16] As a result, this type of consumption became more and more visible since the group using these drugs was already considered deviant. Moreover, within this particular group it was common to inject the substances, which increased (in the eyes of the general public) its marginal and deviant character. The social problems and criminality were more and more seen as effects of drug use, even though they often already existed.

In the mid 1960s the more traditional forms of amphetamine use (for medical purposes) became increasingly rare.[17] At the same time, amphetamine use became an integral part of the criminal subculture. The number of people considered drug addicted, in other words being dependant on an illicit drug, continued to rise in the second half of the 1960s. For this reason a Narcotics Drug Committee (*Narkomanvårds-kommittén*, sou) was created that held an investigation into drug use. In its two reports published in 1967, the committee estimated the number of drug addicts was 3,000 in the county of Stockholm and 6,000 in the entire country. The majority of them were injecting amphetamines; the use of opiates was relatively rare at the time.[18]

3.3 The Experiment of Legal Prescription of Drugs (1965-1967)

For two years, from 1965 to 1967, Sweden had an experiment of legal prescription of narcotics drugs to users. In recent years, this experiment has become relevant again because of the recently (re)launched international debate on legal prescription of drugs like heroin. The Swedish experiment is often referred to as a failure or catastrophe: legal prescription of narcotic drugs would lead to more drug use per person, it would result in an increasing number of new addicts, etc. In more general terms the legal prescription of (any) drug is seen as a defeat and an act of surrender. In

Sweden the experiment is often presented as the immediate or contributory cause of the 'drug epidemic' that developed. In Swedish drug policy pamphlets, this conclusion is used as the basic argument against a liberal drug policy. In the ongoing international discussion on decriminalisation and legalisation of (some) drugs, the experience is sometimes referred to as one of the very rare examples that has been studied and documented, indicating where legal prescription or more liberal tendencies of drug policy can lead to.

The Swedish experiment of legal prescription has been surrounded by misunderstandings. Part of the confusion is related to the influence of Nils Bejerot, one of the 'founders' of the restrictive Swedish drug policy. In his various writings and speeches Bejerot has tried to find proof for his theory of the disease-like epidemic character of drug use. Bejerot believed that the prescription experiment has been the root of the drug epidemic that Sweden has suffered. Other, more recently published studies, however, have criticised Bejerot's thesis severely.

This section will discuss the nature of the experiment, its effects and the conclusions that can be, and have been drawn from it. The secondary goal of this analysis is to untangle some of the misunderstandings that surround the experiment.

The experiment

During two years, from April 1965 till May 1967 narcotic drugs were prescribed to drug addicts in Stockholm. There is some misunderstanding about the nature of the project, which is sometimes presented as a carefully considered plan that was monitored and evaluated. However, the project was never meant as a scientific experiment, but was merely a project that grew out of some medical doctors' practical work. The project was supported by the then dominant social movement in the field of drug policy, the client organisation RFHL, that had been involved in initiating the experiment. The fact this was possible, must be seen and understood in the context of the 'liberal' 1960s when there was a strong plea to have a more permissive attitude towards non-medical use of narcotic drugs.[19] It was only later that the project received official support by the health inspectorate. Because of the non-scientific status of the project, there has never been a control group, which makes it impossible to make a scientific evaluation or to draw anything but very limited conclusions.[20]

At the start, in April 1965, the experiment included ten drug addicts to whom narcotic drugs would be prescribed. At the end of 1965 this number had grown to 60, in 1966 and 1967 around 100 patients participated in the project. Most patients participating in the project belonged to a criminal subculture. During the two year period a total of 120 patients had participated in the project for at least three months. The substances that were prescribed were methadone, morphine and primarily amphetamines, for oral as well as intravenous use.

In the beginning about ten physicians were involved in the project, but by the end of 1965 only one physician remained, the same person who had initiated the project, police doctor Sven-Erik Åhström. For most of the time the experiment lasted, Åhström was the only person writing out prescriptions. Åhström was known to be very outspoken, with liberal ideas about drug addiction and treatment. He was of the opinion that the patients themselves were responsible for the dosages they were taking, he delegated part of his work and responsibilities to a few patients that were permitted to prescribe and distribute as well, and he allowed patients to take drugs home for several days and, if this quantity ran out earlier than expected, they could come back and ask for more.

Because of its liberal practices, the experiment became more and more controversial. Halfway through the experiment, when all the physicians except Åhström had abandoned the project, it was no longer supported by the client organisation RFHL. The police regularly found people with legally prescribed drugs that were not participating in the project, which meant that a lot of the prescribed substances were leaking out. Other criticisms concerned the high mortality among the participating patients and the fact that the crime figures did not decrease, as had been expected. When in April 1967 a 17-years old girl not taking part in the project died from an overdose of amphetamine and morphine that had been administered by one of the patients, the experiment finally came to an end. During the two-year period a total of four million dosages of amphetamine (15 kilos) and 600,000 dosages of opiates (3.3 kilos) had been prescribed to 120 patients.[21]

Conclusions and Consequences

During the 1960s an increase in drug use occurred in Sweden. New drugs such as cannabis and LSD appeared on the market and were used by an increasing number of young people especially. At the same time there was an increase in the use of amphetamine and opiates, the latter being a rarely used drug in Sweden.

Nils Bejerot, a police doctor working in Stockholm, decided to conduct a study into the relationship between drug use and drug policy in Stockholm in the period 1965-1970. Working as a psychiatric consultant to the Stockholm police force since 1958, he became supervisory medical officer at the detention centre in Stockholm where all people arrested for crime were held in custody.[22] Bejerot decided to start a study into the occurrence of injection marks on the arms of arrested people, assuming that this group was well suited to be studied: the identity of the arrested people could be determined with accuracy and intravenous use could be simply and objectively observed.[23] The method followed was simple: trained nurses would inspect the arm veins of every person arrested for crime and taken to the police premises in Stockholm.

One of the goals of this investigation was to "organise a study of a possible connection between drug policy in general and the spread of intravenous abuse in the arrest population which we knew from experience was highly infected".[24] The prescription experiment was of special interest since it enabled a comparison of a permissive drug policy, the period 1965-67, with a more restrictive drug policy, the period prior to 1965 and after 1967. This was very relevant to Bejerot since he believed that drug use had an epidemic and contagious character: "once a group of abusers has formed and a drug culture has arisen in society, the availability of the drugs is the most important factor in the spread of this form of abuse. [...] According to this theory, society must follow a restrictive drug policy for both preventive and therapeutic reasons".[25]

In the data Bejerot presented in his dissertation over the period 1965-70 he found changes between 'permissivity' and 'restriction' in Swedish drug policy reflected in the rates of intravenous drug use.[26] In other words, he found data supporting his hypothesis that the 'permissivity' had led to an increase of intravenous drug use, in other words an epidemic-like spread effect. Bejerot found a remarkable expansion of intravenous drug use among arrested people during the liberal or permissive period. In 1965, 20% of arrested people were intravenous drug users, this figure rose to 25% in 1966 and 33% in 1967. The increase was particularly high among the youngest and oldest detainees. When after 1967 a (gradual) shift occurred towards a more restrictive policy, Bejerot observed a decreasing percentage of intravenous users among the arrested people. Hence, Bejerot saw his hypothesis confirmed.

Bejerot's hypothesis and corresponding findings have been greatly influential in the Swedish drug policy debate. His role within this controversy has gradually shifted from an extremist in a marginal position to the 'founding father' of the restrictive Swedish drug policy. Bejerot's analysis of the 1965-67 experiment is still important today, in the sense that his argument is widely accepted by government officials,[27] and is written down as such in government documents.[28] The negative experience with this prescription experiment is one of the reasons why the Swedish authorities are still reluctant to increase the number of opiate users receiving methadone. Since the two-year experiment of 1965-67 there seems to be a shadow hanging over legal prescription experiments.

Although Bejerot's thesis that the prescription experiment has had a fatal, triggering effect on the further spread of drug use is not valid in scientific terms, the idea is still widely accepted today. Bejerot's influence is surprising since his ideas and conclusions are rarely shared by other members of the scientific community, both in Sweden and internationally. On the contrary, Bejerot's assumptions and conclusions have been thoroughly analysed and criticised.

Discussion
Bejerot's analysis has been the target of criticism from several scientists. The first criticism is that Bejerot's injection mark figures are based on police statistics. As is often the case with police figures, one should hesitate to draw but limited conclusions from these data. Their limitation is that one is never sure whether they reflect real societal developments or merely police activities. In any case one cannot, as Bejerot has done, use the data as a (scientific) indicator for the incidence of drug use.

A second criticism is that, if a rise in the number of arrested people with needle marks is observed, one cannot immediately conclude that this is related to drug policy. One should never exclude that other factors are also (or even more) significant. Lenke & Olsson have pointed out that the increase in detainees with injection marks observed in 1965 was not the immediate cause of the legal prescription experiment, but that other more general developments in this period should be held responsible. There was indeed a rise in observed needle marks, but this figure had already increased before 1965. It is much more probable that the rise should be seen in the context of a larger and longer-lasting development: the already growing drug use of the 1960s. Thus, the rise in needle marks should be regarded as reflecting this instead of being linked to the prescription experiment. This conclusion is endorsed by the fact that in the period 1965-67 intravenous drug use was not only rising in Stockholm and Sweden, but in most European countries and the Western world at large. It is too simple to suppose here a direct causality between the experiment and the increase in drug use, without looking at the wider international and socio-cultural context.

The third and probably most fundamental criticism to Bejerot's arguments concern the statistical significance. The Norwegian researcher Ole-Jorgen Skog, who made a thorough analysis of Bejerot's findings, also including later data (1970-77), found that there was no evidence for the hypothesis that the change from a liberal to a restrictive policy in 1967 had any reducing effects.[29] If the Box-Jenkins time series analysis is applied, a common technique to measure correlation over time, it is found that the correlation is not statistically significant.

Apart from these more fundamental arguments, there are some other points of criticism concerning the effects of the experiment on health and criminality. With regard to health it is sometimes said that the legal prescription experiment resulted in a high death rate of eleven deceased people in the follow-up study in December 1969. However, Lenke & Olsson, after a closer look into the (original) data, have concluded that the number of deceased was only four. Seven of the eleven people died after the project had terminated.[30] There is also some confusion on another point, namely criminality. One of the aims of the project was to decrease criminality, supposing that the drug users would no longer have to commit crimes to finance their habit. However, it is often said that the project did not have this desired effect and that, instead, drug offences aside, it would have led to an increase in other types of crime.[31] Apart from the fact that the desired effect of crime reduction is probably too ambitious, because most participants belonged to a criminal subculture, such an analysis also neglects other facts. Lenke & Olsson have made the observation that in 1969 the Committee on the Treatment of Drug Abuse wrote that many of the patients involved in the project had spent at least part of the year *prior* to the project in prison, and were therefore physically incapable of committing crimes.[32] Considering the fact that amphetamine use at the time developed primarily within a criminal subculture with drug use and criminal behaviour are integral parts of the life style, it may come as no surprise that a rise in criminal acts was observed when some of the patients left prison and entered the project.

3.4 The Definition of a Social Problem: 1968-1980

In the mid 1960s drug use was increasingly considered a problem. However, there was no clear-cut idea of the real nature of the problem and the way it could be tackled. Lindgren has identified the three drug strategies of 1960s: the legalisation strategy, the treatment and reform strategy, and the control and sanction strategy.[33] In the years 1965-69 a debate arose as to which of these strategies would deal with the problem in the most effective way.

Legalisation was the least influential of the three strategies, although this policy option was receiving a lot of attention in the media and was being advocated by some influential individuals.[34] Proponents of legalisation had some impact in the way that their points of view contributed to the prescription experiment of 1965-67, but when the experiment ended, the legalisation option faded away. The treatment and reform strategy had many advocates, especially since it was inspired by criticism of the capitalist society. Concordant with the social symptom theory, drug addiction was seen as a consequence of worsening social conditions. The treatment and reform strategy had some influence, especially during (a part) of the

1970s. Generally though, this strategy was more successful in the debate than in practice.[35] The scheme that seems having had most influence was the control and sanction strategy.

In the period following the prescription experiment, the foundation was laid for the (restrictive) drug policy as it is today. However, it was not only this experiment and its perceived consequences that led to a more restrictive drug policy. The Committee on the Treatment of Drug Abuse (*Narkomanvårds-kommittén*) that was installed in 1965 after signs that drug use was on the increase, published four reports in the period 1967-1969 which have had a large impact on the policy of the late 1960s. The reports gave the government a clear definition of the drug problem and the 'tools' to deal with the problem. The Committee on the Treatment of Drug Abuse first published two reports in 1967, the first on the treatment issue, the second on repressive measures. The second report served as a basis for the Narcotic Drugs Act that came into power in 1968.

To measure the extent of drug use in 1967 the Committee on the Treatment of Drug Abuse conducted a case-finding survey in the Stockholm metropolitan area. This survey found about 2,500 individuals to be either injecting drugs, or otherwise taking drugs on a regular (daily) basis. Making allowances for the unreported cases, the number of 'heavy drug abusers' was eventually estimated at around 3,000, while the number of in the country as a whole this was estimated at 6,000.[36] These drug users, in the survey defined as 'heavy drug abusers', could be considered compulsive drug users or dependant drug addicts, of whom a majority was injecting amphetamines or other central stimulants.[37]

In the two reports published in 1969, the committee published more recent data on the extent of drug use based on surveys. The number of 'heavy drug abusers' in Sweden was now estimated at 10,000. The most commonly used drug was amphetamine, used intravenously. The committee also observed the life time prevalence of drug use among the young people in the Stockholm area to be 17%, while the national figure was only 2%. Although the committee considered most (forms of) drug use as not problematic since it usually only had a temporary character, the increasing number of drug addicts was regarded as a serious problem. It is interesting to note that the committee made a comparison between illicit drugs and licit drugs like sedatives and alcohol.

The committee considered excessive use of sedatives (like sleeping pills) to be less dangerous than that of illicit drugs. Furthermore, sedative use was considered less dangerous since its use was in most cases moderate. The social consequences of excessive sedative use were considered less significant. Consumers are no delinquents, since they can obtain their product legally in pharmacies. When it comes to the comparison between alcohol and illicit drugs, the committee considered drug addiction a bigger problem than alcoholism. The first reason is that the committee considered that an individual could become more easily dependant on drugs than on alcohol. Secondly, drug addiction is believed to place people in anti-social environments, whilst alcoholism is better known in a social perspective through the existence of habits and customs. Thirdly, the harmful effects of alcohol are better known than those of drugs and, finally, drug addicts have a much more negative image in society than alcoholics do.[38] The interesting thing to note is that most reasons that are given here to consider drugs to be more dangerous than alcohol, depend on the place they have, or that is attributed to them in society. In other words, these reasons are in essence *social* factors, largely independent from the properties of the substances concerned.

To tackle the drug problem the Committee on the Treatment of Drug Abuse proposed a series of measures of two types: measures aiming at a reduction of the addiction phenomenon and measures with the objective to prevent circumstances that might lead to an individual taking drugs. The proposed measures to reduce drug addiction consisted of both demand and supply reduction measures. The Narcotic Drugs Act, coming into power in 1968, was part of the latter. As shall be explained in this section, Swedish drug legislation has undergone many changes since its inception. It is interesting to note that sometimes other data than that of 1968 are referred to as turning points in Swedish drug policy.[39] For example, the late 1970s are also mentioned in this respect as it was in this period that the government officially adopted the policy to strive for a drug-free society. Although this moment can certainly be regarded as an important step in the development of Sweden's drug policy, it did not express much of a change, but was merely a reinforcement of the policy already in place. The Narcotic Drugs Act, coming into power in 1968, should be regarded as the basis of the Swedish drug policy as it still is today. It laid the foundation for a policy with close interaction between prevention, control policy and treatment.

The Narcotic Drugs Act does not make any difference between different types of drugs; all substances registered as narcotics are treated identically, without a formal distinction between soft and hard drugs.[40] The drug legislation introduced a categorisation of offences based on three levels with different penalties according to the gravity:

- Minor drug offences, punishable with a fine;
- Normal drug offences, punishable with a fine or imprisonment up to two years;
- Major drug offences, punishable with an imprisonment up to four years.

(*Note:* in time the penalties have become more severe)

Fines in the Narcotic Drugs Act are based on 'day fines', as is the case for most fines in Sweden. These fines are income-related and are fixed at a varying number of days, depending on the seriousness of a crime.

The regulations in this legislation did not yet criminalise drug use. All other drug related acts were in fact considered drug law violations. Notwithstanding the relatively severe nature of the law, the legislator's primarily goal was not to punish drug users but to help and treat them. This explains why there are different categories of offences and why a normal drug offence can also be punished with a fine, a necessary condition to drop a case.[41] To define the gravity of the offence several factors are relevant: whether the individual is working as a 'professional', the quantity of the drugs involved, the type of drugs, etc. Not only was drug use not criminalised, limited possession for personal use was not prosecuted either. As laid down in the Prosecutor General's guidelines, three grams of cannabis was the limit for waivers of prosecution in 1968.[42] For amphetamines, the limit to waive prosecution was 100 tablets.[43] The main reason behind dismissing these offenders was to avoid unnecessary conflicts between law enforcement measures and treatment possibilities.[44]

As shall be explained, the law gradually became increasingly repressive from 1968. As Lenke & Olsson have put it: in the late 1960s the control and sanction strategy was revitalised. In 1969, the *Riksdag* (Parliament) increased penalties for major drug offences from four to six years. The main objective of these measures was to reduce the supply of drugs, thereby using more severe penalties as a deterrence for dealers. In 1972 these penalties for major drug crimes were considered insufficient and were increased again, this time to a maximum of ten years. The reason for harshening penalties in 1972 was not that the drug problem was increasing. On the contrary, indicators showed that the number of drug addicts had remained stable since 1968, which was interpreted as the effect of the repressive measures. Hence, by harshening penalties once more, the idea was to apply the same remedy again.[45] In the same period the possibility of compulsory care was increased and the drug control policy was strengthened by putting the majority of tranquillisers and sedatives on the list of narcotic drugs.[46]

Notwithstanding the harshening of the drug legislation, the general idea behind the drug policy was still not aimed at arresting and punishing drug users. In 1972 the limit for waivers of prosecution of small possession of cannabis could be enough for a week's consumption.[47] During most of the 1970s, police activities were focused on the more serious drug crimes, and not so much on consumers and street dealers. Combatting street dealing was considered a secondary objective and a relative leniency was shown towards drug users.[48]

One of the reasons behind this policy was that the focus of the drug policy was still being hotly debated during the 1970s. A strong body of opinion regarded drug abuse as a consequence of adverse social conditions.[49] Therefore, it was thought, drug policy should focus on measures to improve social conditions instead of combatting drug use and street sales. In comparison to today's standards, the attitudes towards drug use and (small scale) street dealing were relatively liberal.[50] However, this does not imply the drug policy in general during this decade could be characterised as 'liberal'. Generally speaking, the drug policy in the 1970s did not deviate basically from the previous decade and public efforts were mainly put on control measures instead of treatment and social policy measures.[51]

3.5 The Pursuit of a Drug-Free Society: the 1980s

In the mid 1970s heroin found its way into the Swedish drug market. The substance was being used to some extent in Stockholm and the southern city Malmö. However, heroin use was limited in Sweden, both compared to the number of people taking amphetamines, and compared to the extent of heroin use in many other European countries. A national case finding study that was conducted in 1979 found between 10,000 and 14,000 heavy drug abusers in Sweden (average: 12,000). Heavy drug abusers are defined here as "either injecting or using drugs in some other way daily or virtually every day".[52] With respect to the extent and the development of experimental drug use, one has to refer to data of surveys that are carried out among 9th grade school children (15-16 years old) and (male) military conscripts (18 years old).[53] The prevalence figures will be extensively discussed in chapter six.

If the prevalence data of grade 9 students and military conscripts are combined, one can observe, depending on the figures one refers to, a stabilisation or decrease in experimental drug use during the 1970s. This trend continued in the 1980s when the prevalence figure dropped even more. Generally though, it is safe to say the main decrease in drug use occurred during the 1970s. It is interesting to see that official publications rarely mention these trends, but tend to emphasise drug use was still high during the 1970s, and only went down in the 1980s. In *Drug Policy – The Swedish Experience* one reads for example: "During the 1970s, experimental drug use steadied at a relatively high level. From about 1980 onwards it declined noticeably among young persons."[54] There is however, as shall be discussed later in chapter six, not much evidence that this statement reflects the real trends.

In this section it shall be shown that, although there are no clear indications the drug problem was on the increase in the 1970s and 1980s, drugs were perceived as a growing problem in this period. One could make a comparison with what happened in the United States in the early 1980s, when Reagan became president and declared the 'war on drugs'. Although the prevalence of drug use was declining in the 1980s, 'drugs' was presented as a growing problem.[55] The American answer consisted of a war on drugs: tougher penalties for drug law violations and more law enforcement. In broad terms, the development of Swedish drug policy was similar. The perceived 'threat' of drugs and the moral panic that surrounded it, would gradually lead to a shift towards an increased law enforcement approach with sharper penalties for drug law violations.

In 1976 a new coalition government, composed of Centre, Liberal, and Conservative Parties, took office. It was a rather different situation, since this was the first time since 1932 the Social Democrats were not in office, a position that was to last till 1982. During these years, the non-Socialist government made drugs a much bigger issue than previous governments had. From 1977 onwards, the Swedish drug policy would have a more restrictive character. In that year the government appointed a committee to "recommend further measures to curb the acceleration of drug abuse".[56] Following the committee's recommendations, the Riksdag decided in 1977 that the aim of Swedish drug policy would be a drug-free society.

It may come as a surprise that a country adopts such a far-reaching, idealistic goal, which is in many eyes considered as unrealistic. In Sweden however, the drug-free society is seen as a realistic option. The reason for this, in some respect, unrealistic pursuit, can partly be found in Sweden's positive experience with the welfare state and its firm belief in being able to change society. As discussed in the previous chapter, Sweden's history in the twentieth century is remarkable in the sense that the country transformed itself from one of the poorest to one the richest countries in Europe. One of the legacies of this achievement is the deeply rooted conviction that Social Democratic 'social engineering' is capable of changing society and solving its problems.

It is sometimes stated that the change in policy that occurred around 1980 was a shift or break compared to the 'liberal 1970s'. It has already been briefly mentioned that this was not really the case. As Lenke & Olsson have put it, "In the public discourse, it is even claimed that this turn constitutes a break with the policies of the 1970s, which today rhetorically is labelled as liberal. No doubt new and stiffer law enforcement policies did imply a more restrictive or even repressive drug policy, but to say, in a qualitative sense, that this constituted a totally new policy is doubtful".[57]

Lenke & Olsson stress that the foundation of the restrictive drug policy was laid in the late 1960s; what happened around 1980s can best be described as a "strengthening of certain policy measures already being an important part of the entire drug policy".[58] Parliament's decision in 1977 to strive for a drug-free society resulted in a number of changes. For example, possibilities of waivers of prosecution were being restricted. The new guidelines introduced in 1980 only made dismissals possible if the possessed drugs were destined for personal use and under the condition that the amount was so small that it cannot be subdivided anymore. In practice, this meant at the most one joint (up to one gram) or not more one dose of amphetamines (0.1 or 0.2 grams). However, possession of heroin, cocaine, and morphine were excluded from being dismissed, because these substances were considered to be more dangerous.[59] Interestingly, cannabis and amphetamines had been placed in the same category. In the Prosecutor General's guidelines it was written that (new) scientific evidence about the harm of cannabis use justified a stricter line with respect to cannabis.[60] The new guidelines are clearly reflected in the number of registered drug offences, that rose from 22,500 in 1979 to 68,000 in 1982.[61]

In 1981 the minimum sentence for major drug offences was raised from one to two years imprisonment. As described previously, the maximum sentence for this category of drug offences had already been increased to ten years imprisonment in 1972. At the same time the maximum penalty for normal drug offences was raised from two to three years imprisonment. Another change in 1981 was that the amount of drugs was no longer relevant to the gravity and, hence, categorisation of a drug offence, now it was the nature of the offence, in other words the degree of seriousness.[62]

On the care and treatment side a change was to take place as well. In June 1981 Parliament passed a new social welfare legislation: the Social Services Act. This law was supplemented by two bills, one on compulsory care for children (LVU), and another on compulsory care of alcohol and drug abusers (LVM). From this moment on there would be more legal opportunities to put people into treatment against their will, or under the pressure of possible coercion, to direct them into voluntary treatment.

The conservative coalition had already introduced drugs as an election theme during the 1976 campaign. During the 1982 election campaign the

Social Democrats adopted the same tactic and made drugs one of their important themes. The Social Democratic Party declared through deputy Prime Minister Carlsson, the *Folkhemmet* (the people's home) to be 'clean of drugs'.[63] The use of this very symbolic expression, traditionally used to depict the social welfare state, demonstrated the importance the Social Democrats attributed to the question. When the Social Democrats returned to power in 1982, with an almost absolute majority in Parliament, they reconfirmed the aim of the Swedish drug policy as it had already been formulated by Parliament in 1977: the pursuit of a drug-free society. The government appointed a drugs committee to make proposals to combat drugs.

Someone that seems to have been influential in the way the drug policy developed in the 1980s was Gertrud Sigurdsen, Minister for Health and Social Affairs. One could say she introduced a new way of looking at drugs, in a certain manner of speaking a new theoretical model or even paradigm. It is, however, difficult to say whether she really introduced a new way of thinking or whether she adopted a trend that was already going on, and had been introduced earlier in the 1960s and 1970s by Nils Bejerot. In any case, Sigurdsen emphasised the dangers of drugs and its properties, for example by saying it 'could happen to any family'. In essence, this was a break with the traditional social welfare theory, the so-called symptom theoretical perspective, that used to emphasise the socio-economic conditions of the people (like poor housing conditions) as explanatory factors for social problems, like alcohol and drug abuse. As a matter of fact, Sigurdsen was criticised for adopting this new approach by the working class temperance association *Verdandi*. Sigurdsen is also said to be responsible for the decreasing role of the client organisation RFHL in the 1980s, although it had been the dominant social movement in the field of drugs during the 1960s, and still was influential in the 1970s. Sigurdsen found herself also increasingly at odds over the alcohol and drug policy with some members of the government commission responsible for keeping an eye on the operation of the new compulsory treatment Act (LVM) passed in 1982. This led in 1986 to the replacement of the commission's liberal chairman who was replaced by a senior member of the Parents Against Drugs (FMN), one of the militant social movements in the field.[64]

In 1983 a change of a different nature occurred in the Swedish drug legislation. Whereas before tougher penalties had been the way of pursuing a stricter drug policy, this time the area covered by criminal law was being increased. More acts were now criminalised, such as acts that could facilitate a drug deal. Together with these changes in the penalty area, the legislator presented data on 'the actual drug use situation'.[65] This drug situation was presented as an underlying cause of the rise in criminality. By doing this, the actual 'drug situation' became, de facto, unacceptable, even though drug use among young people had not increased, nor were the more severe forms of drug use on the increase.[66]

In 1985 the Narcotics Drugs Act underwent a new series of changes. Minor drug offences, until that moment only punishable with a fine, could now also lead to an imprisonment of up to six months. Simultaneously, the possibility of a fine was excluded when it came to normal drug offences. Thus, from this moment on, normal drug offences would automatically lead to imprisonment. In the same year there was a debate as to whether drug use alone should be criminalised. 1985 was also an election year and the issue almost became an important election theme, exactly what the Social Democrat government wanted to avoid. Eventually, criminalisation of drug use did not take place because the Social Democrats were opposed to the idea. The government said it wanted to wait for the results of a study the Public Prosecutor was asked to conduct on the question of criminalisation of drug use. This report was published after the 1985 elections, won again by the Social Democrats. According to the Public Prosecutor's report there was no practical reason for criminalising drug use.

The discussion about criminalising drug use returned in the 1988 elections. In this year drugs became an important issue in the campaigns. The Social Democrats won the elections and came into power again. Although the party traditionally had not wanted to take any action in criminalising drug use and to take a tougher line on drugs, they gradually shifted towards a (more) restrictive policy, both influenced by the political process and other parties, managing to make drugs a political issue. Eventually a compromise was found: drug use would be criminalised, but the penalty would be a fine, instead of imprisonment. The background of criminalising drug use was that society would make clear it was an unacceptable activity, which would in particular have a important psychological and symbolical effect upon young people.[67] The debate on the criminalising of drug use was not over yet though, as there were still people arguing imprisonment should be the punishment.

When in 1991 a new conservative government coalition took office, led by Carl Bildt, it promised to be tougher on drugs. Bengt Westerberg, Minister of Health and Social Affairs and leader of the Liberal Party, declared the punishment of drug use by a fine did not go far enough; it should be punishable by imprisonment, because this would enable urine tests to be carried out (since these tests can only be required when the offence committed is an imprisonable one).[68] It would take another two years before this measure was implemented. Eventually it was in 1993 that drug use was made punishable by a maximum of six months imprisonment. The reason for this more severe punishment was not the desire to imprison drug users, but to be able to detect (the offence) drug use more easily. This can be done by imposing a urine or blood test on someone who is under the suspicion of having used drugs. All this means is that the police now has more opportunities to discover (past) drug use without actual possession. This means in practice that, without discovering any drugs on an individual, but on the basis of suspicion of being under the influence of drugs, the suspected individual can be taken to a police station where a urine or blood test is imposed.

If the 1980s and the early 1990s are compared to the more liberal 1960s and 1970s, one can observe a number of important changes. In the 1980s drugs became a political issue, in the sense that it was a theme of discussion during election campaigns. Whereas in the beginning it was basically the non-Social Democratic Parties asking for a more restrictive approach, gradually the Social Democratic Party also shifted to a law enforcement approach, both under the influence of (the success of) other parties demanding a tougher stance on drugs, and under the influence of pressure groups (see next chapter).

Not only were the drug laws being sharpened, more importantly the 'nature' of the law enforcement policy was changing. In the 1960s and 1970s the priorities of police actions were concentrated on the dealer, in other words on the supply side. The drug users were more or less left in peace. In the late 1970s, this situation was reversed; the emphasis was now put on the drug users. Therefore, from that moment on, going into the 1980s and 1990s, drug users become the 'target' of police actions. This new approach was effectively the application of Nils Bejerot's theories. According to Bejerot, the drug user is the only indispensable link in the 'drug chain' and the element that keeps the keeps the 'engine' going. If the drug users can be prevented from taking drugs, the whole system will eventually collapse. The impact of Bejerot is shown by the words spoken in 1991 by Bengt Westerberg, the then new Minister of social Affairs and Health and leader of the Liberal Party.

> "The government considers that the present law concerning the punishment for drug offences does not go far enough. The 1988 law that criminalised all use of drugs was like 'hitting air'. Since the punishment is fines only, the police have no right to demand urine tests and cannot therefore prove that someone has misused drugs. We considers that consumption should be regarded as similar to all other ways of handling drugs. Consumption is the motor of the whole drug carousel."[69]

3.6 Conclusion

This chapter has given an overview of the Swedish drug experience. It has been shown that Sweden had a relatively long history of the use of central nervous system stimulants. Introduced in the late 1930s, amphetamine could be legally bought over the counter in pharmacies. They were used as slimming pills or to increase the mental and physical capacities. The majority of the consumers were 'normal' people who occasionally used central stimulants in a functional way and did not develop problems. In the 1940s the number of users was estimated at 200,000, which was 3% of the population. A small group of around 200 users was taking higher doses and were considered excessive users. Because of this abuse, increased regulations to prescribe amphetamine were implemented. This opened the way to other central nervous system stimulants being used like phenmetrazine and methylphenidate. Similar to amphetamine, most users used occasionally and a small number of people were consuming excessively which eventually led to stricter regulations. There were, however, still liberal prescription procedures, which meant that people could procure central stimulants relatively easily. Moreover, central stimulants could be bought over the counter in other European countries like Spain, that was becoming a popular holiday destination.

The control measures that were introduced to limit consumption resulted in the fact that most middle and upper class users simply stopped taking central stimulants. A group that remained outside the effects of the control measures were the excessive users, many of whom belonged to a criminal subculture. Not only were they taking the substances in large quantities, they also used them in a different way: not orally, but intravenously. The more traditional forms of amphetamine use became increasingly rare, whilst in the criminal subculture, use became an integral part of this subculture. This resulted in a situation where the deviance of this subculture was seen as a consequence of amphetamine use, whilst this deviant behaviour was actually already in place. The development of the consumption of central stimulants from the late 1930s to the mid 1960s could be described as the transformation of a socially accepted medicine used by many, and different kinds of people, to an illicit drug basically consumed in a deviant environment.

Unfortunately, the period of the legal use of central stimulants has not been extensively studied. An interesting conclusion might be drawn from this period though. Generally speaking, consumption was socially accepted and not considered a problem. Even substance abuse was not considered as deviant, but was seen as an individual problem that had to be cured by medical science. This situation can be compared with the use and abuse of opium and morphine in the period before this started to be seen as a problem. These substances were regarded as legal medicines that were both used and abused. However, because of the legal status they had, abuse was not seen as deviant behaviour as it is today, under a regime that does stigmatise use. Hence, the way drug use and abuse are being perceived, are to a certain extent dependant on the formal status they have: licit or illicit.

In this chapter the experiment of legal prescription of drugs to drug addicts from 1965-67 was extensively discussed. A small group of around

120 people, many with a criminal background, could legally obtain narcotic drugs. However, the experiment is surrounded by many misunderstandings and myths. For example, it is often believed to have been the origin of the Swedish drug epidemic, but scientifically speaking, there is not enough proof to suggest a causal relationship, especially if one looks at the wider international context. In the Western word at large drug use was on the increase, irrespective of experiments or the drug policy that was applied. However, the conclusion drawn from it was that the experiment was alleged to have triggered drug use, which was one of the reasons to adopt a more restrictive approach in the late 1960s. The other one was the publications of the reports of the governmental Committee on the Treatment of Drug Abuse that showed the drug problem was on the increase.

In 1968 the Narcotics Drugs Act came into power. In the 1970s and 1980s the act underwent a gradual harshening. A difference was that in the 1970s the focus of the police activities was the supply side of the drugs, whilst in the 1980s the police targeted the street dealers and drug users. In 1977 the government (the first non-socialist government since 1932) adopted the goal of the drug-free society. Throughout the 1980s 'drugs' were increasingly perceived as a social problem, although there were no clear indications the problem was on the increase. Drugs also became a political issue, mainly under the pressure of the conservative parties, and one can observe an increasing 'moral panic' on drugs. In 1989 drug use was criminalised with a fine, and in 1993 drug use was made punishable by an imprisonment of six months.

4 Understanding Swedish Drug Policy

4.1 Introduction

To understand the Swedish drug policy as it is today, it is insufficient to look solely at the Swedish drug experience. Drug control systems do not always result from the experiences a country has had with certain mind-altering substances. Drug control systems can be very complex entities, sometimes (also) serving goals other than one would suspect at first sight. Therefore, to get a real, in-depth understanding of the Swedish drug control system, other aspects should be taken in consideration as well.

In the first section a brief overview of alcohol use and alcohol policy will be given. This overview is by no means complete. The field of alcohol use and the policy that has been applied to limit consumption is very complex. A lot of reputable alcohol research is being done in Sweden and other Scandinavian countries. This section will only discuss those aspects of the Swedish alcohol tradition that are relevant as background information to understanding the drug policy. It may seem logical for a country with a strong temperance tradition to have a restrictive policy on illicit drugs.

However, having an understanding of the alcohol policy is not sufficient to comprehend the drug policy. For example, the comparison between the drug policy and alcohol policy does not hold completely; it is not their aim to strive for an alcohol-free society, but Sweden does strive for a drug-free society. Another difference is that the Swedish alcohol policy could be labelled 'rational'. The drug policy in Sweden, however, can hardly be given the qualification 'rational'.

The paradox of Swedish drug policy is that the Swedish drug problem in itself is relatively small, as compared to other European countries, but it is perceived by public opinion as a very large social problem. The expression 'moral panic' is probably best suited to describe this situation. Opinion polls show that people actually perceive drugs as one of the main threats to society, far above other social problems like unemployment, the environment, racism, etc. In the previous chapter it was shown how the Swedish drug legislation underwent a gradual harshening, although there were no signs that the magnitude of drugs as a social problem was growing. The question that arises is why are people so 'afraid' of drugs and why are they susceptible to the moral panic that surrounds it. Why would a society that defines itself as being rational, make such seemingly irrational decisions?

After discussing both the alcohol consumption and alcohol policy, the role of the popular movements that are active in the field of drugs will be discussed in section 4.3. In chapter two the important role of popular movements in Swedish society in general was described; now one will see that some popular movements have played an essential role in shaping Swedish drug policy as it is today. In section 4.4 the ideological and scientific foundations of the Swedish drug policy will be discussed. In essence one finds here the justifications for conducting a restrictive drug policy. A lot of attention will be paid to cannabis since the most 'prevention' and 'opinion formation' on drugs concentrate on this substance. Prevention and opinion formation are two of the main elements of the drug policy, and form an integral part of the school programmes in Sweden. At the age of seven some children get their first drug prevention education, and by the age of twelve almost every child has been informed about drugs. This chapter will end with a discussion about the function that the drug policy is serving in Swedish society.

4.2 Alcohol in Sweden

Alcohol Consumption

To understand a drug policy it is interesting to look first at the way alcohol has been dealt with, the most familiar and commonly used intoxicant in Western countries. In the case of Sweden both the way alcohol has been used throughout time, and the policy that has been applied in regulating alcohol use, are essential elements to interpret its drug policy.

Sweden is said to belong to the vodka belt, the zone stretching from

Europe to America including countries like Canada, Russia, Poland, and the Scandinavian countries. The most common intoxicant that was traditionally used in these countries was alcohol, especially the strong or hard liquors. One of the main reasons these countries traditionally used stronger liquors is because wine could not be produced and beverages like beer and ale could not be stored and were difficult to distribute.[1] Thus, Sweden has a tradition of drinking vodka (*snaps*).

It is a popular misunderstanding that Swedes drink a lot of alcohol. However, compared to many other (European) countries, the total consumption of pure alcohol per capita is not very high.[2] Alcohol consumption in countries with a beer or wine tradition is generally higher. However, an important feature of alcohol consumption in Sweden is that it has a "culturally-established drinking pattern" in which alcohol is widely used "as a means of intoxication rather than a table drink".[3] Sweden is generally said to having typical Nordic intoxication oriented drinking habits. In other words, when it comes to drinking, the aim is to get drunk. As a matter of fact, the expression 'drinking' in Sweden already expresses that a state of drunkenness will probably be reached. This is sometimes said to mean that Swedes are not able to use alcohol in a controlled or moderate way. It is often said by Swedes that for some reason or the other they are unable to do this.

The explanations for the Swedish consumption pattern that are generally given vary; naturalistic, climatological, and social factors are involved. It is sometimes said that the intoxication oriented consumption pattern is one of the inheritances of the fierce and wild Viking spirit, a theory that could be described as naturalistic. A second explanation puts the emphasis on the climatological factors (the cold, dark climate), in other words boring natural conditions that, in the spirit of Montesquieu, would have led to the Swedish melancholic psyche and, consequently, has generated a desire for intoxication.[4] Another, third possible reason that helps to explain the drinking pattern has to do with the traditional work mentality of the Swedes in which the (social) drink functions as a 'reward' for the work that has been done. Traditionally, many Swedes working in the woods were away from home for a long period of time. Coming home, a glass would be raised for the end of the working period, and the start of leisure time.

Even today Swedes are very strict in making the distinction between work and leisure time, and drinking is, for most people, limited to the weekends. As a rule, Swedes drink alcohol on Friday and Saturday nights (not on Sundays since Mondays follow...). The separation between the working week and the weekend is also defined as most people buy their alcohol for the weekend on Friday afternoon, after work. Because of the fact that liquor stores (*systembolaget*) are state controlled and have limited opening hours (namely only on weekdays) it is not possible to buy alcohol during the weekends, except low alcohol beer available in the supermarkets. As a rule, the quantity that is bought on Friday afternoon should be the amount required for the weekend. As a result, few Swedes keep alcohol at home during the week.

It is puzzling why so many Swedes buy their alcohol on Fridays, which may mean they have to queue. Why not shop on Wednesday or Thursday when there are less people in the *systembolaget?* One could also wonder why they only buy the amount they need for their weekend consumption. It is sometimes thought, especially by non-Swedes, that the explanation is that Swedes are unable to control their alcohol: having it at home during the week, would inevitably lead the Swede to reach for the bottle. Consequently, as some kind of self protection measure, Swedes buy alcohol on Fridays, for the weekend. However, it is more likely that alcohol marks the start of a period of leisure time, which explains why Swedes buy their alcohol on Fridays.

A possible explanation of the Swedish intoxication oriented drinking pattern that is rarely mentioned has to do with Swedish culture and mentality, for which alcohol use can be very functional. The Swedish drinking pattern seems particularly appropriate in regard to the shyness and inhibitions of Swedes. These traits might be understood by looking at the social rules and obligations Swedish society generally imposes upon people. The (internalised) social norms in Sweden, prescribing how one is supposed to behave, are oriented towards controlling feelings and not expressing too much emotion. The fact that one does not often see Swedes laughing easily or losing their temper are indications of this restrained emotional display. Foreigners report the Swedes to be 'cold' and the Swedes even see themselves as 'stiff'.[5]

The behaviour of the – normally – emotionally disciplined Swedes can change dramatically when alcohol comes into the picture. Things that people are usually not 'allowed' to do, now suddenly become possible or can be overcome. As Daun has put it:

"One of the social and psychological functions of drinking in Swedish culture is to lessen the individual's fear of making a fool of him – or herself – for example the anxiety people feel about saying the wrong thing. Instead, under the influence, it is permitted to be 'too' aggressive, 'too' sentimental, 'too' loud or gay. The individual then never – or seldom – is accountable for breaking the norms. [...] What matters to the drinker is less the psychological effects of alcohol than the 'cultural ticket' to a freer and more irresponsible pattern of social interaction."[6]

In this respect, alcohol can be functional in the way it is used as a means of 'stepping out' of the social control system and letting one's hair down. When alcohol is used, people are more or less excused to do things they would, under normal conditions, not be allowed to. This 'deviant' behaviour that manifests itself after drinking, is not interpreted as being the person's responsibility, but alcohol is blamed on causing this 'strange' conduct. Therefore, alcohol can be used as an excuse for this 'irresponsible' behaviour.

This hypothesis might be confirmed by the fact that it seems that Swedes are not really as drunk as they appear to be. To some extent they seem to be acting or dramatising their drunkenness. Alcohol can be useful to reach this state. The fact of being or seeming drunk, 'allows' people to do things that would otherwise, without alcohol, be socially unacceptable. In this respect it is relevant to note that public drunkenness and the corresponding behaviour, are more or less socially accepted in Sweden, at least to a much larger extent than in other (non Nordic) Western countries.

Notwithstanding the drinking habits of the Swedes, things are slowly changing though and becoming more similar to the patterns in the rest of Europe, especially among young people. It should not be forgotten this is the case in other fields as well. Ironically, recently a new expression has come into use to describe a new alcohol consumption pattern that is developing in Sweden: 'European drinking'. This term is used to define drinking one or two glasses after work, without reaching a state of drunkenness.

So it appears that an end may come to the traditional intoxication-oriented drinking pattern of the Swedes, or that this pattern will at least be modified. It would be wrong to think that the new drinking pattern would mean that a form of self-regulation will suddenly develop. There has actually always been some form of self-regulation. What it comes down to is that alcohol and drinking alcohol are now gaining different *functions*. When discussing alcohol consumption patterns with Swedes, they tend to reconcile relatively easily to the 'fact' they cannot control alcohol. It is almost seen as an unalterable fact of life. Yet, this argument is not very convincing considering that Swedes are generally very self-disciplined. For example, considering the working conditions and the high degree of freedom and responsibility employees – even those in the lower ranks – have, it is hard to imagine Swedes would be undisciplined to such an extent they could not be able to handle alcohol. This situation in which one actually shirks one's responsibility, is sometimes explained by the external control model that has characterised Swedish alcohol policy since the nineteenth century. In other words, because of the external control policy, people have hardly learned to deal with alcohol in a 'responsible' way. What seems of much more importance than these possible explanations of traditional drinking patterns, is that for one reason or the other, the function of alcohol simply was to get intoxicated. This is now slowly changing.

Alcohol Policy
The aim of Swedish alcohol policy is to reduce the total consumption of alcohol. The reason for having this policy is to reduce the social and medical damage that results from alcohol consumption. The general strategy of limiting alcohol consumption is to restrict the availability of alcohol. The main means to reach this goal are the state monopoly on alcohol and the price mechanism.[7] Before going into that question, the background to understand this policy will be discussed, such as the temperance movement, the restrictive alcohol policy during the twentieth century, and the total consumption model that gives the scientific basis of the actual alcohol policy.

It has been pointed out that Sweden belongs to the so-called vodka belt, the zone of countries with a tradition of stronger liquors like vodka. In the nineteenth century the temperance movement would get a foothold in Swedish society and be of great influence. It is for this reason Sweden is one of the (nine) temperance cultures: the English speaking cultures of the us, Canada, the uk, Australia, and New Zealand; and the Nordic societies of Finland, Sweden, Norway, and Iceland.[8] It is interesting to note that in all these countries, historically, people drank a considerable portion of their alcohol as distilled liquor (mainly, vodka, gin, rum, or whiskey). Another characteristic of these cultures is that they are predominantly Protestant.[9] Again, it should be noted that temperance cultures are not the heaviest drinkers; today they consume significantly less pure alcohol per capita than non-temperance societies.[10]

The goal of the temperance movement was to achieve total abstinence of alcohol and a complete ban on alcohol. The temperance movement was particularly strong at the end of the nineteenth century, and was one of the main social movements of the time, having strong links with the labour movement. Temperance movements emphasised the damaging properties of alcohol. For example, it was argued that alcohol destroyed a drinker's abilities of self-control and self-discipline, and that it would weaken the higher and moral portions of the brain. "Temperance supporters in the nineteenth century also maintained that alcohol was an inherently addicting drug (the way people often think of heroin today), and that it eventually enslaved people."[11]

Despite their influence and strong popular roots, the temperance movement has never managed to achieve total prohibition in Sweden. Eventually the outcome was a restrictive system by state monopoly on alcohol sales. In 1917 the 'Bratt System' was introduced, based on the propositions of Dr Ivan Bratt. This system consisted of a government monopoly on the sale of alcohol, and a ration book entitling people to buy alcohol up to a certain quota. The control system led to an increase in alcohol prices, especially of the strong liquors. Rules were strict, the minimum age to get a ration book was 25 and before it was issued an examination was carried out to establish whether the applicant was abusing alcohol and whether his financial position was satisfactory. The authorities could reduce the ration or withdraw the ration book if a person was not purchasing in conformity with the rules.[12] Generally the husband as head of family was the ration book holder, having the right to buy up to four litres of spirits a month. Married women had no ration books, whilst single women received a smaller ration.[13] Furthermore, the supply of alcohol was restricted in restaurants, in particular for women and young people.[14] This also explains why Sweden has never developed a working class restaurant culture.

In 1922 a referendum was held on the question whether Sweden should have a total ban on the sale and consumption of alcohol, in other words an alcohol-free society. A very small majority of 51% voted against this ban. The ration system had actually led to a drop in the support for total prohibition. The temperance movement had from its inception been against this ration system, since it was advocating total abstinence. It was in this period, the 1920s and early 1930s, that society's control was the strongest with home inspections, anonymous information-gathering, and databanks.[15] The ration system experienced growing criticism, especially after the Second World War. For example, it was claimed that the ration system created an artificial demand for spirits.[16] Following this claim, it was thought alcohol consumption would reduce if the ration system were abolished. Eventually the system was abolished in 1955. Abolition of the ration system did not, however, lead to a decrease in alcohol consumption. During the first years after the abolition of the ration book system there was an steep increase in consumption, but increased taxations in 1956 and 1958 meant to curb the increase, brought consumption down to its former level.[17] In the 1960s and 1970s alcohol consumption would see another increase, until it reached its peak in 1976 with 7.7 registered litres pure alcohol per capita.[18] After 1976 the trend shows a slow decrease in the registered alcohol consumption finding a 'stabilised' level of about six litres per capita (of the population over 15 years) in the late 1980s and 1990s.[19] It should be remembered that the alcohol consumption figures just given, only show the registered alcohol sales. Obviously, unregistered alcohol consumption, consisting of both imported and home-made alcohol, is alleged to be substantial, since prices are high and alcohol is not easily available. Unregistered alcohol consumption are assumed to be about 25-30% of the registered alcohol sales, which makes the total per capita (pure) alcohol consumption to be around 8 litres.[20] With these figures it should be borne in mind that the temperance movement has not yet died out in Sweden; it is believed that between 10% and 12% of the adult population do not drink at all.

Despite the abolition of the ration book system in 1955, several important parts of the restrictive alcohol policy have remained in force until today. The main mechanisms in limiting total alcohol consumption are availability and price. The *systembolaget*, the State-owned alcohol retailing outlets, are central to the implementation of the alcohol policy. These outlets have the monopoly of all alcohol sales, except lighter beer not containing more than 3.5% alcohol, which can be bought in supermarkets. There are 395 *systembolaget* in the whole country, and they are open until six p.m. on weekdays. Hence, during the weekends it is not possible to legally buy stronger beer, wine or liquors, except of course in bars, restaurants, and clubs. The sale of alcohol in the *systembolaget* is restricted to people of 20 and over, whilst 18 year-olds are allowed to buy in a bar. The fact that alcohol is restricted for teenagers, means that many procure alcohol illegally. The secret way that this is done, can remind one of the way people buy illicit drugs in other countries. The fact that the alcohol on the black market is usually the strong, home-made liquors containing 40 or 50% alcohol, means in practice that some teenagers start drinking strong liquors instead of weaker alcoholic drinks like beer and wine.[21]

The State monopoly on alcohol sales also makes it possible to have a price policy, which forms another essential mechanism of Swedish alcohol policy. The goal of high taxes is not only to limit total alcohol consumption, but it is also used to encourage people to consume weaker alcoholic drinks like beer and wine, by putting a high tax on strong spirits. Hence, the price mechanism is used to achieve a different consumption pattern in which people are drinking 'more' weak alcohol to the detriment of the traditional strong liquors.

Besides the instruments of availability and price policy, there is a ban on advertising and information is spread about the health risks of alcohol use. Alcohol preventive measures are for a large part in the hands of the popular movements and other non-governmental organisations such as youth groups, sport clubs, scouting, education organisations, unions and church organisations.[22]

The actual Swedish alcohol policy finds its scientific basis in a WHO report that dates from 1975: *Alcohol Control Policies in a Public Health Perspective*.[23] The alcohol policy that was to be implemented in 1977 after the recommendations of the *Alcohol Policy Commission* was founded on the theoretical model of this publication: the total consumption model, which suggests a correlation between the total alcohol consumption and the total damage caused by alcohol, such as liver cirrhosis, pancreatitis, certain types of cancer, alcoholism and cancer.[24] Furthermore, it is alleged that the more individuals are drinking, the more people will change from moderate drinking to heavier forms of drinking and alcoholism. Conversely, the less people drink, the less the alcohol damage will be. Since it is assumed that alcohol consumption is influenced by its availability, the implication is that the policy should focus on limiting availability.

The total damage caused by alcohol is, of course, difficult to measure and varies according to drinking patterns. Statistics show clearly that in wine cultures, medical injuries like liver cirrhosis are common. On the other hand it is true that in countries that have intoxication-oriented drinking patterns, where one drinks on fewer occasions, the medical damage is generally lower, but the 'social costs' might be higher. In Sweden a clear correlation has been observed between violence and drinking, as alcohol is involved in 70% to 80% of all crimes of violence. A criticism of the Swedish alcohol model could be that it focuses too much on the medical costs, and not enough on the social costs, which are much more difficult to quantify.

In 1993 a research team has studied the possible effects of a reduction of alcohol prices in Sweden.[25] If the prices were to be adjusted to the Danish level (meaning a price reduction of 50% for beer, 25% for wine, and 15% for spirits), it is estimated this would entail a growth of pure alcohol consumption of 1.5 litre per capita per annum. This rise in alcohol consumption was supposed to lead to a 13% increase in fatal accidents, a 14% increase in suicides, a 18% increase in murders. Furthermore, alcohol-related deaths would rise with 1,000 a year and the number of assaults by 5,000.[26]

Despite being modified over time, since the nineteenth century the Swedish alcohol policy has been restrictive and the emphasis has been placed on external control rather than on individual self-control. As mentioned before, things are changing. A shift is currently taking place from the external control model to another system in which internal control is inevitably going to play a more prominent role. This is partly due to an apparently natural development in which one moves from intoxication-oriented drinking patterns to more moderate 'European drinking'. It is also important to note that alcohol has become much more available in Sweden over recent years. For example, today there are many more bars than a few years ago, the reason being that the rules to obtain an alcohol license have been relaxed. Until a few years ago catering establishments were obliged to serve food to get an alcohol licence, and for restaurants the restriction was that 70% of the turnover had to be food-related. Today one can see more bars and restaurants serving alcohol, as long as they serve some kind of food. With this increased availability of alcohol, a bar culture is developing.

Concomitant with these developments, consumer prices for alcohol have dropped over recent years. Thus, alcohol has become more widely available at a cheaper price. In this way, the Swedish alcohol policy is becoming more similar to more liberal alcohol policies. Of course, these developments cannot be separated from Sweden's joining of the European Union in 1995. The EU and its regulations make it increasingly difficult to have monopolies, like the Swedish state monopoly on the sales of stronger alcohol beverages. During the negotiations for EU membership, Sweden had to give up its monopoly on wholesaling, distilling, imports, and exports of alcohol. The monopoly of the *systembolaget* on the sales to restaurants also came to an end. Only the monopoly of the *systembolaget* for retailing was retained.[27] These political developments imply it is inevitable that Sweden will gradually move towards an alcohol policy with less emphasis on external control, and more importance attributed to internal self-control.

4.3 Popular Movements and Lobby Groups

In section 2.5 the role of Sweden's popular movements was discussed. It has been shown that these popular movements play an important role in Swedish society at large. Popular movements, irrespective of the field they operate in, play an essential role in Swedish society in which they are highly integrated. Every popular movement is eligible to receive a subsidy from the Swedish State. To be called a Popular Movement, the organisation must be nationally established and have many local branches throughout the country.

Traditionally, a number of popular movements are active in the field of alcohol, like the several temperance movements that exist. It previously has been stated that in the nineteenth century they were, together with the Labour Movement and the Free Church Movement, among the first important popular movements in Sweden. Today, temperance movements still exist, but they have lost a lot of the impact they once had. Temperance movements are slowly dying out, the membership is falling, and the movements are basically composed of elderly people.

Popular movements active in the field of drugs play a more active role. They actually have played a vital part in the development of the Swedish drug policy. One could even say that these popular movements can be regarded as being the driving force behind the development of a stricter drug policy. As a matter of fact, the Swedish drug policy cannot be understood without taking into account the role some of these Popular Movements have played, and are still playing.

In this section the main non-governmental organisations active in the field of drugs will be discussed: RFHL, RNS, FMN, the Carnegie Institute, and ECAD. This section does not give a broad description of all these popular movement, their organisation and history.[28] The relevant organisations will first be discussed briefly, which will be followed by outlining the role they have played at various times. Besides the social movements, some of the other lobbying groups, like European Cities Against Drugs (ECAD), the Carnegie Institute and their 'coalitions' will also be discussed in this section. This overview is to give an idea of the importance of lobbying and pressure groups in shaping Sweden's drug policy as it is today.

In the 1960s the main popular movement working in the field of drug policy was the Swedish Association for Assistance to Drug Users (RFHL), in short a client organisation. The majority of RFHL is composed of (ex-)drug users. RFHL was founded in 1965, the same year the prescription experiment started, which was supported by the RFHL. In the 1980s RFHL became involved in therapeutic communities. As a result it became partly a treatment institution. As compared to the other popular movements working in the field of drugs and the general viewpoints held about drugs in Sweden, RFHL can be considered as a progressive organisation. It has been a supporter of needle exchange programmes, and it has been opposed to compulsory treatment and the criminalisation of drug use. Generally speaking, RFHL is one of the rare organisations that is not part of the broad consensus in Swedish society about the drug policy.

During the 1970s and especially the 1980s a great shift took place. RFHL lost a lot of its influence and power in favour of three other popular movements that developed as the most influential popular movements in this field. These three organisations are Parents Against Drugs (FMN), Hassela Solidarity, and the Association for a Drug-Free Society (RNS). These three organisations have different points of departure, but are all striving for the same principles in the field of drugs: a drug-free society and a correspondingly strict drug policy. These movements can be regarded as the main driving forces behind Sweden's drug policies. They have actually managed to get their principles of a drug-free society adopted by the Swedish authorities. Still today, FMN, Hassela Solidarity, and RNS play an important role in shaping Swedish drug policy, or keeping it as it is.

Parent's Against Drugs (FMN) was founded in 1968 and is basically composed of parents of drug addicts, primarily mothers. FMN is a national organisation having about 40 local branches and a few thousand members. FMN's main activities are supporting parents of drug addicts, the setting up of self help groups and organising training courses. FMN also had two therapeutic communities and hundreds of 'centres' for drug addicts, such as family care centres. Although FMN is merely working on a local level, it can be considered an important pressure group on the national level, trying to get its views through to politicians and influencing public opinion. On the national level FMN has the same objectives as RNS (a restrictive drug policy), but FMN is less militant and also shares some of its ideas with RFHL, like e.g. the client's perspective. The person who was for a long time the central figure of FMN is Johan Danielsson, but he recently ceased these activities.

Hassela Solidarity is a popular movement that was founded in 1969 by the former military and teacher K.A. Westerberg. In that same year an 'educational' community was founded in the village Hassela, 350 kilometres north of Stockholm. Today Hassela has four communities in Sweden; two in Hassela, one in Värmland (near Gothenburg), and one on the main island on the east coast, Gotland.

The idea of the Hassela communities is not to 'treat', but to 're-educate' problem teenagers from the age of 13 to 21. Teenagers with psychological problems or psychiatric disorders are excluded from the Hassela programmes. A majority of the teenagers was taking drugs and/or (to a lesser extent) alcohol, many having a criminal background. In recent years, 60% to 70% of the students had a (second generation) immigrant background, many coming from the working class suburbs. Hassela considers that taking drugs is "like doing the wrong things in life", and Hassela is there to "learn how to live an ordinary life".[29]

Most students in the communities arrived there through LVU, the compulsory care programme for young people. It is the social services that decide to what kind of institution the young people are directed, one of the possibilities being Hassela, for which the social services have to pay 1,600 to 1,700 kronor a day (US$ 210). To lower the costs, a city can negotiate a larger contract with Hassela. For example, the city of Stockholm has a contract for a 'standard' eight places in the Hassela communities. These communities are actually companies that make their income by fulfilling contracts with social services from local communities. All four companies joined the popular movement *Hassela Solidarity*.

The four Hassela communities have a total number of about 65 students (as they are called) and about 40 staff members. To be re-educated, the students stay in one of the Hassela communities for a period of 12 to 15 months. This period is generally followed by a supplementary course of

12 months, which consists of a semi-independent life outside the community, in the Hassela village.

In each community the students and the Hassela staff try to live and work as one big family. Education takes a prominent place within the Hassela programme. If the students are not going to school or are having other types of education (like leadership education), they work within the community. The rules in the communities are very strict. For this reason Hassela has received a lot of criticism in the past and has been sometimes labelled 'Fascist'. It is known that the tough approach has 'destroyed' some former students. In the 1970s Hassela is said to have adopted a less tough approach. Hassela justifies its policy though by pointing out its high success rate.[30]

Since it was founded by Westerberg, Hassela has had a clear working class and social democratic background. Hassela supports working class moral and values and does not hide that one of the goals of the educational programmes is to transform the students into 'normal citizens', in other words, 'workers' or social democrats. Coercion is accepted in this process. In fact, when it comes to drug use, Hassela considers compulsory treatment or education certainly justified, or even necessary, to stop a person taking the substances.

Except offering re-education, Hassela plays an active role in the field of drug policy, especially in carrying out its ideas about the necessity of a restrictive drug policy. For this reason Hassela not only offers prevention programmes in some hundred schools in Sweden, but more importantly Hassela tries to influence public opinion and politicians. Compared to the size of the organisation, its 2,000 individual members, and its main activity, which is re-educating approximately 60 students a year, Hassela is tremendously influential. One of the reasons for Hassela's power and influence is that it shares its ideological background with the Social Democratic Party. The close links between Hassela and the Social Democratic Party can be illustrated by the fact that former head and the 'brain' behind the organisation, Vidar Andersson, is today a member of parliament for the Social Democratic Party. As a politician Andersson plays an important role in drug policy debates and has recently, in 1997, been appointed the expert on drug policy by Prime Minister Göran Persson.

Hassela has such good contacts that they deal directly with the politicians and not with lower-ranking civil servants. One should not forget Hassela is obliged to maintain good contacts with politicians, since it is financially dependent on treatment funding, that is sanctioned by politicians. However, good political connections are insufficient to explain Hassela's impact. To be influential, the first thing that counts is to be backed by public opinion. Hassela has a very strong lobby and is selling its work and ideology in a refined way, by using leftist, social democratic rhetoric. For example, Hassela claims that "intoxicated, ignorant and disorganised people are easy to manipulate and oppress and quite often they do not take any part in the creation of a future society", and states further that "it is beyond doubt that the existence of drugs is one, if not the one, cause of the drug problem".[31] Hassela clearly states that the basis of its activities is the struggle for democracy, solidarity, equality, and justice. In this struggle for a better society, Hassela opposes very strongly any drug legalisation initiatives, that are considered 'easy solutions'.

To reach many people Hassela has a very active public relations policy and has good contacts with the Swedish media. To see the attention Hassela gets, one would think the movement is much more important and greater than it actually is. Someone who has a key position in the Hassela movement is Torgny Peterson, today chiefly working as the director of *European Cities Against Drugs* (ECAD). In the past Peterson was the chairman of Hassela. Today, he is still playing a key role as the man behind, and responsible for, many of their publications and public relations activities. Peterson is also Director of the *Hassela Nordic Network* (HNN), the international branch of Hassela whose aim is to prevent the legalisation of drugs.

Another very influential popular movement active in the field of drugs is the *Association for a Drug-Free Society* (RNS). Apart from being influential, RNS is also the most militant popular movement in this field. As the name indicates, RNS strives for a drug-free society. RNS was founded in 1969 by Nils Bejerot, the police doctor who has already been discussed in section 3.3 as the person who wrote about the (alleged) effects of the legal prescription experiment, from which he drew the conclusion that it was actually the origin of the Swedish drug epidemic (see also the following section). Bejerot had always been opposed to the experiment and wanted an organisation to fight for a restrictive drug policy. Yngve Persson, a retired union activist and Social Democrat got the RNS organisation together.

RNS is a popular movement with a somewhat revolutionary and combative character, once described by its founder Bejerot as a guerrilla movement.[32] As such RNS does not accept any government funding, although it is entitled to it, as a popular movement. Therefore, RNS is dependant on the contributions of its members. Thanks to an active membership policy, partly consisting of going from door to door, RNS has experienced a growing number of members in the 1990s, totalling 18,000 today. Most are passive members, paying 200 kronor (US$ 25) a year for which they also receive the RNS magazine. One could wonder why an organisation demanding a stricter drug policy in a country that already has a strict policy, manages to attract such an increasing membership. The first answer to this question is that, although drug use in Sweden does not manifest itself on a large scale in comparison to other European countries, drug use is on the increase in the 1990s, which would 'necessitate' more controlling measures. The second explanation has to do with the Sweden's recent EU membership. The EU joining was exploited by RNS by presenting Europe as a danger where evils like drugs are coming from, eager to threaten the secure, drug-free Sweden and from which the legalisation lobby derives, which should be fought against.

Just like Hassela, RNS achieves its potential of influencing the general public on drug questions, for which it maintains a very active lobby. RNS not only has members writing articles to newspapers, but also organises petitions, and local and national demonstrations, resulting in a powerful lobby on both the local and national government level.

It was mentioned previously that the role of the popular movements discussed in this section, is vital for understanding the gradual harshening of Swedish drug policy. Popular movements like FMN, *Hassela Solidarity*, and RNS are constantly trying to get support for their ideas for which influence on the general public is essential. Good contacts with the (popular) media are, of course, elementary in this process. They know how to play on people's feelings in a refined way, for example by using traditional Social Democratic rhetoric and by capitalising on the declining *trygghet* (security) Swedes are facing in the 1990s. As has just been pointed out, the situation is often presented as if the Swedish haven is being threatened from the outside, in particular by (continental) Europe, where drugs are alleged to be coming from.

As a result of their influence on the general public, popular movements have managed to win political power. They can put drugs on the political agenda, and, consequently, put pressure on politicians. Because of this constant pressure, a process has been set in motion that is now almost impossible to stop. Drugs has almost become a national issue, to such an extent that it is nowadays impossible for politicians *not* to be tough on drugs; if they were, they would soon find it to their political cost. This can be illustrated by the fact that if politicians do not take a tough stance on drugs, for example during speaking engagements and political campaigns, they will receive criticism from the popular movements, that will use their influence and power to attack the soft attitude on drugs. As Per Johansson of RNS points out, "if you want to stay in power, you can not say you want a more liberal approach to drugs. It would be your political death".[33] This situation has developed to such an extent that even the word 'liberal' has gained a negative connotation. To 'eliminate' someone who does not agree with the success of the Swedish drug policy, it is sufficient to label that person a 'drug liberal'. With such a qualification one is powerless in drug debates, and one loses all credibility.

In Sweden there is no real political rift on the drug issue; both left and right wing parties support the restrictive drug policy. This was, however, not always the case. During the 1980s it was the conservative party that seized the opportunity to capitalise on the drug issue and put it on the political agenda. One could say, this set a process in motion in which drugs were to become an increasingly political issue, especially during election campaigns. Once again, it should be noted that the politicians are under constant pressure from the popular movements. When in motion, it is almost impossible for parties not to take part, even the Social Democratic Party that, at first, did not want to take more restrictive measures. This became very clear during the 1980s, when drugs were to become a political issue.

In the previous chapter a description was given of the gradual harshening of drug legislation. Following the experiences of the conservative parties during the 1976 election campaign (which they won), the Social Democrats, for their part, also made drugs a major election theme the year of the 1982 elections. When elected to office, they appointed a committee to investigate how the drug problem could be tackled more effectively. Among the issues brought up by the committee, was the question whether drug use should be criminalised. When the committee broached this issue, a consensus was far from reached. There were some tendencies wanting to criminalise drug use, the main reason being to show a clear stance on the unacceptability of drugs use, but the government's committee struck a different note. It was of the opinion this would make treatment and care more difficult and rejected criminalisation.

FMN and RNS soon reacted by demanding the criminalisation of drug use, what RNS especially had always wanted. As shall be discussed in the next section, RNS founder Bejerot considers the drug user to be the irreplaceable and weak link of the drug chain, from which follows that drug policy should focus on hitting the drug user. This viewpoint was supported by the right-wing opposition and some Social Democrat MPs. FMN and RNS then organised a petition asking for the criminalisation of drug use, claiming that they had collected almost half a million signatures. Even more significant was an opinion survey indicating that criminalisation was supported by 95% of the population.[34] Another step in this campaign for criminalising drug use was a march from the province of Dalecarlia (in central Sweden) to Stockholm, a reminder of the past when farmers marched to the capital to have their demands heard.[35] Notwithstanding the pressure that was applied, the Social Democratic government was not willing to give in.

In the following elections of 1985 the drug issue returned to the political agenda. The conservatives promised to criminalise drug use when it came to power. The Social Democratic Party, realising how the drugs issue could be capitalised upon, tried to avoid the issue becoming an election theme and said it wanted to wait for the results of the Public Prosecutor's study. This though, was not accepted by their opponents like FMN and RNS, that replied by organising demonstrations. When the Social Democratic government took power after the 1985 elections, it still did not want to criminalise drug use, one reason being this was what the Public Prosecutor had recommended in his study. This decision caused another wave of debates and criticism. Under the pressure of the popular movements and the opposition, both backed by public opinion, the government eventually was obliged to criminalise drug use.

Besides dealing with popular movements, attention should also be drawn to some other factors, such as the lobbies of both the treatment sector and the police, and organisations like the Carnegie Institute, and European Cities Against Drugs (ECAD). Although less important and influential than FMN, Hassela, and RNS, their role should not be underestimated.

Since treatment is as one of the pillars of the Swedish drug policy, a substantial amount of money is allocated for drug treatment. Most treatment in Sweden takes place in drug-free treatment centres, many of which are located in rural areas. As shall be discussed in section 5.4, the emphasis of treatment in Sweden was put on long-term, in-patient programmes. It was by no means exceptional that a person was put in drug treatment for a period of two years. Because of its size, the treatment sector, among which one also finds Hassela, is inclined to have a very strong lobby. In the second half of the 1980s the treatment lobby became strong, since HIV and Aids started to manifest themselves. The treatment sector could 'use' these threats to ask for more money to be allocated for drug treatment, in which it succeeded. Because of the HIV threat, huge sums of money were made available to find every intravenous drug user in the country. In this situation, the treatment sector, the social workers and the police had shared interests. One could say they formed some kind of 'coalition' to ask for more resources to be able to tackle the problem.

The criminologists Leif Lenke & Börje Olsson have described the growing influence of the police lobby. For example, in the 1960s the police, already unhappy about the legal experiment, seized the opportunity that was offered by the conclusions that were drawn by (police doctor) Bejerot to ask for a stricter approach. When a national police board was created in 1965, the police gained a stronger lobby and became an important factor in influencing Swedish drug policy.[36] Bejerot's conclusions were "given massive support and promotion by a police organisation that probably has no equivalent in Western society when it comes to the degree of centralisation and political influence in society".[37] Moreover, Lenke & Olsson state that the "organisation's central bureaucracy numbers over 1,000 people, which constitutes a substantial force for lobbying due to its strong connections with the media, especially the tabloid press".[38]

It is interesting to see that the police increasingly worked together with a research centre, the *Carnegie Institute*. Founded in 1982 the aim of the institute is to carry out research on questions like drug use, criminality and other related issues, and to spread this information. Nils Bejerot became scientific director, a position he was to hold until his death in 1988. Another key person in the Carnegie Institute was Carl Persson, who was head of the national police from 1965 to 1978.[39] The current director is Jonas Hartelius, who is said to carry the message of his 'intellectual father' Bejerot further. Hartelius is often consulted by the police and judicial system to give 'scientific' facts about drugs. The police and the Carnegie Institute seem to have formed some kind of 'coalition', considering the fact that the Hartelius has, in his capacity of expert, written many articles about drugs in the police magazine.

The Carnegie Institute does not want to publicise where it obtains its funding.[40] Yet, the budget must be substantial, given the fact the institute has a research programme that has resulted in 26 books since 1982, and the fact that it hands out awards to individuals who have proved themselves praiseworthy in the fight against drugs. In 1993 the journalist's prize went to RNS journalist Pelle Olsson, who made two trips to the Netherlands the following year, resulting in the book *Holland och Narkotikan – Tre dog en blev galen* ('Holland and Drugs – Three died, one got crazy').

The most recently established organisation founded in Sweden and playing an active role in the drug policy area is *European Cities Against Drugs* (ECAD). ECAD was founded as a reaction to the 1989 Frankfurt Resolution, that pronounced itself in favour of the decriminalisation of cannabis and a harm reduction approach. The consequence was the foundation of European Cities Against Drugs (ECAD), based on the Stockholm Declaration. ECAD adheres to a restrictive drug policy, and is opposed to discussions on both the decriminalisation of cannabis and heroin distribution.

Founded in Stockholm in 1993, ECAD was getting funding from Swedish government institutions, like the National Institute of Public Health, the National Board of Health and Welfare, and the Ministry of Social Affairs. An office in the City Hall of Stockholm was put at the disposal of ECAD by the City of Stockholm (one of the members) till the year 2002. Today, ECAD no longer gets funding from Swedish State institutions; it now depends on the contributions of its 178 members, consisting of both cities and villages. The contribution varies from £150 to £6,000 a year, depending on the size of the 'city'. ECAD's budget today is around two million kronor (US$ 250,000).[41] ECAD is particularly strong in Scandinavia, Greece, and non-German-speaking Switzerland. Moreover, ECAD has a large number of European capitals amongst its members, like Berlin, London, and Paris.

ECAD has an office in which three people work. Apart from a secretary, there is Torgny Peterson, the chairman, and Åke Setréus, the director. Both Peterson and Setréus work for ECAD on a part-time basis, positions they combine with key roles in other organisations. Peterson is also acting director of the international branch of Hassela, the Hassela Nordic Network (HNN), whilst Setréus works in a government institution, the National Board of Health and Welfare, where he is responsible for allotting money to organisations working in the field of drugs. Hence, he was in also the position to allocate money for ECAD in the first years of its existence.

Another key person in ECAD and one of its founders, is Carl Cederschiöld, who also represents the (conservative) opposition as first vice president of the municipal executive board of Stockholm and Vice Mayor of Stockholm. His wife, Christina Cederschiöld, is also active in the field, among other things through her work as a member of the European Parliament for the conservatives.

As has been shown in this section, several pressure group and lobbying organisations are relevant to understand Swedish drug policy and its gradually increasingly restrictive character. The police, mainly since there is a national police force, has played its part in this development. More important has been the role of pressure groups that were discussed in this section. Since 1996 the Swedish National Police has had a new commissioner, former minister Sten Heckscher. Heckscher does not have the reputation of being tough on drugs. Towards the end of 1996 he gave an interview to RNS magazine *Narkotikafrågan* in which at one point he said to the interviewer: "why are you always so terribly repressive?" and "why do you always want a lot of things done to people who have not committed any crimes?"[42]

Considering the different organisations that have been the driving forces behind the Swedish drug policy as it is today, the observation has to be made that the hard core drug-fighters wanting a drug-free society actually consists of a small circle of people. Whereas in the past someone like RNS-founder the late Nils Bejerot played a crucial role in the origin of the restrictive drug policy (see also next section), a person like Torgny Peterson has now assumed this role, making sure this approach is not relaxed.

The popular movements have got what they wanted; they have succeeded in getting the Swedish government to adopt their goal of a drug-free society. In this respect one could wonder why the popular movements have not stopped or relaxed their fight for a drug-free society and a restrictive drug policy. The reason is that Sweden's EU membership is considered as a threat to the restrictive Swedish policy, since more liberal tendencies are perceived to be coming from the continent. This explains why the popular movements continue their struggle, not only in Sweden, but even more so in Europe. Since Sweden has joined the EU, Swedes have become known for the fanatic way some of them fight against any drug liberalisation initiatives. In the eyes of the other member States, Swedes may make a strange impression and it does happen that in European meetings and debates Swedes make fools of themselves by the almost religious approach with which they treat the drug question. The Swedish authorities are now placed in a dilemma. The authorities are unhappy their country is sometimes taken to be represented by militant drug fighters, whose status is not always clear. For example, when ECAD directors Peterson and Setréus are making their case in Europe, they are sometimes thought to be representing Sweden or the City of Stockholm. This confusion is, of course, partly due to the double functions they occupy, like the case of Setréus who also works for the National Board of Health and Welfare. To their European interlocutors it may not be clear that the Swedes they speak to, are even to Swedish standards considered fanatic and 'extreme'. There are signs the Swedish authorities are unhappy about the militant way an organisation like ECAD 'represents' Sweden in Europe.

4.4 Ideological and Scientific Foundations of the Restrictive Model

In order to understand the Swedish restrictive drug policy, it is essential to point out some of its ideological and scientific foundations. This section will discuss some topics that are relevant here: the theories of Nils Bejerot, and two matters concerning cannabis, the stepping stone or gateway hypothesis, and the scientific evidence meant to prove how dangerous cannabis is.

The Theories of Nils Bejerot

Nils Bejerot has already been mentioned in the previous chapter as the person who conducted a study on the needle marks of police detainees in Stockholm. Over the years Bejerot has played a very active role in the Swedish drug policy debate. Since he appeared on the scene in the 1960s he has argued for a more restrictive drug policy. The previous section described how Bejerot founded RNS, one of the main Swedish organisations and lobbying groups that strives for a restrictive drug policy.

In the beginning Bejerot was not taken very seriously and did not have much influence. He wrote many articles and gave interviews in newspapers, especially in the popular press (tabloids), rarely in the more serious newspapers. Bejerot was very fanatical and the people saw him as an angry old man, for this reason he was disliked by many people.[43] In the course of time, Bejerot's influence grew, to an extent he became a national celebrity. This can be shown by the fact that when his house was burnt down by some angry drug addicts, most newspapers printed this as front page news.

Bejerot has explained his concept of drug use and addiction in his dissertation and other publications.[44] He distinguishes several types of addictions, of which the *epidemic addictions* take the most prominent place and are most relevant with regard to illicit drugs. His definition of epidemic addictions is the following: "Mainly among young, psychologically and socially unstable persons who, usually after direct personal initiation from another abuser, begin to use socially non-accepted, intoxicating drugs to gain euphoria".[45] The point of departure for this definition is the scientific meaning of epidemics, which basically means that a disease has a unusual high incidence defined in time, place and persons and compared with previous experience. Bejerot however, goes further in his concept of epidemic addictions since this definition does not mention contagion, an aspect Bejerot considers of eminent importance when it comes to illicit drug taking. He considers that epidemics of drug abuse have a high psycho-social contagiousness whereby "the availability of the drug is the most important factor in the spread of this form of abuse, once a group of drug abusers has been formed and a drug subculture has arisen in society".[46] This means that one drug user can 'contaminate' another person with similar psychological and social characteristics. This explains the expression Bejerot uses for the spread of drug use, psycho-social contagion, that could also be described as peer pressure. Contagion (c) can be considered as a function of susceptibility of the individual (s) and exposure (e), which can be put in the following formula: $c = s \times e$.

According to Bejerot the drug epidemic spreads quickly, and over longer periods even an exponential growth can be observed. Bejerot has stated that "in most countries" it has been possible to observe such an exponential growth.[47] He mentions the examples of Sweden, where intravenous amphetamine use doubled every thirteen year between 1946-1965, and England where between 1959-1958 the number of heroin users doubled every sixteenth months. One of the 'problems' of the drug epidemics that Bejerot describes is that they do not respect international borders. Again, he refers to the Swedish epidemic of intravenous amphetamine that spread quickly and extensively: after developing in the 1940s in the centre of Stockholm, it spread rapidly to the rest of Sweden (Gothenburg in 1956), and to other countries, such as Finland (1965), Denmark (1966), Norway (1967), and Germany (1972).

Since drug use as it is described by Bejerot has a contagious character, the spread of the epidemic is difficult to tackle. Considering the formula, Bejerot suggests that susceptibility of the individual is difficult to influence. Exposure on the other hand, can be limited by policy. Therefore, society must have a restrictive drug policy to limit general exposure to illicit drugs, which means in practice that the prevalence, and more especially the incidence of drug use should be kept down.

With regard to the policy that should be applied to drug users, Bejerot argues as follows. The policy should target the drug user, since the drug user is the irreplaceable element of the 'drug chain'. Moreover, the danger is that the drug user encourages other people to use drugs as well. Drug dealers can and will be replaced by other dealers in the event of them being arrested. The drug user on the other hand is not replaceable, but can be considered as the motor of the system. To break the chain it is therefore important to target the drug users: "We have to accept the painful fact that we cannot win decisive advances unless drug abuse, the abuser and personal possession are placed in the centre of our strategy."[48]

Bejerot does not believe in repressive law enforcement measures for drug users, but believes that drug users have to take responsibility for their behaviour. With regard to Swedish drug users, he suggests a punishment of one month clearing the forest for the first offence of drug possession, two months for the second, etc. Furthermore, Bejerot believes governments are not able to tackle the problem without popular support, which can be achieved through "broad political agreement and massive information which leads to something like a popular uprising against drug epidemics."[49]

The Stepping Stone Hypothesis

This hypothesis, also known as the gateway hypothesis, basically means that cannabis use will 'automatically' lead to the use of other drugs that are considered more dangerous. One of the most well-known advocates of the stepping stone hypothesis is the controversial scientist Gabriel Nahas, who states that "it appears that the biochemical changes induced by marijuana in the brain result in a drug-seeking, drug taking behaviour, which in many instances will lead the user to experiment with other pleasurable substances".[50] Thus, Nahas argues that cannabis use is likely to 'automatically' create a desire for other drugs, and he furthermore states that "the risk of progressing from marijuana to cocaine or heroin is now well documented".[51]

The stepping stone hypothesis has probably been one of the most widely discussed topics in drug policy debates over the last decades. A lot has been written about it and there is no need to repeat those discussions here. What is important to realise, is that over the years the stepping stone hypothesis has lost a lot of its influence and today is hardly taken seriously by most specialists. The main reasons for this is the absence of any scientific indications – in a biological and pharmacological sense – that support this thesis, nor is there any empirical evidence suggesting such a relationship. It is acknowledged though that, under certain social conditions, a (substantial) number of cannabis users might indeed start using drugs like amphetamines, cocaine, or heroin. If this occurs, it is generally thought, it is not as much due to the substance cannabis, but merely to the circumstances under which cannabis is taken, as in the case of certain subcultures. All things considered, there is more reason to believe it is because of the illegality of cannabis and the way society reacts to its use, or the fact that cannabis use occurs within specific subcultures, that people might progress from cannabis to other drugs, rather than attributing this shift to the pharmacological properties of cannabis.

The objective of this section is not to discuss the stepping stone hypothesis in detail. What is most relevant, is to realise that in Sweden a lot of value is given to this hypothesis. Whereas in most Western countries the stepping stone hypothesis has lost ground and no longer plays an important role in most drug policy debates, it certainly does in Sweden. The impact of this theory has to be placed in the perspective of the influence people like Nils Bejerot and Gabriel Nahas have had in Sweden. These two men, who were personal friends as well, are highly respected by the advocates of a drug-free society. Their theories, although not taken very seriously in mainstream scientific circles, both internationally and in Sweden, are used as a justification for being restrictive on cannabis. In fact, the Swedish drug policy actually focuses on cannabis, since it is alleged 'drug careers' start with this substance.

In this perspective it is relevant to come back to the scientific basis of the Swedish alcohol policy, the total consumption model. This model assumes a relationship between the total consumption of alcohol and the total damage caused by alcohol. The model also suggests that the more individuals are drinking, the more people will change from moderate drinking to heavier forms of drinking. Hence, from a public health point of view the best option is to keep the number of drinkers as low as possible.

It is important to understand this claim, as it is supposed to be valid for illicit drugs as well: the more people start experimenting with drugs (cannabis), the larger the number of drug addicts, and the greater the total damage for society will be. As a result, drug policy should focus on limiting total drug consumption of drugs, to start with any drug experimentation, which in practice means preventing cannabis use. Although at first sight it seems logical to translate the total consumption model of alcohol to the field of illicit drugs, this argument could be considered somewhat naive and unrealistic.

First, the major difference between alcohol on the one hand, and illicit drugs on the other, is the latter being illegal. As a result, a quality control is absent when it comes to drugs. Since illicit substances are in many cases mixed with other substances, that are in some cases more harmful than the illicit drug itself, combined with the fact that the consumer is not aware of what he is actually taking, one could also assume that the harm of a substance increases with its illegal status.

Secondly, another important difference between alcohol and illicit drugs is that the harm caused by alcohol is basically the same – although there exist many different forms of alcoholic drinks. Illicit drugs on the other hand, consist of a wide range of different illicit drugs, each having its own properties to which different 'kinds of harm' can be attributed. Hence, when it comes to illicit drugs, there is no clear correlation between total consumption and total harm.

If one wants to apply the total consumption model to illicit drugs, one could also argue in a very different way. Since one of the objectives of alcohol policy is to achieve a shift from the consumption of stronger liquors to lighter alcohols like beer and wine, all based on the reduction of total harm, it could logically follow drug policy should try to achieve a shift to the consumption of 'lighter drugs'. In any case, whereas the

Swedish alcohol policy could be labelled as 'harm reduction', the drug policy certainly cannot. On the contrary, one could easily argue the Swedish drug policy *increases* harm. Not only is the mortality among drug addicts in Sweden very high (see 6.6), one could also argue that by limiting the availability of a an illicit drug like cannabis, one opens the gate to experimenting with more dangerous substances, either licit or illicit. For example, among 16 year-old school students the prevalence of solvents (like glue and thinner) is actually higher than the prevalence of cannabis.[52]

Finally, one has to wonder to what extent drug use can really be influenced by drug policies. Although it is very tempting to suggest drug use can be affected by policy, one has to question if this really is the case. The American experience, where one observes a repressive drug policy together with a prevalence of drug use that is probably higher than anywhere in Europe, and where increased law enforcement measures have not lead to a decrease in drug use, lead one to think drug use cannot easily be influenced. In this respect it is interesting to note that when the first report of the *European Monitoring Centre for Drugs and Drug Addiction* (EMCDDA) was presented, the director Georges Estievenart has stated that international, cultural factors are much more relevant in explaining drug use than law enforcement measures.

The Dangers of Cannabis

Besides pointing out the risks of cannabis use as a gateway to other drugs, the danger of the cannabis itself is often referred to as the reason for having a restrictive policy on all drugs. Since the goal is a drug-free society, the logical consequence is that any drug use is unacceptable. This means that most effort is put into preventing any experimentation with drugs. Since cannabis generally is the first illicit drug that is encountered, in practice the emphasis is put on preventing cannabis use. As a consequence, cannabis is in a way the 'target' of drug prevention activities, justified by the alleged danger of the properties of this substance.

It is not uncommon in Sweden that a convention on drugs begins by stating there are 'hundreds or thousands of scientific articles' that show how dangerous cannabis is. In many of the interviews that have been conducted it also appeared that many people refer to 'studies' that show how dangerous cannabis actually is, but when asked in detail about these studies, most of the time the question remains unanswered. The dangers of cannabis that are usually referred to are cannabis psychosis, lost of fertility, genetic modifications (which can also affect descendants), disturbances of the sex hormones, the flashback (the cannabis high can coming back at an unexpected moment), and a higher chance of suicide.

Cannabis psychosis is often presented as the major risk of cannabis use. A second danger of cannabis use that is often heard concerns the correlation between violent deaths and cannabis use. A study conducted by Jovan Rajs of the Department of Forensic Medicine, and Anna Fugelstad of the St. Görans Hospital (both based in Stockholm), who carried out autopsies on the brains of deceased people, allegedly found a correlation between traces of cannabis in the brain and violent deaths such as suicide, murder, and accidents. These violent deaths were supposedly caused by the completely unexpected and impulsive behaviour of the cannabis users. In a paper written by Jovan Rajs for the Ministry of Health and Social Affairs, one reads: "People who have used cannabis on its own, without simultaneous consumption of other substances, have frequently died in connection with impulsive and unforeseen acts of violence. The predominant form of death is suicide".[53] These findings have been used in a recent prevention video, issued by the National Institute of Public Health, where a person suddenly falls from a balcony after having smoked a joint at a party. In Mariaungdom, a clinic for teenagers in Stockholm, the social workers go as far as to say that when young males are taking cannabis, they do not develop physically and remain having a 'baby skin'. When cannabis use is stopped, the physical development would restart.[54] The reason for this restraint in the development would be the decreasing production of the male sex hormone testosterone.[55]

Other things which are highlighted concern the addictive character of cannabis, both physically as well as mentally. The period in which cannabis dependence develops is said to be matter of weeks or months, and to kick a cannabis habit would be as difficult as with a cocaine and heroin addiction.[56] In any case, looking at all the prevention and information material about drugs, a difference between the so-called soft and hard drugs is not being made, nor does one get a realistic idea about the possible dangers of cannabis. The latter can be explained by the fact that only drug scare messages seem to be 'allowed'.

Pointing out the possible risks of cannabis use seems to have had its impact on people, since 'ordinary' people who have been spoken to, often refer to these risks, and mention them as one of the reasons for not having tried cannabis. An important reason many people are 'aware' of the dangers related to cannabis use is that all parents of 8th grade (14-15 years old) school children, receive the *Hash Book* that is issued by the National Institute of Public Health.[57] What is surprising, is that there hardly seems to be a need to know the contents and facts of these 'studies' on which the drug scare messages are given; referring to them seems to be sufficient for the sake of drug prevention. In this respect it is relevant to note that this information is rarely spread by scientists specialised in this field, but is dominated by representatives of the popular movements, social workers, and the police. In a manner of speaking, they have the monopoly on spreading information about cannabis. This can mean in practice that a policemen tells school children about the effects of cannabis on the brain.

The information that is given is rarely based on scientific facts, or is presented in a wildly exaggerated fashion. One gets the impression the danger of cannabis is merely a 'construction' serving a higher goal; one has decided cannabis to be evil, so the arguments that can justify this standpoint are collected. However, there are changes occurring in this respect. In 1996, the National Institute of Public Health decided that the contents of the *Hash Book* had to be based on scientific facts, which is why most of the drug scare messages have been removed from the book. It will take time though before the more scientifically based information about drugs will penetrate society, since the information that was previously spread has left its traces in the sense that people are still somewhat 'brainwashed'. In this respect it should not be forgotten that the *Hash Book* is not the only provider of information on drugs; so are the popular movements, the police, treatment centres, and social workers.

The extremely negative effects that are being attributed to the properties of cannabis, cannot solely be explained by the struggle for a drug-free society, a goal that seems to justify means like 'horror campaigns'. The question remains how it can be that internationally respected medical reviews like the *British Medical Journal* and *The Lancet* declare that cannabis use, even in the long run, is not very harmful, whilst in Sweden it is said the use of this substance is very dangerous, which could be supported by scientific evidence.[58]

The alleged danger of cannabis as one is told in Sweden, may not only be based on 'myths' and 'constructions'. What is important to realise here, is that most of the existing knowledge about cannabis in Sweden is based on *clinical* experiences. Physicians generally do not always realise to what extent an epidemiological problem is involved, namely that their observations and impression of a certain phenomenon or symptom can be distorted by the fact these impressions are based on clinical selection. This may be seen with regard to phenomena and symptoms the physician is familiar with, but when it comes to the use of illegal substances, he may not always realise his observations are not representative, but are only clinical selections of this phenomenon. Patricia & Jacob Cohen have demonstrated the differences that can appear between a clinical selection of certain illnesses and its epidemiological occurrence. They called the bias resulting from this 'the clinician's illusion'.[59] In the case of cannabis use in Sweden, it is highly probable that most knowledge is based on clinical observations that do not necessarily say much about cannabis use in general. A publication that is used in Sweden and is often referred to is Thomas Lundqvist's *Cognitive Dysfunctions in Chronic Cannabis Users Observed During Treatment.*[60] Lundqvist who works at the Drug Addiction Treatment Centre of Lund University Hospital, studied approximately 400 patients with chronic cannabis use (consuming hash containing 6-8% THC), who all displayed the seven criteria of cannabis dependence according to the definitions of DSM III and DSM IV. Lundqvist found various brain impairments and cognitive dysfunctions among cannabis users. However, while looking at the typical client profile of the patients, one can come to the conclusion that the patients by no means match the adjective 'normal' or non-deviant, simply because these patterns of use are not part of the observations. The typical client profile is as follows:

"S(he) has problems finding exact words to describe what he really means; has limited ability to enjoy reading, motion pictures, theatre, music, etc.; has feelings of boredom and emptiness in daily life, loneliness, being misunderstood; externalises problems and avoids accepting blame; is certain that he functions adequately, is not able to examine his own behaviour critically; has feelings of being incapable and unsuccessful; is unable to maintain a dialogue; has difficulties with concentration and attention span; has fixed opinions and pat answers to questions; makes statements like 'I am different, other people don't understand me, I don't belong to the community'; doesn't plan the day; thinks he is active because he has many ongoing projects, which are seldom finished; has no daily or weekly routine."[61]

This 'typical client profile' makes it clear that the patients described by Lundqvist neither represent a cross-section of the general population, nor are there indications that they are representative of cannabis users in general. For example, this clinical picture is completely different from the average cannabis user in Amsterdam that emerges from a population survey. According to the data from this survey the 'average' cannabis user in Amsterdam is relatively highly educated.[62] In any case, it is safe to say that no conclusions about cannabis use in general can be drawn on the basis of Lundqvist's selective, clinical data.

The question is actually whether the chronic cannabis users as observed and described by Lundqvist are representative for chronic cannabis users in general. Bearing in mind the typical client profile and the different dysfunctions that are mentioned, a entirely different picture of cannabis users appear in other studies that outline chronic cannabis use.[63] Two possible explanations can be considered. The first possible explanation is that (chronic) cannabis users in Sweden can be considered to be 'heavy smokers'. This hypothesis is not improbable since alcohol use in Sweden is traditionally characterised by a consumption pattern oriented towards intoxication. It is conceivable this pattern can also be applied to cannabis, since people have not 'learned' to use intoxicants in a moderate fashion. Unfortunately, from the researcher's point of view, it has not been possible to observe cannabis use in an 'open atmosphere' to determine certain possible specifics with regard to cannabis use in Sweden as compared to other countries, which could test the validity of this argument. Nevertheless, the conversations that were held with cannabis users would lead one to think that cannabis use in Sweden, as seems to be the case in Denmark, are much more oriented towards intoxication than in the Netherlands.[64] According to some social workers it is quite common for a cannabis smoker to consume around a gram a day.[65]

A second possible explanation for the extremely negative consequences being attributed to cannabis use, based on clinical evidence, has to do with the fact that cannabis use in itself is already considered very deviant behaviour. Because cannabis use in Sweden is completely marginalised, in other words deviant, most 'normal' people will not even try cannabis. Its use is so socially unacceptable that those who have tried, will only tell their most intimate friends. In conversation with Swedes who had tried cannabis, many of them had done so outside Sweden. An important consequence of the deviance attached to cannabis use, is the effect that those who do try cannabis, and especially those who continue to consume it, are fundamentally people who were already deviant. Furthermore, because of this deviance, it is unlikely 'normal', moderate cannabis consumption patterns will (easily) develop. The barrier to use cannabis is made so high that most normal citizens will not even think about it. On the other hand, those who have crossed the barrier – again, probably people already on the margins – know they have transgressed the norms, meaning they are now 'on the other side', where normal norms do not exist at all, and there is no longer any need to develop such norms, just because they are already deviant. The norms that may exist once one has crossed the barrier, are those of the subculture one becomes a part of. To summarise, by marginalising cannabis use and attributing many dangers to its use, in a way creates a 'self-fulfilling prophecy'. The negative effects attributed to (the deviant behaviour) cannabis use will, in a manner of speaking, be proved by those who consume.

4.5 *The Function of a Restrictive Drug Policy*

In discussing drug policies one should not be under the impression that decisions are taken on rational grounds. Still, some questions remain unanswered. For example, how can it be that people are so vulnerable to the drug scare messages, as they seem to believe them? One of the reasons people believe the information that is given might be that Swedes are not used to drugs, especially those who live in rural areas. On the other hand, drugs are not completely alien to Sweden. In the late 1960s and early 1970s some people tried cannabis and many more have seen or known people who have tried. And, in those decades drug use was not as deviant as it today, which would suggest that people have experienced cannabis as not being as dangerous as it is often portrayed. Besides that, nowadays people travel more, which means there is more exposure to ideas and experiences of other countries. Yet, the reality is that many people do believe in cannabis dangers like hash psychosis, a higher risk of suicide, and second and third generation effects. The explanation probably has to be sought in the relationship Swedes have towards the State, which is basically a positive one. As demonstrated in chapter two (*Understanding Sweden*), most people have experienced the virtues of the State and 'the system', which lead to a situation in which one is trusting and tends to believe what one is told from 'above'.

Another question that arises is how is it possible that drugs are perceived as one of the biggest threats to society, and why do drugs provoke such extremely strong reactions, to a degree that the State adopts the goal of a drug-free society? According to Henrik Tham, Professor in Criminology at Stockholm University, these strong reactions have to be seen "in light of the notion of drugs as a contagion that can afflict anyone at any time and that is sweeping through younger and younger age groups in society".[66] Furthermore, the risks related to cannabis are seen as especially serious as a gateway to the use of heroin and other hard drugs, which in turn could lead to extensive criminality, marginalisation, and death.[67] The question is how can it be that drugs and drug users scare people so much and why are the reactions to drugs in Sweden so fierce. Opinion polls show that people consider drugs as one of the major threat to society, far above other social problems like unemployment and racism. Drugs as a problem falls into a different category from all other social problems; they are almost seen as *the* threat, and people's main enemy.

It is difficult to pinpoint what exactly is the cause of the Swedish 'drug panic'. Several factors can be mentioned in this regard. In the 1960s and 1970s the famous Swedish documentary maker Stefan Jarl made three documentaries that may have contributed to the negative image that drugs have.[68] His first film, entitled *Mods*, was about 'people outside society', a film that gave a somewhat romantic image of drug users. At the time of his first film, Jarl did not yet know in what direction his subsequent films would go. A few years later, in the second film, the same drug users appeared to be becoming worse and some had even died. The third film, called *The Social Inheritance*, was about the next generation, for example the children of the drug addicts from the first two films, some of whom were also using alcohol and drugs. Jarl's documentaries have had a tremendous impact in Sweden. Most people, except the younger generation, have seen these films. They have contributed to the very negative opinions that exist about drugs.[69]

The media have also played their part in contributing to the image of drugs that exists among the general public. Bergmark & Oscarsson have analysed the descriptions of drug and drug users in fifteen different daily newspapers in the period 1981-1983. They show that newspaper articles, when discussing drugs, tend to stress the psychological and physical consequences of drug use: "there is a strong emphasis on the changing of the individual drug users, both mentally and physically".[70] Bergmark & Oscarsson conclude their analysis by stating that it is not an insurmountable task to outline the contents of the 'governing images' in the press, the analysed articles can be summarised fairly briefly and succinctly:

"The abuse of drugs leads to extensive alterations of the abuser's body and mind in an obviously negative way; psychosis, distorted reality conception, anxiety, apathy, brain damage, impaired immune defence, genetic lesions, and so forth, are all possible consequences of drug abuse. The governing image of the abuser in the press seems to be a person more or less 'out of his mind' and at the same time a 'physical wreck'."[71]

In a more recent article on criminal policy, Henrik Tham makes a similar point. Tham states that it is "clear the media have been very active in the definition of drugs as a major social problem". He points out that four daily newspapers together have published more than 12,000 articles on drugs in the period 1981-1991.[72]

Not only have the media played an important role in highlighting the public concern about the drug problem, the government has played its part as well. In the previous section it was shown that a central element of drug prevention campaigns consists of pointing out the dangers of drugs. In practice, the focus is then placed on cannabis since this is often the 'first' illicit drug people encounter. More generally, 'drug prevention' and 'opinion formation' are central elements for the drug-free society to prevent people trying drugs. The impact of these drug prevention campaigns should not be underestimated. It has already been said that all parents of 8th grade school children (14-15 years old) receive the *Hash Book*, a book in which the dangers of cannabis are presented. As a matter of fact, drug prevention in schools starts at a much earlier age, sometimes at the age of seven. When children reach the age of twelve, most have taken part in a drug prevention programme.[73] In the 7th grade, when children are 12-14 years old, the ANT-courses start: courses on Alcohol, Narcotics, and Tobacco. From then on, the course forms a recurring element of the school curriculum which is addressed one day every year. The main aim of the course is not to inform the school children in a differentiated and rational way about the real effects of these substances, but to teach them about the dangers of drugs, which is often done in a dramatised manner lacking a scientific basis. The goal of these drug-scare messages is, of course, to frighten children into not experimenting with drugs. Besides drug prevention programmes that are part of the school curriculum, the government also has other anti-drug campaigns. Moreover, the government is not the only party involved in spreading drug prevention information, so too are social movements (Hassela, FMN, RNS), the police, and social workers. The impact these different programmes have had, is that most 'ordinary people' really do perceive drugs as something evil. The campaigns seem to have had such impact that, when the drugs topic is discussed with Swedes, they usually come up with what they have been taught about drugs. In this respect, the information campaigns seem to have had the desired effect.

A good way to understand people's reactions to drugs, is to look at how the society reacts to deviance in general. As has been pointed out in earlier chapters, Sweden was a relatively homogeneous society on the outskirts of Europe where one was familiar with most social problems. In this respect, drugs is something strange and unknown, which makes it understandable that they trigger violent reactions and fear. Related to this is the tradition of the welfare state, meaning that there is a firm belief in the social engineering capacities of society. It was thought that the social problem 'drugs' could also be eliminated, for example, by offering care and treatment to the drug users. However, drug users still exist and it has proved very difficult to keep drug addicts 'clean' from drugs. In a manner of speaking, drugs was something the welfare state had no influence over and could not cope with and 'solve', thus showing the restrictions of the welfare state's social engineering capacities.

Den gode fiende (The Ideal Enemy) is in academic circles regarded as one the best books written about the background of drug policies in Scandinavian countries.[74] This book was published in 1985 and written by a Norwegian professor in criminology at the University of Oslo Nils Christie, and the late Kettil Bruun, a Finnish professor in alcohol research at Stockholm University. Christie & Bruun describe drugs and drug addicts as the ideal or perfect society's 'enemy'. They characterise Scandinavian drug policy as a 'war' fought with an escalating intensity and claim that Sweden is one of the 'hawks' in this war.[75] Christie & Bruun state that this war against drugs is merely a symbolical war, fought against the easy target of drugs, drawing attention away from other social problems in society. The reactions that followed the publication of the book revealed that for many people there was indeed a war going on.[76]

Since a problem becomes a problem only when it is defined and conceived as such, Christie and Bruun define the drug issue as the ideal target to be defined as a major social problem or enemy. The explanation why it is precisely on 'drugs' that the war is declared, and not 'unemployment' or 'alcohol', comes down to one thing: the lack of power. According to Christie & Bruun the 'perfect' social problem has the following traits:

nobody defends the enemy; the struggle against the problem gains a lot of kudos; the costs connected with the battle become a burden mainly for non-privileged groups; and the lifestyle of the majority is not disturbed. Finally, the ideal enemy is of the kind that it can explain other problems in society, such as problems among youth groups, poverty, criminality, and homelessness. Drugs tend to be an answer that leaves the powerful elite and the great majority of people alone, distracting attention away from other, urgent social problems. In short, drug users are an ideal 'enemy' or scapegoat to blame social problems on and to draw attention to.

In line with *Den gode fiende*, Swedish criminology professor Henrik Tham has analysed the Swedish restrictive drug control model and the 'function' of drugs as a social problem. In the article *Drug control as a national project: the case of Sweden*, Tham discussed the question of why in Sweden the reactions against drugs are so strong, although data are showing the problem is limited and not on the increase. For this purpose he has analysed the drug debate in the media, in platforms of political parties, and parliament during the 1980s and early 1990s. Eventually Tham concludes that the struggle against drugs is so strong and widespread because it serves "the function of strengthening a threatened national identity in a situation where the traditional 'Swedish model' has come under increasingly hard attack from both inside and outside the country".[77] Tham's analysis clearly shows that in Sweden drugs are often perceived as one of the major social threats to society. The debates around drugs are centred on two central themes: the dangerous quality of the substances and the extent of the problem. Additional themes are 'morality', the 'people', 'consensus', and 'Sweden and abroad'.

In the Swedish drug debate references are often made to morality. The clearest example of the moral approach to the drug problem is, of course, the definition of a drug-free society which makes all illicit drug use unacceptable. As Tham point out, a crucial aspect of this moral standpoint is to define 'liberalism' in a ferociously derogatory manner.[78] This situation has developed in such a way that 'liberal' has indeed gained a negative connotation, as it effectively means not subscribing to the concept of the drug-free society. Even comments about drugs that in some way or the other do not follow the official line, or do not adhere to the doctrine that all drugs are very dangerous, can be labelled 'liberal' or 'drug liberal'.[79] Such a classification is sufficient to be paralysed in a drug debate. The morality concept could be traced back to the traditional working class values, of which the drug users lifestyle is the opposite. For example, in RNS magazine *Narkotikafrågan* references are often made to the decadent and hippie culture of which drugs could be part.[80] The way Hassela presents drugs also makes open drug use as seen as an attack on the traditional working class values of order, discipline, solidarity, and decent behaviour. This idea was legitimated ideologically in the 1970s when Jan Myrdal, one of Sweden's leading intellectuals, who wrote that drug addicts are disruptive to the general morality and that criminality and drug use prolong the oppression of the working class. They must first lift themselves out of their 'lumpenproletariat' before they can be seen as comrades.[81]

Tham's thesis that the struggle against drugs and the aim of a drug-free society as a means to reinforce the national identity, is also based on the fact that drugs are often presented as a threat to the Swedish society. "The idea that the entire society is facing a threat has come to mean that it is the Swedish society itself that is at risk. Swedishness is expressed in the indignation that drugs are spreading to what is typically Swedish – our small towns and rural areas."[82] In this perspective, the struggle against drugs gains another dimension, surrounded by a large degree of moral panic. For example, the chairperson of the Christian Democratic Party, Alf Svensson, stated that the Swedish national radio and television should transmit regular prime-time broadcasts with information about drugs. Swedish television granted the police and customs time slots to announce a telephone number where people can give anonymous tips about drug crimes.[83] Tham ends his analysis by concluding: "Drugs [...] have come to represent something more than themselves. Drugs have been perceived as an attack on cherished 'Swedish' values. In a period of national uncertainty, the struggle against drugs has been broadened into a more general national project for the defence of 'Sweden'."[84]

The threat of drugs is often portrayed as something coming from outside Sweden. As Tham points out in his analysis of the media coverage, a recurrent theme is that drugs come from abroad and are alien to Sweden. "[...] the enemy image and the struggle's popular support have taken on a clear national(istic) complexion: drugs represent an attack on the King-dom of Sweden – both culturally and territorially."[85] Newspapers, in par-ticular the tabloids, tend to emphasise the foreign origin of both drugs and drug dealers. This 'relationship' between drugs and foreigners has even led the newspapers to abandon their tradition of not publishing names and photographs of suspects. Tham mentions that the tabloid *Expressen* carried a month-long special about drugs, including articles on a Greek organising consignments of drugs whilst in one of Sweden's pris-ons, a shipment of heroin from Turkey, the leaders of a international crime syndicate, the role of the Iranian security police in the trade, the 'deadly harvests' in Thailand, and Chinese triads. One member of Parlia-ment, who later became Minister of Defence, claimed on television that Sweden should be protected from drugs and terrorist immigrants.[86]

Not only are drugs alleged to be coming from abroad, so are the ideas of a more liberal approach to the drug problem. The 'European debates' about decriminalisation, legalisation, and harm reduction are seen as threats to the restrictive Swedish drug policy. Therefore, the membership of the European Union could, in the long run, mean that Sweden has to adapt its drug policy to the rest of Europe. As described in chapter two, EU mem-bership was a very delicate matter and the political decision to join the EU was preceded by a referendum and a long and fierce debate. Ironically, several of the 'hot issues' in this debate had to do with drugs, both licit and illicit: alcohol, *snus*, and drugs. The alcohol debate centred on the State monopolies on alcohol (see 4.2) and the fact that membership allowed more alcohol to be legally imported from other member States. *Snus* is a smokeless tobacco, somewhat similar to chewing tobacco, that is used quite widely in Sweden.[87] Since the EU at first did not allow *snus*, mem-bership would imply *snus* to be declared illegal. This prospect led to a lot of protests, such as people having stickers on the car bumpers saying 'EU? not without my snus'. Eventually Sweden was allowed to keep *snus*. Drugs was another hot topic in the debates about the EU. It was thought that EU membership meant that more drugs would come into the country, resul-ting in more drug use and drug addicts. As a matter of fact, the increase in drug use in the 1990s (see 6.2) is often attributed to the EU membership.

An important reason a majority voted for EU membership was that the referendum had been preceded by a referendum on the same question in Finland. The positive outcome of the referendum in the neighbouring country of Finland probably had a positive effect on the Swedish decision. In a referendum in Norway held later, the outcome was negative. If the Norwegian referendum had preceded the Swedish one, the outcome in Sweden could have been very different. Today, Swedish opinion about EU membership seem to be predominantly negative. The many changes Swedish society has undergone in the 1990s are attributed by some people to the EU membership. This holds true not only for drugs and the increase in drug use, but also for the economic crisis, the rise in unemployment, and the decline of the welfare State. As indicated before in this section, drugs seem to have become the 'symbol' of the changes Swedish society is experiencing.

As an EU member, Sweden has proven to be a active promoter of a restrictive drug policy. Supposing that attack is the best form of defence, it tries to fight against the liberal tendencies as they are perceived to exist on the European mainland. EU membership has also resulted in re-activating popular movements like FMN, Hassela, and RNS. Since the Swedish authorities adopted the goal of a drug-free society government, it was no longer necessary to be (very) active in Sweden. The Popular movements are now concentrating on Europe. The activities of *European Cities Against Drugs* (ECAD) should also be put into this perspective. Although ECAD does not represent official Swedish standpoints, and sometimes takes positions that are even to Swedish standards extreme, the fanatic way the Swedish policy is being promoted abroad, should be interpreted as a way to maintain the restrictive drug policy.

4.6 Conclusion

To understand Swedish drug policy one has to look at a wide range of factors. First of all, the attitudes towards alcohol, the traditional intoxicant, were discussed. Both the traditional consumption of alcohol, the function of alcohol, and the alcohol policy were described. Unlike what is often thought outside Sweden, the consumption is not at a high level as compared to most other Western countries. The difference is that alcohol use in Sweden traditionally has a typical Nordic intoxication-oriented drinking pattern. Hence, in practice drinking often means getting drunk, although in recent years this is changing and 'European' drinking patterns are becoming more widespread, especially among young people. In fact, this means that alcohol use is getting a different function from its traditional one.

It is important to realise that Sweden is one of the temperance cultures, countries where the temperance movement gained a foothold in the nineteenth century. The Swedish temperance movements' aim was to achieve a total ban on alcohol. Due to the influence of the temperance movement, Sweden traditionally has had a restrictive alcohol policy. In 1922 a referendum was held on the question of whether Sweden should become alcohol-free, which was rejected by only a very small majority. From 1917 to 1955 Sweden had a ration system on alcohol. After 1955 several important elements of that restrictive alcohol policy remained, such as the State monopoly on the sales of alcohol. Except low alcohol beer not stronger than 3.5%, alcohol has to be bought in one of the 395 State-owned *systembolagets*, which are restricted to people of 20 years and over. This also means there is a (substantial) black market of alcohol.

The alcohol policy is based on the 'total consumption model', a scientific model of alcohol policy. The aim of the alcohol policy is to limit the total consumption of alcohol since this would reduce the total harm caused by alcohol. The main mechanisms that can be used are availability and price. Sweden's joining of the European Union meant that it had to give up some aspects of its restrictive policy. In the 1990s alcohol has become increasingly available in Sweden, for example in restaurants, and the number of bars has increased as well.

Swedish attitudes towards alcohol are relevant since a restrictive alcohol policy makes a restrictive drug policy a logical option. Moreover, the total consumption model on which the alcohol policy is based, is thought to be valid for illicit drugs as well. By limiting the total consumption of drugs, the total harm caused by drugs is alleged to be lower as well. However, it was shown that this correlation is far from clear when it comes to (different) illicit drugs.

The attitude towards alcohol and the alcohol policy, however, are not sufficient to understand the attitude and policy towards illicit drugs. In this chapter it was shown that several organisations, lobbying groups, and sometimes individuals have played an important role in shaping Swedish drug policy as it is today. Popular Movements and pressure groups like FMN, Hassela, and RNS have played a essential role in this respect. Because of their strong lobby activities and the refined way they play on people's feelings (of insecurity) they have managed to influence public opinion and put drugs on the political agenda, which has resulted in a situation that if a politician is 'soft' on drugs he will do so at his political cost. The pressure groups should be considered as the driving forces behind the restrictive drug policy.

The founder of RNS, Nils Bejerot, can be considered to be the founding father of the Swedish drug policy. His theories of the epidemic and contagious character of drug use, served as a basis for the policy that was implemented. Other scientific bases of the restrictive model are the stepping stone hypothesis and the dangers that are attributed to cannabis. It was shown that these dangers are often presented in a much exaggerated fashion and not always based on sound, scientific knowledge. Moreover, the available knowledge of cannabis in Sweden is often based on clinical experiences. Considering the very deviant character of drug use in Sweden, this has to some extent led to a situation of self-fulfilling prophecy.

Finally, an important factor in understanding Swedish drug policy is to look at the *function* of the fight against drugs in Swedish society. Opinion polls show that there is a large degree of moral panic about drugs in Sweden. Drugs are seen as one of the main threats to Swedish society, far above other social problems like unemployment. A part of the explanation why drugs trigger such violent and irrational reactions in Sweden may be that in a historical sense Swedes are not very familiar with intoxicants other than alcohol; drugs were something 'strange' that the welfare state could not easily cope with. However, since a social problem becomes a problem only when it is defined as such, the real explanation should be sought deeper. Drugs provide a welcome vocabulary of attribution; several Scandinavian authors have shown that drugs are, in essence, the ideal social problem which can be used as a scapegoat on which to blame other social problems. The fight against drugs in the 1980s and 1990s has become so fierce because, in a time of increased insecurity and the decline of the welfare State, it has come to symbolise the protection of what is 'typically Swedish'. This explains why the 'threat' of drugs is often presented as something alien to Sweden and coming from abroad. Newspapers tend to emphasise the 'foreign' origin of both drugs and drug dealers. This helps to understand why, since Sweden has joined the European Union, it fiercely defends and markets its restrictive drug policy. The liberal tendencies concerning drug policy that are perceived on the continent, are considered a threat.

5 Swedish Drug Policy in Practice

5.1 Introduction

Swedish drug policy is built on three pillars: prevention, control measures, and treatment. Although all drug use in Sweden is unacceptable, the policy aim is not to punish people. By offering care and treatment the drug user should become drug-free and be rehabilitated and reintegrated into society. The policy holds up a positive ideal, although it sometimes falls short in practice.

There are many myths surrounding the Swedish drug policy. For example, outside Sweden it is sometimes thought every drug user the police identifies, is arrested and directed to social workers who work in close collaboration with the police. Then the social workers direct the individual to treatment, if necessary compulsory treatment. As said, it is indeed the case that the goal of the Swedish drug policy is not to punish people but to offer them help and treatment. For this reason Sweden invested huge amounts of money in treatment, especially in in-patient treatment centres in the Swedish countryside where people were treated for one to two years. However, as will be shown in this chapter, the reality is different.

This chapter gives a description of the Swedish drug policy in practice. The element prevention and 'information formation' was already discussed in the previous chapter (section 4.4). This chapter will focus more on the 'drug practice'; What kind of drugs can one find in Sweden? How easy or difficult is this? What happens if the police catch a drug user? What will the punishment be? Besides giving a brief description of the treatment system (in 5.4), this chapter will also discuss other aspects of the drug policy in practice. Part of the research carried out in Sweden consisted of fieldwork, which included visits to 'drug sites' and conversations with (former) drug dealers and drug users. This fieldwork was conducted in Sweden's main cities: Stockholm, Gothenburg, and Malmö. Together with information from other sources, this enables us to give an idea about the drug situation in practice.

5.2 Drugs in Sweden

As was the case in most Western countries, drug use increased during the second half of the 1960s in Sweden. Besides the group of injecting drug (amphetamine) users, other drug use also increased as well, in particular in the second half of the 1960s. Cannabis became the most widely used illicit drug, especially among young people. The use of LSD and opiates was relatively rare. It has already been pointed out that Sweden makes an exceptional case in Europe as amphetamine, instead of heroin was the most widely used drug among drug addicts. Broadly speaking, this situation has remained the case until today. A new development is that heroin use is on the increase, not only among (former) amphetamine addicts, but also among young people with no 'addiction record'. This has developed to such an extent that in 1996 in Stockholm amphetamine and heroin seemed to balance each other out. Cocaine will not be discussed, since cocaine use in Sweden is relatively rare. The main reason for this is, of course, the 'traditional' use of amphetamine, a stimulant drug stronger than cocaine.

Amphetamine
As pointed out in chapter three (*The Swedish Drug Experience*) Sweden has a 'history' of the use of central nervous system stimulants (CNS). These amphetamine-like drugs were used widely by 'ordinary' people without posing too many problems. Central stimulants were easy to get and were used by a great majority of the consumers to lose weight or as a stimulant drug (e.g. students in periods of exams).

Amphetamine use started to be considered a real problem in the 1950s and 1960s when young people started using it, most of whom belonging to a criminal subculture. Stricter regulations meant to limit use, led to a situation in which consumption among 'ordinary' people indeed decreased significantly. On the other hand, stricter regulations did not have much effect on amphetamine use by young people in a criminal subculture. In essence, this situation could be characterised by a gradual marginalisation of the amphetamine users. The fact that the use of drugs by people belonging to a criminal subculture was considered a problem and 'threat' to the establishment, was reinforced by the fact that the way they administered the drug was intravenously. Furthermore, this type of drug use became very 'visible' since this group of users was already deviant.

Although changes are occurring and heroin use is on the increase in Sweden (see 6.2 and 6.3), one can still say the 'average' drug addict is a male intravenous amphetamine user. In the 1970s and 1980s most amphetamine was said to originate from the Netherlands, but its role of supplier has become less significant. In recent years the provenance of drugs has shifted to Poland where approximately 85% of the seized quantities originates from, as against 15% from the Netherlands.[1] There is reason to believe that producers and smugglers from other Eastern European countries are also 'active'. Some years ago Polish amphetamine was called 'Pig's Speed' (*gristjack*) because of its poor quality. Hence, people preferred the Dutch speed. Reports from drug addicts are that the quality of the Polish amphetamine has improved. Police sources indicate the Polish amphetamine has a purity between 80% and 100%.[2]

The price of amphetamine is approximately 300 kronor a gram, approximately US\$ 37.[3] If amphetamines are bought in larger quantities of ten grams the price is approximately 1500 kronor, hence 150 kronor a gram. Contrary to heroin, amphetamine is not so much of a 'street drug' in Sweden, although it can also be bought in places like Stockholm Central Station. It is more common to buy amphetamine in apartments, and (illegal) bars where larger quantities like ten grams are bought that can serve for several days. Hence, amphetamine users usually wait until they have a greater amount of money to be able to buy larger quantities like ten grams that will serve them for a few (two, three) days.[4] Unlike heroin addicts, they usually do not score for one or two doses.

Amphetamine use among drug addicts is in many cases episodic, meaning the substance is taken during a certain period, which is followed by a rest period of some days, which basically consists of sleeping. The phase of drug taking varies from three days up to a week or even a week and a half, depending on the individuals mental and physical health. During the 'drug-taking period' amphetamines are injected several times (4-6) per twenty-four hour period. The drug user is very active and rarely sleeps or does not sleep at all. During the first days of this phase the drug user hardly eats, but afterwards he starts eating in a normal way. Drinking on the other hand is very common, especially beer. Since amphetamine addicts hardly sleep in their 'active period', they have all kinds of nocturnal activities. The several drug addicts that have been interviewed, used to spend their nights hanging around outside, driving around in cars, or drinking beer in a pub. Many amphetamine addicts stay at home though, to drink beer and to watch television, such as sports programmes and blue movies.

It is common to become paranoid when taking large quantities of amphetamine without getting much sleep. Paranoia is also the reason many addicts spend most of their time at home. When the active period reaches its end the paranoia often manifests itself in a stronger from. This marks the beginning of the rest period during which one sleeps for several days, depending of course, on the length of time one has been awake. Many addicts take some heroin as a downer before going to sleep. For some people the cycle restarts as soon as they wake up. Others stay abstinent for a while, whilst other users consume limited amounts for a certain time.

In recent years a number of amphetamine addicts has 'shifted' to heroin. Unfortunately no specific research has been done on this subject, so it is not possible to explain this phenomenon. A possible explanation could be that amphetamine use in the long run is too exhausting both mentally and physically, considering the lifestyle of amphetamine addicts as just described. The increase in heroin use among (former) amphetamine addicts could also be related to the increased availability of heroin, leading to more experimentation with it. In any case, whereas before the amphetamine and heroin consumer groups were completely separated, to a degree it is sometimes said they 'hated' each other, today, it is no longer a question of two completely separate worlds.

Heroin
Heroin arrived on the Swedish market around 1975. It was used by some people, but amphetamine stayed by and large the most widely used drug by addicts. There are, however, some geographical variations in this re-

spect. In the capital Stockholm, amphetamine use is indeed much more common among drug addicts. In Gothenburg, in the west of Sweden, heroin use was, until a few years ago, almost non-existent; by definition a drug addict was taking amphetamine. In the more Europe-oriented city of Malmö in South Sweden on the other hand, heroin use was more common than it was in Stockholm.

Heroin in Sweden used to be white South East Asian heroin (heroin No. 4), called *smack* in Sweden. According to some sources it is brought in from Thailand and to a lesser extent from the Philippines; other sources presume there might be a Chinese connection. The heroin is brought in by Asian and Swedish couriers; the latter case being facilitated by the increase in tourism and the Swedish/Nordic colony in Thailand and the Philippines.[5] Other, more recent transport routes are said to go through China and Russia, up to Finland and the Baltic states before reaching Sweden. Most heroin users prefer white heroin over brown, basically because white heroin can be easily injected, which is the most common way of administering it in Sweden. The brown (Turkish) heroin from South West Asia (heroin No. 3) is, just like everywhere else in Europe, only available in base form, meaning it is only soluble if an acid like lemon is added. Although white heroin is still the most popular form of heroin, it recently has lost part of its market share to brown heroin, since the latter has become cheaper.

Until a few years ago the prices for brown and white heroin were the same: 500 kronor for one dose of 0.2 gram, usually 'packed' in a capsule. The price of a gram usually was 1500 kronor. In recent years there is cheaper, brown heroin on the market. This is said to be due to the import of heroin by people who are closer to the 'source' than the Swedish importers, like Albanians (from Kosovo), Iranians, Iraqis, Kurds, Turks, and 'Yugoslavians'. The police talk about three main routes: couriers travelling through East African countries (from the airports of Dar es Salaam and Nairobi), Eastern European routes (from the Czech Republic and Slowakia through Poland to Scandinavia), and via Russia.[6] The purity of heroin in Sweden is generally between 15% and 25%.[7]

The availability of cheaper brown heroin is particularly evident in Sweden's main drug scene for the past 20 years: in the *Sergels Torg* square, also known as the *Plattan*. Many dealers of different types of (ethnic) background can be found here selling drugs, heroin in particular. Since 1996, Gambians dominated the street trade by reducing the price from 500 to 300 kronor for one capsule (0.2 gram), and 700 to 800 kronor for one gram. Although heroin is the main product sold here, it is also possible to buy amphetamine, cannabis, methadone (200 kronor a pill), rohypnol (10 kronor), and injection needles.

Sergels Torg or *Plattan* is an ideal location for dealing since it is a big square in the heart of Stockholm's city centre, with an interchange of trains and subways. As a result, *Plattan* is both a general meeting place and a place where many people pass by every day. For many years it has been a thorn in the flesh of policy makers that right in the capital's main square, drugs are being sold, and both addicts and dealers can be found 'hanging out'. In January 1996, a special police action was started aimed at 'cleaning' Plattan from drugs, drug dealers and drug users. As a result of the special police actions that have taken place, today there are less drug addicts and drug dealers than previously and the phenomenon has spread throughout the city. The police actions have not managed to rule out street dealing at Plattan. Although the police has three shifts of policemen each consisting of eight officers that are constantly working in Plattan trying to 'disturb' the market, dealers can be found at any time around Plattan.

It should be noted Plattan is especially a market for the most marginalised drug addicts.[8] Those who are better off, or have better connections, do not go to Plattan, but buy their drugs in apartments. Since pagers and especially mobile phones have become widely used in Sweden, it is increasingly common that these are used for buying and selling drugs.

In the various suburbs that were visited in Gothenburg, Malmö, and Stockholm, heroin seems relatively easily available. Unlike the situation in the city centres, hardly any police can be found here. Several social workers that were interviewed, mentioned 'many' young people smoking heroin (chasing the dragon), sometimes combined with rohypnol. According to reports it is also easy to get raw opium in these areas, due to the presence of people coming from opium producing and consuming countries such as Iran.

Cannabis

In the 1950s and early 1960s cannabis in the form of marihuana was used in small confined groups of jazz musicians and intellectuals. In later stages marihuana was 'replaced' by hash, as was the case in most European countries. Today cannabis in Sweden is, in most cases, Moroccan hash, whilst marihuana has become relatively rare. Marihuana found in Sweden may have been imported from Africa (West Africa), Asia, or South America (Columbia). It is also reported that there is local, non-professional marihuana production. Hash arrives in Sweden from various sources. It is reported that Moroccan hash comes in through several European countries. According to police sources, Denmark and the Netherlands are important source countries for hash arriving on the Swedish market. A consignment of 20-50 kilos in a private car is seen as the 'classic example', to which can be added that this occurred less frequently in the 1994 police statistics.[9] According to a hash dealer operating at the middle level (2-5 kilos), hash also comes in from Germany and Spain. Different kinds of 'groups' and people of both Swedish and foreign origin are involved in the importation of hash.

There are indications that the hash on the Swedish market is of a relatively low quality (as compared to, for example, hash in Denmark) due to the fact that it is adulterated. The wholesale kilo price of average hash is approximately 35,000 kronor (approximately US$ 4,400). When hash is bought in 'cakes', quantities of 100 to 125 grams, the price per gram is 45-50 kronor. The retail price of hash usually is 60 kronor a gram, which is normally bought at five grams at a time (for 300 kronor). In the 1970s and to lesser extent in the 1980s it was possible to buy hash on the streets, but this has become increasingly difficult due to police actions directed at the street level. In Stockholm the central subway station T-centralen used to be a known sales point for cannabis, but increased police efforts moved the retail market to apartments and parks. Since police efforts follow the market movements, it also has become more difficult to buy hash in the parks. For example, in the Stockholm parks Valsaparken and Humlegården nowadays one hardly finds any hash dealers; only in the Kungsträdgården park can one still buy hash. It is quite common that hash dealers in parks also sell other products, such as amphetamine. The retail sale from apartments has probably become more important as a result of the increased police efforts aimed at the street trade.

Hash in Sweden is usually smoked in a pipe, called a *digger*-pipe (named after the type of pipe that is used). When smoked, a little or no tobacco at all is added. Moreover, conversations with people familiar with different 'smoking cultures', lead to think that quite a few Swedish hash smokers can be considered 'heavy smokers'. As mentioned in section 4.4, it is not unlikely since the 'traditional' alcohol consumption pattern is oriented towards intoxication, this pattern can also apply to cannabis. Although less common than pipe smoking, hash is also smoked in the form of (big) joints. It seems that the latter have similarities to what can be observed in Denmark; joints usually contain a lot of hash (0.5-1 gram) and not much tobacco (half a cigarette). The latter could validate indications that on many occasions hash smoking in practice means heavy smoking.

5.3 The Practice of Police and Justice

Police Activities

In 1994 Sweden had 17,632 police officers. As the total population is 8,8 million, this means that there are 200 police officers per 100,000 inhabitants. Compared to other Scandinavian countries, Sweden maintains a relatively large police force.[10] Since in practice all police officers are occasionally working on drug cases, it is difficult to determine what proportion drug issues take up of the police activities. According to Eva Brännmark of the Swedish National Police Board, 500 to 800 police officers are working full time on drugs, which would be 2.8% to 4.5% of the total number of police officers.[11] The police yearbook on the other hand, states that investigation of drug-related crimes takes up 12% of its daily working hours, which would represent approximately 2,000 police officers.[12]

As discussed in section 3.4, the focus of law enforcement policy shifted around 1980. Part of this change was, naturally, the adoption of the goal of a drug-free society. In the 1970s, the policy of the police was directed at combatting big dealers and the import of drugs. Drug use was not criminalised and small possession of cannabis and amphetamine was dismissed. In the 1980s this policy changed; waivers of prosecution were restricted and the emphasis of law enforcement was now put on 'disturbing the market', in other words the street dealers and the drug users. In fact, this shift implied the application of Nils Bejerot's theories who considered drug users to be the most vulnerable in the 'chain' of drugs, out of which theory would follow that the drug policy should focus on drug users instead of on drug dealers. The shift in policy that occurred around 1980 is clearly reflected in the police arrests. Between 1970 ands 1982 the number of drug offences rose from 22,500 to 68,000.

To make it clear that drug use was an unacceptable activity, drug use was criminalised in 1988. However, since the penalty for drug use was a fine, it was difficult to detect drug use without drug possession being a question. Hence, some argued there should also be the possibility of a prison sentence, the main reason for this being this would enable body examinations to be carried out. As described in section 3.5 it was especially the right-wing Liberal Party that was advocating stiffer penalties for drug use. When the Liberals came to power in 1991 (in coalition with the Conservatives and the Centre Party) they indeed took this stance. After only two months in office, in November 1991, Bengt Westerberg the then new Minister of Health and Social Affairs and leader of the Liberal Party, declared at a RNS meeting that the police should be allowed to do urine tests to prove that someone had been using drugs. In line with Bejerot, on this occasion Westerberg claimed drug consumption to be "the motor of the whole drug carousel".[13]

Two years later, in 1993, the penalty for drug use was increased to a prison sentence of up to six months. Since July 1993, the police have had a means at their disposal to force people suspected of having used drugs to undergo a urine or blood test. The police guidelines are such that a person can be taken to a police station on the suspicion of being under the influence of drugs, without there being a question of any disturbance, for example to a third party. The actual law in force makes it possible to detect people under the influence of drugs, drug recognition experts (DRE's) instruct police officers on how to recognise signs if someone has drugs in their body.[14] The police is waiting for a new law that will allow it to test 'any' person without reason.[15]

Not everyone in the police force is convinced of the effectiveness of the urine tests, but since the role of the police is to enforce the law, and the authorities have decided is should be implemented, the urine test is not really a subject for discussion within the force. Generally the police's far-reaching powers to perform a urine test are justified by stating that it enables the police to detect new drug users, after which they can be put into treatment. It is asserted that many drug users who were previously unknown, have been found thanks to the urine test. According to Eva Brännmark of the Swedish National Police Board the urine test has also helped to find drug dealers: drug users undergoing a test would give names of their dealers.[16] Other police sources however, like police officers working at the street level, declare that drug users give names of dealers if tip-off money is offered to them. But, this practice is not connected to the urine tests, but is a more general police method for which a budget is available. The tip-off money varies according to the nature and quantity of the drugs: for a tip leading to a find of ten capsules (approximately two grams) of heroin the money to be paid to an informer will be 500 kronor. For larger quantities like 350 grams of heroin, a sum of 10,000 kronor will be 'awarded'; two kilos of hash can lead an informer to receive 7,000 kronor.[17]

As already mentioned in the previous section, in January 1996 a special police operation was begun in Stockholm. The operation entitled 'Together against drugs' was created with the aim of 'cleaning' the streets of drug addicts, in particular the central *Plattan* square, Sweden's most visible drug scene. In a period of two months, 500 people were brought in by the police working at *Plattan*.[18] The police is almost permanently present at *Plattan*; a total number of 24 police officers work in three shifts at *Plattan*, meaning there are always eight operative. Because the police are almost always present they know exactly who the drug addicts are and who are the drug dealers.

Since the police officers are familiar with most of the faces they see, they can easily detect 'newcomers'. If a new face appears, (s)he is immediately approached by the police and asked about the purpose of his or her presence. The police's attitude in this respect is not so much 'tough' but more 'social'. The officer then asks if the approached person has used any drugs. If the answer is negative, but the officer suspects the person has used drugs, (s)he is taken to the police station. The police states that these actions enable them to find and 'help' drug users, especially teenagers using drugs – in other words teenagers slipping further, of which drug use is a sign. Taking them to the police station to undergo a urine test, makes it possible to intervene at an early stage before it is 'too late'.

If a person is suspected of having illicit drugs in their body and is taken to the police station, a small instrument is first used for verification. This device can test traces of one drug at the time, a procedure that takes a minute-and-a-half. If the person confesses to having used drugs, the urine sample is sent to the police laboratory where a second, more serious test is done which takes sixteen minutes. The laboratory then sends back the test result to the police station, from where a fine will be sent by mail to the drug user. The fine depends on the income of the individual, but is generally between 500 and 1,000 kronor.[19]

In 1993, when the urine tests were introduced, around 1,300 urine tests were performed in Sweden. In 1994 and 1995 this figure rose to respectively to 6,000 and 9,000. In the period from January to June 1996 5,500 urine tests were conducted in Sweden. The total cost on a yearly basis of the urine tests is six million kronor.[20]

Originally the aim of the urine test was to find drug use among people who were not 'known' or registered as drug users. Also the General Prosecutor recommended that the urine tests should be used to find young drug users, the urine tests should not to be applied to the 'old addicts'. As previously said, when the tests were introduced 'new' drug users were indeed being found. However, in the course of time this has somewhat changed. The drugs market has adapted itself to the police presence and has partly moved elsewhere. Since the police, due to its massive presence in the areas where drugs are, as is the case at *Plattan*, it knows in many cases exactly who the drug addicts are. A urine test is not necessary to have this confirmed. As a result, the police practice with regard to the urine tests has partly changed in the sense that many 'suspected' drug users who are taken from the street to undergo a urine test, are in fact the 'old' drug addicts who were already by and large known to the police as such. Hence, in daily practice, the tests are used to disturb the market and to make drug use more difficult. It is only in rare cases that these drug addicts are directed to treatment after the test, as the official policy indicates. The drug addicts for their part, see the urine test as something like harassment. Although the police officers who work on the street level know that few new drug users are now found through the tests, they justify their work by pointing out the few young drug users that are found.

Another 'target' of the police activities with regard to drugs concerns rave parties. These parties were introduced in Sweden in 1989 in the city of Gothenburg. From Gothenburg the rave scene spread to other cities in Sweden. Rave parties are considered a problem by the police since drugs are being used at these parties, especially by young people. The most commonly drugs being used by some rave party visitors are amphetamine, ecstasy, hash and LSD. The price for an ecstasy tablet is 200-300 kronor, the price of a LSD dose is 70 kronor. Because of the lower price of LSD as compared to that of ecstasy, LSD is said to be more common among teenagers.[21] In 1996 the police actions against rave parties throughout Sweden were reinforced.

It was in Gothenburg where the police started targeting rave parties, resulting in 500 arrested people since 1989.[22] Although the Gothenburg police targets the dealers at rave parties, visitors to rave parties are taken to the police station as well to undergo urine tests. From September to November 1996 around 75 party visitors were drug-tested, most of whom were positive. The most commonly detected drugs found in the urine were amphetamine and hash; ecstasy and LSD were also commonly found. It was not unusual that people were found to be positive for benzodiazepines (sleeping pills), especially at after parties.[23] In a few cases party visitors tested positive on heroin. This heroin use was probably taken for similar reasons as benzodiazepines, namely serving as a 'downer'.

The police operations against rave parties culminated in early February 1996 with a raid on a rave party in suburban Stockholm. One night, 90 policemen raided a party at the 'Docklands', a rave club that had opened its doors six months before. The party organisers belonged to an organisation called *The Freedom Front*, having generally 'liberal' views.[24] Around a thousand people were at the rave party, and when the police raided the place, everyone was forced to leave immediately. Hundreds of people were forced to go outside into the cold winter night only dressed in T-shirts, and were not allowed to get their coats.[25] Eventually 72 people were arrested and 48 'drug samples' were found at the raid, later named 'razzia' by the press.[26] A week later, on February 17, the police raided 'Docklands' again when (only) 300 visitors were present. This time two people were arrested. Following this raid, the police forbade the organisation of any more parties at 'Docklands', a decision that was later reversed by the court.[27]

The Judicial Practice

Swedish drug legislation has three categories of drug offences: minor, normal and major. It depends on both the nature of the substance and the quantity that is possessed in which category the offence falls. The following table 5.1 shows the gravity distribution, based on the Prosecutor General's directives.

Table 5.1 The categorisation of drug offences according to substance and quantity

	Minor	*Normal*	*Major*
Amphetamine	up to 6 g	6,1 g -250 g	250 g or more
Cannabis	up to 50 g	51 g up to 2 kg	2 kg or more
Cocaine	up to 0.5 g	0.6 g - 50 g	51 g or more
Heroin	up to 0.39 g	0.4 g - 25 g	25 g or more

The question to be asked is what happens to someone found guilty of drug offences. A person who was tested positive on the urine test and confesses to having used drugs, will be punished with a fine, even if this occurs several times. Fines in Sweden are called 'day fines', based on the offender's income. Theoretically the amount varies from 900 to 150,000 kronor. The lowest fine of 900 kronor can, in special cases, be halved to 450 kronor, the absolute minimum. The drug addicts that were interviewed and who had been in this situation several times, usually received a fine of 450 kronor.

When it comes to drug use and possession of small quantities falling in the category of minor offences, imprisonment up to six months is an option. However, in these cases imprisonment is rare, the usual penalty is a fine. However, the latter is only true when it the offence is committed for the first or second time. For example, a drug user who has been arrested a few times for drug use or small possession, every time being in the possession of one capsule of heroin, is likely to be sentenced for one month.[28] When a person is found *selling* or is presumed to be selling a small quantity of drugs (falling in the category minor drug offence), imprisonment follows in every case. Although the legislation itself does not make this distinction between drug use on the one hand and drug dealing on the other hand, this difference is made in practice.[29]

Normal drug offences are punishable with a fine or an imprisonment up to three years. The actual penalty largely depends on the nature of the substance, the quantity and the 'circumstances'.

Major drug offences are punished with a minimal sentence of two years. The maximum penalty in this category is ten years, which is applied in following cases: one kilo of heroin or more, at least two kilos of cocaine, and ten kilos of amphetamines or more. In the case of recidivism, the penalty can be increased by another four years. In some cases another four years can be added, making the highest possible sentence for a drug offence eighteen years. In the Swedish judicial system someone is normally released after having served two-thirds of their prison sentence.

In recent years the number of drug offences has been around 30,000 a year. This does not, however, lead to a similar number of convictions. One reason is that the offender remains undetected or not proven guilty; another reason being that one offender may commit a number of offences, resulting in a single, combined penal sentence.[30] The number of offenders convicted for drug law violations in recent years in Sweden, was between 4,000 and 5,000 a year. When looking at figures of drug law violations in Sweden, especially if they are compared with the statistics of other countries, it is important to realise that these figures do not include smuggling (regarded as an offence against the Act on Smuggling), but only comprise offences against the Narcotics Drugs Act.

No precise figures were found about the application of the Narcotics

Drugs Act in practice. Some observations can be made though on the basis of the available data. Drug offences can be punished by a fine and/or imprisonment. The 4,000 to 5,000 convicted drug offences every year have in the years 1990, 1991, and 1992 resulted in about 1,400 cases (approximately one in three) resulting in unconditional prison sentences.[31] This implies that in about two-third of convicted drug offences the penalty is a fine or a conditional imprisonment. Of the 1,400 unconditional prison sentences, approximately 250 were for a period of over two years.[32] Again, offences of the Act on Smuggling are not included here. Since smuggling drugs in Sweden is a very severe offence, the total number of prison sentences for 'drug crimes' should be higher.

According to Arthur Gould, based on a report from the Ministry of Justice, over 6,000 people were sentenced for drug crimes in 1990. 68% of these were minor drug offences. 102 people were sentenced for drug use; 3,700 were found guilty of possession.[33] These figures probably refer to all drug related offences, hence both offences on the Narcotics Drugs Act and the Act on Smuggling. Other figures are given in a publication from the National Institute of Public Health. Here one reads that in 1993 there were 7,229 indictments for drug offences. Of these drug offences, 69% were minor drug offences, 26% normal drug offences, and 5% major drug offences. Moreover, of these 7,229 people indicted for drug offences, cannabis accounted for 41%, 37% amphetamine, and 8% opiates.[34]

Drug Seizures
The quantity of drugs seized in Sweden is relatively low. This is probably due to various reasons, the most important one being Sweden's geographical position.

Table 5.2 The quantity of seized drugs in Sweden (in kilos)

	1990	*1991*	*1992*	*1993*	*1994*	*1995*
Amphetamine	107.9	103.7	120.6	142.0	210.2	278.6
Cannabis	601.0	638.9	375.9	536.4	457.4	527.2
Cocaine	8.8	225.9	60.9	13.7	28.8	3.7
Heroin	11.7	10.9	24.6	21.9	21.0	30.9

Source: CAN (1997)

Drugs comprise a big part of the total judicial activities. Although precise figures have not been found, drugs are said to rank second after 'economic crimes'. The judicial system has had its budget cut and was reorganised in 1996. There are indications that not everyone in the judicial system is satisfied with the 'burden' of drug cases on its system and the tendency towards more law enforcement and stiffer penalties. However, for those who do not subscribe to this tendency, they state it is the government who is 'pushing' more law enforcement measures. The government for its part, is being put under pressure from public opinion that considers that if a tight rein is not kept on drugs, the result will be more drug problems.

5.4 The Treatment System

As described previously, the goal of the Swedish drug policy is not to punish drug users, but instead, to offer help and rehabilitation. Drug treatment is one of the three basic elements of the Swedish drug policy, and a lot of financial resources are allocated for it. This section does not intend to give a complete overview of the extensive treatment system in Sweden, but will (only) highlight some of its major aspects. A more complete overview is referred to in other sources.[35] Therefore, this section will focus more on recent developments that have occurred in the field of drug treatment in Sweden. The major changes that have taken place in the treatment system in Sweden in the 1990s, have been so radical that one could even question whether the extensive treatment system as it has existed for a long time, and as is still sometimes presented, is still relevant to the situation today.

A key expression to an understanding of the treatment system in Sweden is the 'caring chain', signifying the different elements of the treatment system, like outreach activities, detoxification, out-patient care, and institutional care. Social workers play a key role in this chain. They are the ones who, in their outreach work, identify drug use and, in principle, determine if the drug user is eligible for drug treatment, and if this is the case, what type of treatment. Of course it is not only the social workers but also the institution they are working for, the municipal social services, that have a central role in the caring chain. The social services not only decide about treatment, but have to pay for it from their municipal budget as well.

Different types of drug treatment exist in Sweden and different kinds of distinctions can be made in this regard. Berglund et. al. for example, state that two main types of treatment can be distinguished that developed in Sweden since the middle of the 1960s. One type of programme is the milieu-therapeutic type that was developed in the UK by Maxwell Jones, which has a democratic, non-hierarchical structure. The other type, called the 'Hassela-pedagogics', which was to some extent inspired by the Russian educator Makarenko.[36] The drug treatment programmes in Sweden could also be distinguished in another way, namely in voluntary care and compulsory treatment. Voluntary treatment consists of (in-patient) therapeutic communities, (out-patient) open care, and foster or family care. Compulsory treatment consists of two types, LVM for adults and LVU for young people. Hassela falls also into the second category since most of their clients have come through LVU. A description of the Hassela programmes is referred to in section 4.3.

Of the different forms of drug treatment, therapeutic communities (TC's) have for a long time been the most dominant. Communities are based in the rural areas of Sweden, where it was not uncommon for a drug addict to spend a period of two years. Many of the treatment institutions are non-governmental: 65% of all institutional care is privately run.[37] This implies they have to sell and market their services to the government institutions, either at the national level (the Board of Health and Welfare), or at the local level (the social services). This also means treatment institutions have to compete with each other, especially in times when economies have to be made.

One of most discussed forms of drug treatment in Sweden is compulsory treatment. Compulsory treatment is based on two Acts: the LVM Act (Care of Alcohol and Drug Abusers Special Provisions Act) for adult abusers, and the LVU Act (Care of Young Persons Special Provisions Act) for young people (teenagers). LVM and LVU are not applied to drugs, but also to alcohol (and solvents) and other problems, for example in the domestic situation. As a matter of fact, LVM is used more for alcohol than for drugs. Both LVM and LVU fall under the remit of the National Board of Institutional Care (SiS). The Board is responsible for all the LVM and LVU homes in the country. Nationally there are 25 LVM homes where around 780 adults are housed, and 25 LVU homes with 580 young people.[38] The staff in each home varies from 15 to 100. In all, the Board employs around 3,000 people. The 1994-95 budget was 1.2 billion kronor.[39] If someone undergoes compulsory treatment, the board pays only a part of the costs; two-thirds of the costs, which amounts to 1,900 kronor a day, is paid by the social services of the municipality in which the person lives. The period during which someone is put in compulsory treatment is six months. Until 1988 the maximum period for compulsory treatment had been two months.[40]

The purpose of LVM is to protect someone who is considered as an abuser of either drugs, alcohol or solvents from himself or others. "The purpose of intervention is not to coerce the individual through a complete programme of rehabilitation, but instead, through short-term intervention, to overcome a life-threatening situation and motivate the individual for continuing care on a voluntary basis".[41] Hence, LVM is not as much a real treatment, but merely used as a means to get someone into (voluntary) treatment. It also happens that social workers threaten to put someone into compulsory treatment, with the assumption that the person will prefer to go into 'voluntary' treatment.

Contrary to popular belief (especially outside Sweden) the compulsory treatment for drug addicts in Sweden is on the whole quite uncommon and is relatively rarely applied. For drug using teenagers on the other hand, the option of LVU is used much more. It also happens that compulsory treatment is used as a 'threat' to force someone into ordinary, 'voluntary' treatment.

The treatment sector underwent major changes in the second half of the 1980s. In 1985 it was found that 142 drug users had become infected by the HIV virus. In 1986 another 204 persons were discovered to have contracted the virus through intravenous drug use.[42] The government introduced a motion stating that drug addicts were a key group that could spread the infection.[43] It should be noted that at the time both heroin and amphetamine were in most cases used intravenously.

Unlike many other European countries, the Swedish government did not decide to introduce a harm reduction policy as a way to prevent the spread of HIV. The Swedish government decided that in view of the menace of HIV and Aids, the aim of the drug policy was to reach all intravenous drug users with detoxification, sampling, and treatment.[44] Hence, social workers were 'sent on the streets' with the aim of finding all drug addicts, who could then be directed to treatment centres. This government standpoint led to very substantial sums of money being allocated to drug policy in 1986 and 1987. Several dozens of millions kronor, up to 70-80 million kronor extra, were made available for this purpose. It was the National Board of Health and Welfare that was responsible for distributing the money for more information, more outreach activities of social workers and especially more treatment homes. The police also received extra resources, since it was responsible for detecting drug users as well.

Because so much money was made available for treatment, it was relatively easy to open new treatment centres. In the second half of the 1980s a large number of treatment centres sprang up in different parts of Sweden, like for example residential treatment centres. Furthermore, numerous joint projects were started by the social services and prison and probation authorities.[45] This period that was to last until the 1990s could be called the 'golden age' of the treatment sector. There was enough money available to put someone into treatment for a period of two years. In many cases this was in a therapeutic community. Because of all the resources that were put into drug treatment, many people found employment in this sector, which resulted in it having a very powerful lobby. "The expansion of treatment facilities for drug abusers, mainly as a result of the HIV threat, had given a large group of professionals a vested interest in institutional treatment".[46]

The huge sums that had been made available to find drug addicts and have them treated, lasted for about four years. The feared epidemic of the spread of HIV did not, in fact, occur. This had probably been partly due to the attention that was given to the risk of HIV as soon as the epidemic was discovered among intravenous drug users. Another, sometimes neglected reason why HIV did not spread as rapidly as expected, was the simple fact that Swedish intravenous amphetamine users share needles to a much lesser extent than heroin addicts do. It has already been mentioned that most drug addicts in Sweden use amphetamine.

In the 1990s the treatment sector would once again undergo changes. As a matter of fact, the picture of the Swedish treatment system as it is sometimes presented, seems to be no longer applicable to the present situation. The economically difficult situation of the Swedish economy has changed the picture dramatically. Not only have the drug treatment and detoxification clinics suffered from budget cuts, but actually the whole medical sector and psychiatric sector at large has. Several clinics have been closed, or have been reduced in size. Generally, detoxification and psychiatric care has seen their number of places reduced to approximately half the number as compared to the late 1980s. For example, in 1990 there were five detoxification clinics in the Greater Stockholm area. In 1996 it was planned to cut this to only two clinics. The general psychiatry department of St. Görans hospital, one of Stockholm's main hospitals had 13 units in 1990, each with 15 beds. Due to the economic crisis, this number was reduced to seven units in 1994; in 1997 only four units were to remain.[47] When looking at the number of people in treatment institutions, the changes become apparent. Whereas in 1989 there were 19,000 people in treatment centres (for both alcohol and drugs), in 1994 this number had dropped to 13,000. In the same period, the number of people in compulsory care dropped from 1,500 to 900. Due to the budget cuts, 90 treatment homes were closed between 1991 to 1993.[48]

An important development in the 1990s that affected the treatment system was that the way it was financed changed. As a matter of fact, a different financing system was introduced in the social sector: *beställare – utförare*, literally 'order and carry out', meaning that all kinds of services now have to be 'bought and sold'. The background to the introduction of this system was, of course, the policy of retrenchment. It was decided to introduce this new way of financing in 1988 but it really took effect in the early 1990s. In this new system the social services, in practice the responsible local politicians, have become responsible for the money that is allocated for treatment. As a result, it is no longer the specialists who decide if a person gets treatment or not, this now falls under the responsibility of the local politicians, the local city board, or their staff.

Not only has the voluntary treatment system been subject to changes for the last few years, compulsory treatment has undergone changes as well, albeit not for exactly the same reasons. Although no precise figures were found as regards to this, the impression exists that the number of people put in compulsory treatment is (rapidly) falling. In any case, this is what has been observed in the municipalities of Stockholm and Botkyrka (just outside Stockholm). However, this has not been exactly the same policy measure as the general decrease in treatment availability. Since July 1994 it is at the local, municipal level of the *socialdistrikt* where is decided whether to apply for compulsory treatment in an individual case. Before 1994 this decision was made at the county level. It is, however, still at the county level (in the county court) where the decision is eventually taken if someone is indeed put into compulsory treatment.

The change in the level of decision making whether to apply for compulsory treatment or not has led to fewer people being put in compulsory treatment. In Stockholm, the effect of the new way of financing can be observed in the statistics of the social services of 1992-1993. The two main effects have been that fewer people are put into treatment, and if they are being treated, the period of treatment has been shortened. In Botkyrka the same phenomenon can be observed, but here there is also another reason that compulsory treatment is applied less than before, namely that it does not have the desired effect which is to protect abusers (see section 6.5). For example, the social services in Botkyrka, hardly use compulsory treatment anymore. The main reasons is that it does not work and it is too expensive, namely 1,900 kronor per day.[49] Since the period of compulsory treatment is in most cases six months, this care is very expensive. The social services of Botkyrka managed to convince the politicians that the money could be spent in a better way. In 1993 the municipality of Botkyrka spent two million kronor on compulsory treatment. Confronted with these figures and the low effectiveness of compulsory treatment, the politicians decided to use this option only in rare cases. In the situation where a drug user receives treatment, this will, in almost all cases, be on a voluntary basis. The municipal budget for treatment (including the housing costs) in Botkyrka is still falling; from the already reduced level of 22 million kronor in 1995, it decreased to 16 million kronor in 1997. For Botkyrka this means it has become rare to put someone in treatment for a period of two years, which was very common in the 1980s and early 1990s.

The overall picture that comes across is that major changes have occurred in the treatment system over recent years, starting approximately in 1991. The main reason for this is the very substantial budget cuts in the sector. Two main consequences can be seen in this respect. First of all, less people are actually undergoing treatment as compared to before. Due to the fact that decisions about treatment have recently started to be taken at a local level, this also means that the opportunities to obtain treatment have decreased. For example, this means that a request to get treatment, will no longer be automatically honoured. It now occurs that people are refused treatment because they have had their 'chance'. Such a response would be unimaginable in the 1980s, when there was place for everyone.

Secondly, the nature of drug treatment has undergone great changes. The duration of treatments has become shorter, and one has observed a great shift from in-patient to out-patient care. These two developments have resulted in a situation in which it is rare today if the treatment period exceeds one year; generally the treatment period is now six months. Due to the budget cuts, use of cheaper (short) treatment programmes like the Minnesota 12-step model have grown considerably, to the detriment of the more expensive, lengthy stays in treatment homes that were characteristic of the 1980s.

Methadone Programmes

Sweden has several methadone programmes. Methadone programmes actually have a long history in Sweden. Influenced by experiences in the USA, in 1966 the first programme was started in the Ulleråker Hospital in Uppsala; this was the first methadone programme in Europe. However, since the legal prescription experiment of 1965-1967 when opiates and especially amphetamine were prescribed to a group of drug addicts, there is a strong reluctance to introduce any more 'legal prescription programmes'.

In the second half of the 1980s, when HIV manifested itself among intravenous drug users, the number of methadone places was increased. In 1985 a methadone programme was started in St. Görans Hospital in Stockholm. Introduction of the methadone programmes did not occur without opposition, especially from the social workers' side. Today there are four methadone programmes in Sweden: in Malmö, Lund, Stockholm, and Uppsala. Officially the methadone programmes are on an experimental basis. The total number of people under methadone treatment may not exceed 500; in 1996 approximately 480 people were in a methadone programme.[50]

All the methadone programmes in Sweden have a high threshold; the criteria to participate in a methadone programme are relatively severe. One has to be at least 20 years old, one must have tried several other forms of treatment, one must have a history of at least four year opiate use (known to the authorities), and one must have chosen the methadone programme oneself. Before entering the methadone programme the patient must first go through a detoxification period of a few days, to make sure the patient is drug-free. The admission criteria are less strict when someone is HIV positive.

The methadone programmes have strict rules, resulting in almost no legal methadone 'leaking out'. Use of other illicit drugs is not permitted and alcohol may only be used moderately. Moreover, the objective of the patients must be to lead a 'normal life', which can be achieved by abandoning the 'drug addict's life style' and by tightening family ties. To obtain methadone, patients must visit the clinic on a daily basis. Under certain conditions this can graduate to once or twice a week.

Urine controls are used to check if the patients respect the rules. If traces of heroin are found, the patient is expelled and excluded from the methadone programme for two years, which happens to around 25% of the patients. The methadone programmes are officially oriented towards total abstinence, which is why the doses are gradually lowered. The patients are not informed about the quantity of methadone they receive, and to what extent their doses are reduced.

Needle exchange

Needle exchange programmes are limited in Sweden. In the light of the goal of the drug-free society and the unacceptability of taking drugs, there is something contradictory about needle exchange programmes. In the late 1980s, in the light of the HIV epidemic, though there was a debate about needle exchange programmes. In 1988 the National Board of Health and Welfare proposed the introduction of needle exchange programmes throughout Sweden, which was adopted by the government. This resulted in fierce protests from pressure groups and professional associations, both in the press and public meetings. The following year, in 1989, the proposal was finally quashed by the Parliament. It was felt that a higher availability of needles would not stop the spread of HIV, on the contrary, it was thought to increase intravenous drug use.[51]

There are only needle exchange programmes in Lund and Malmö, that started respectively in 1986 and 1987. The main objective of starting the programme was to stop the spread of HIV. The programme received a lot of opposition from social workers and from 'Stockholm'. The fact that they exist here is attributed to (the influence) of one person, the late Kerstin Tunving, head of the psychiatric detoxification clinic at St. Lars Hospital in Lund. Officially the needle exchange programme is a scientific project on an experimental basis. Although one could label the programme as a measure of 'harm reduction', it is never called this since this expression has sensitive connotations within the Swedish context.

The needle exchange programme in the Department of Infectious Diseases of the University Hospital in Malmö has around 2,800 people on its files. Every intravenous drug user is allowed to take part in the programme; the only rule is the minimum age of 20. Every year the programme is used by 1,000 people a year, who exchange 12,000 needles a year. Besides the possibility of exchanging needles, the programme also offers general health care. The clients undergo a HIV test every three months, they are vaccinated against hepatitis B, and are offered general medical care. The programme even has a midwife who visits once a week.

5.5 Conclusion

This chapter started by giving a description of the various drugs that are available. The 'typical' drug addict in Sweden uses amphetamine intravenously. The background of the use of central stimulants has already been discussed, in chapter three. Amphetamine use is episodic, meaning the substance is taken during several consecutive days and nights, which is followed by a period of rest for which heroin is sometimes used as a 'downer'. After this, the cycle restarts. In recent years some amphetamine users have changed to heroin. Unlike heroin, amphetamine is not really a street drug; users usually buy amphetamine in apartments. Most amphetamines in Sweden are said to be imported from Poland.

The use of heroin has been relatively rare in Sweden, in the city of Gothenburg in the west it was almost absent. The heroin on the market used to be white, of South East Asian origin. In recent years cheaper brown South West Asian heroin has become more available. In the bigger Swedish cities heroin is relatively easy to obtain. This is particularly evident in Sweden's main and most visible drug scene, *Sergels Torg* in the heart of Stockholm and its surroundings, where drug users and drug dealers can be found almost twenty-four hours a day. The special police actions that were introduced to disturb the market have not managed to curb the activity. A consequence has been that heroin is increasingly sold from apartments and in the cities' suburbs where the police are not very active.

Cannabis found on the Swedish market is usually in the form of hash, which mostly originates from Morocco. Due to police efforts, it has become increasingly difficult to find cannabis on the streets. Here also, the effect has been that selling has moved from the streets to apartments. Hash in Sweden is usually smoked in a pipe, whilst joints are less common. There are some indications that the intoxication-oriented consumption pattern that is found with regard to alcohol, is also to some extent valid for cannabis.

In the 1980s the bias of the police activities shifted from the supply side to the demand side. The aim was no longer to target big dealers, but the drug users, since they are considered to be the motor of the 'drug engine'. In the same decade waivers of prosecution were restricted and in 1989 drug use was criminalised. Since 1993 drug use is punishable by an imprisonment of six months, which means it forces suspected drug users to undergo a urine test. The reason for introducing these measures is that they enable 'new' drug users to be found who were previously unknown to the authorities. Approximately 10,000 urine tests are currently performed in Sweden every year. Although new drug users were detected when the urine test were introduced, the figures show that most (alleged) drug users undergoing urine tests are actually the 'old' drug addicts who are already known.

In recent years there have been approximately 30,000 drug offences per year. Drug offences are classified in three categories, depending on the gravity of the offence: minor, normal, and major. The 30,000 drug offences lead to a lower number of convicted drug offences of 4,000 to 5,000 a year. The large majority of drug offences fall into the 'minor' category which often lead to an administrative sanctions. Generally speaking, judicial practice is severe. A drug offence is always followed by a fine or imprisonment. The lowest fine, such as for drug use detected by a urine test amounts to 900 kronor, which in some cases is halved. Selling drugs automatically leads to a prison sentence.

The main objective of the police activities is to prevent drug use. Officially the policy is to arrest every drug user and to direct this person to a social worker, who is either working directly with the police or working for the social services of the community. The social worker then refers the drug user to a suitable treatment programme. As has been described, there are many different treatment programmes in Sweden, the predominant form consisting of therapeutic communities. Besides voluntary treatment there is also the possibility of putting someone into compulsory care. This much discussed form of drug treatment is, however, not common and is applied in a decreasing number of cases.

The Swedish treatment system as it is often presented was to some extent applicable to the situation in the 1980s, when there were enough financial resources (made) available to place people in treatment for a two-year period. Especially in the latter half of the 1980s, when under the threat of HIV drug users were considered a key group who could spread the virus, huge sums of money were allocated for drug treatment programmes.

The reality of the 1990s is that the economic crisis Sweden faces, has led to substantial cuts in the resources allocated for treatment. As a result, many clinics and sections of hospitals have been closed. Moreover, the length of treatment has reduced substantially. Whereas in the 1980s it was normal for a drug user to spend two years in an in-patient treatment programme, in the 1990s most treatment courses are less expensive out-patient programmes that last several months.

The shift from in-patient to out-patient drug treatment programmes is partly related to a different system of financing. Today, drug treatment is no longer paid for from the national budget, but is now the responsibility of the local social services who have to pay for it from their resources. Since the local authorities have also suffered budget cuts, this has resulted in a situation where it has become increasingly difficult even to get treatment. Furthermore, because of high unemployment it is no longer possible to offer work for everyone. This also means that the Swedish model that wishes to offer a drug addict who wants to kick the habit in a place in a treatment centre and after a period of rehabilitation the possibility of re-entering civilised society where he or she will find work, no longer exists. Given the unemployment rate, it is very difficult, if not virtually impossible for a former drug addict to find work. The budget cuts in treatment programmes imply that the 'caring chain' is reaching less people than before, although the increase in drug use cannot be doubted.

6 Is the Swedish Drug Policy Effective?

6.1 Introduction

Whether a drug policy is effective or not is a very difficult question to answer. The main reason for this being that no standard criteria exist to 'measure' the success or failure of a drug policy. To be able to present the success or effectiveness of one's policy, one needs, of course, some criteria to measure this. However it is often forgotten that these criteria are not always applicable to other countries, because the objectives of a drug policy, assuming countries have a drug policy and corresponding objectives, differ from one country to the other.

As has been stated in previous chapters, Sweden's objective is to strive for a drug-free society. Having this as the main objective, the criteria to measure the effectiveness of the policy should be centred on the prevalence of drug use. In Sweden it is alleged that its restrictive drug policy, especially when it was reinforced in the 1980s, has resulted in a decrease of both experimental drug use and the number of drug addicts. The prevalence and incidence figures of drug use and the success that is attributed to these figures will be discussed in the section that follows this introduction. In 6.3 new patterns of drug use will be discussed, which partly reflects the findings of the visits to drug scenes and underprivileged urban areas.

In the light of the goal of the drug-free society other possible criteria such as the social conditions in which drug users are living, the society's reactions to drug use, and morbidity and mortality rates, are consequently less relevant. As a matter of fact, the high mortality figures in Sweden have rarely played an role in the drug policy debate. The fact that some of the drug users die, seems to be regarded as a consequence of the game the drug user plays. But it is not only the prevalence of drug use that can be an indicator to determine whether a drug policy can be called effective. Therefore, this chapter will also focus on other criteria, since they are generally accepted indicators to determine the effects of an applied drug policy.

Since prevention, control measures, and treatment form the basis of the Swedish drug policy, all three elements will be extensively discussed in this chapter. The control measures will be discussed in section 6.4, treatment will come up in 6.5, and prevention will be discussed at the end of this chapter, in section 6.8.

6.2 Prevalence of Drug Use

Prevalence Figures

Surveys from 1988 to 1993 show that 8-9% of the Swedish population between the age of 16 and 74 has tried drugs at some time (lifetime prevalence).[1] This prevalence is probably a little bit lower than in other Western European countries. Last year's prevalence for drugs use is however relatively low: 0.8.[2]

To look at the development of drug use in Sweden, one can refer to two surveys that are carried out on a yearly basis: one among 9th grade school children (15-16 years old) and one among (male) military conscripts (18 years old).[3] It is on the basis of the progress of these figures that the Swedish drug policy is often called effective. The prevalence of drug use among both 9th grade students and military conscripts seems to have decreased as a result of the stricter policy. The decrease in drug use seems in particular to have occurred in the 1980s, the decade when the drug policy was harshened. These trends are presented in several government publications, sometimes in an emotive way. In *The Hash Book* one reads that the restrictive policy has resulted in lower drug use than in other countries: 5% of the 9th grade students (15-16 years old) had tried drugs in 1993, whilst in Denmark 24% of young people from 16-19 had ever smoked hash, and 17% had smoked in the last year. Aside from the fact that these figures cannot be compared since they refer to different age categories, one can also question the more general assumption that the sharpest decline in drug use occurred in the 1980s when the drug policy was harshened. In *Drug Policy – The Swedish Experience*, one reads for example: "During the 1970s, experimental drug use steadied at a relatively high level. From about 1980 onwards it declined noticeably among young people".4

It is doubtful whether this really is the case. Looking at the figures it is more true to state that the sharp decline has already occurred in the 1970s. It seems that the fall that happened during the 1980s, was only a continuation of an already existing trend. Indeed, in *Trends in Alcohol and Drug Use in Sweden*, a report giving an overview of the existing prevalence figures, one reads:

> "The proportion of 9th grade students who report having used drugs at least once was highest in the beginning of this time period [1971] and decreased markedly during the first half of the 1970s. Among boys the proportion went down from 14% in 1971 to 7% 1975, and among girls from 17% in 1971 to 8% in 1975. During the first years of the 1980s, the proportions remained around 8-9% for both groups. In 1983 they decreased to about 5% among boys and about 6% among girls."5

Henrik Tham has analysed the prevalence figures of experimental drug use among 9th grade students. From his analysis one can derive that there are actually two possibilities, both of which are presented in a graph.6 It is not necessary to show this graph here and discuss its details; what is relevant is that in both possibilities the sharpest decrease in experimental drug use occurred in the 1970s. In the 1980s this trend continued, but the decrease in drug use is less steep than in the 1970s. When these figures are put in a wider context, the Swedish trend fits into the international development of decreasing experimental drug use during the 1970s and the 1980s in particular, not only in Europe, but in the United Stated as well.7 Comparative studies of the German Karl-Heinz Reuband have shown that in several European countries the prevalence of drug use has undergone the same trend, irrespective of the applied drug policy.8 Even in the 'liberal' Netherlands a sharp decrease of cannabis use was observed among school students from the early 1970s into the 1980s.9

The prevalence figures of military conscript gives a slightly different picture. The proportion of military conscripts that declared to have tried drugs during the 1970s varied between 15% and 19%. In the 1980s this figure would drop to 10%, reaching the (lowest) level of 5.8% in 1988. The life time prevalence of both 9th grade students (15-16 year) and military conscripts (18 years olds males) since 1971 are presented in graph 6.1.

Graph 6.1 Life time prevalence of drug use among 9th grade students and military conscripts.

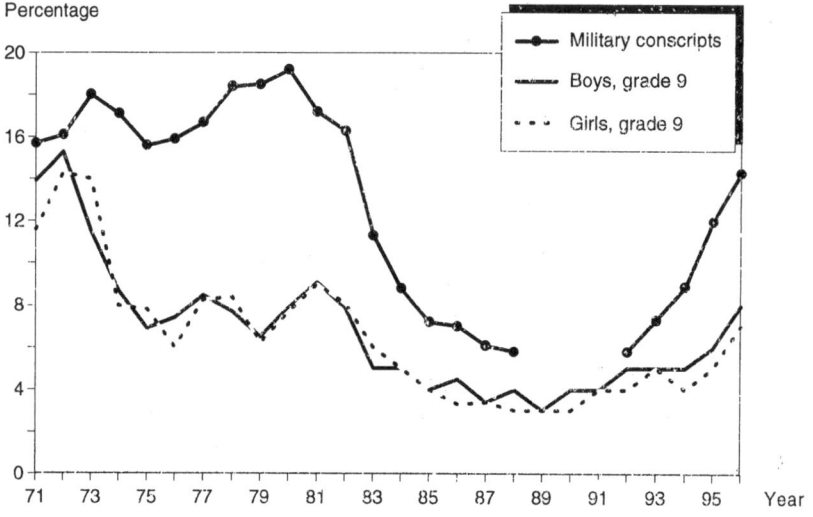

Source: CAN (1997)

There is little doubt the prevalence of experimental drug use has decreased in Sweden during the 1970s and 1980s. That is to say, if one refers to the life time prevalence of the two categories that are shown in the above graph. There are no figures available for older age groups, which means one cannot make a more general observation on the prevalence of experimental drug use. There is reason to suppose that some of the people who experiment with drugs, do so after the age of 15-16 or 18. In the city of Amsterdam, where cannabis is widely available, the average age of first use is 20.[10] The hypothesis that some people experiment at an older age becomes more likely looking at figures showing the life time prevalence of the city of Oslo (see graph 6.2).

136

Graph 6.2 Lifetime Prevalence of Cannabis Use among Young People in Oslo, in Three Age Categories.

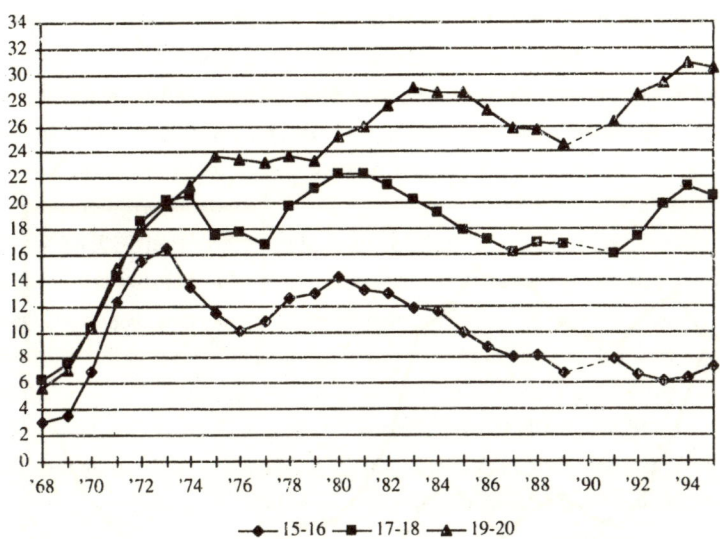

—◆— 15-16 —■— 17-18 —▲— 19-20

Source: Astrid Skretting (1996), p. 45.

The Oslo prevalence figures can, to some extent, be compared to the figures in graph 6.1. It should be noted that the Swedish figures are national, and the Norwegian only refer to the capital Oslo; the prevalence of drug use is usually higher in urban than in rural areas. On the other hand, the Oslo figures refer to cannabis only, whilst the Swedish data refers to all drugs.

The prevalence figures of Oslo might shed a different light on the Swedish figures. When the prevalence figures of the 15-16 years Swedish school students are compared to those of 15-16 years old Oslo youngsters, the similarities are striking. Although the Oslo figures are (slightly) higher, they show the same trend as the Swedish figures. The Oslo figures suggest that if one solely looks at the prevalence of 15-16 years old, the general trend during the 1970s and 1980s is downward. If however, the figures of older age groups are included, a completely different picture results. The Oslo figures clearly show that some of those who try cannabis, do so after the age 15-16; another section of the users starts after the age of 18. Moreover, it is likely that after the age of 20 even more people will try cannabis. As was said, this is also the average age of first cannabis use in Amsterdam.

In Sweden there are no prevalence figure available for older age groups other than 15-16 and 18 years old, but the Oslo figures at least show that on the basis of prevalence figures of 15-16 and 18 years old alone, one cannot make a sound general statement about the prevalence of experimental drug use in general. To make a more general observation on the prevalence of experimental drug use, one could be surprised that so 'many' young people report having used drugs. Considering that in Sweden drug use is considered as very deviant behaviour, and the fact that the 9th grade school students fill in the questionnaire while they are in school, where they feel that they are being observed by their teachers, it is inevitable that there is some underreporting of drug use.[11] Whereas in the 1970s it was, to some extent socially acceptable to say one had used cannabis, in the pursuit of the drug-free society of the 1980s and 1990s this behaviour has become more deviant and socially marginalised, to such an extent it has become a matter one can only discuss with one's most intimate friends.

Graph 6.1 also shows that the downward trend in experimental drug use was reversed around 1991. In the 1990s drug use would gradually increase. The figures show that in the 1990s more 9th grade students experiment with drugs. The highest figure reached so far was in 1996, 8% of the boys and 7% of girls declared having tried drugs. Compared to 1990 and 1991, the prevalence of experimental drug use in this group has doubled in 1996.

It is interesting to note that among 9th grade students the prevalence of solvents (glue, thinner, etc.) has actually been higher than the prevalence of drug use. 11% of the boys, and 7% of the girls declared having used solvents.[12] Furthermore, in 1996 5% of the military conscripts reported having sniffed during the previous two year period.[13] Social workers report that the sniffing of lighter gas is increasing among teenagers. This can sometimes leads to serious accidents; in 1995 three 14 year-old boys died of a an 'overdose' of lighter gas, after a single inhalation using a plastic bag filled with lighter gas.[14]

As expected, the prevalence of experimental drug use among 18 years military conscripts is higher than that of 9th grade students, but the trend is similar. The prevalence of drug use among this group gradually rises from 6% in 1988 and 1992 to 12% in 1995 and 14% in 1996. This means the life time prevalence has doubled since 1992.

Prevalence figures of a survey that is carried out by the City of Stockholm among 9th grade students, also show an increase in the 1990s. Since the prevalence of drug use is usually higher in urban areas, the Stockholm figures are, as expected, higher than the national prevalence figures. Whereas in 1990 8% of these 15-16 years old school students declared having used drugs, in 1996 it was 13%.[15]

To be able to comment on the prevalence of drug use, it is insufficient to look only at the life time prevalence; one should also study more recent use, like last month prevalence. It is interesting to see that among 9th grade students in Sweden last month prevalence has never been high. After the scores of 6% and 7% in respectively 1971 and 1972, this level has never been reached again. Last month prevalence of drug use during the 1970s and 1980s varied between 1-4%. From the mid 1980s until 1994, 1% reported having used cannabis in the last month. In 1995 and 1996 this figure rose to approximately 2%.

Last month prevalence of drug use among 18 years old military conscripts reached its peak in early 1970s with 5%, and gradually declined until reaching around 1% in the late 1980s and early 1990s. The sharpest decline in use was reported in the 1970s, and not in the 1980s as it is sometimes stated. From 1995 to 1996 the last month prevalence among military conscripts increased from 1% to 2%.

The recent increase in both experimental drug use and last month prevalence can hardly be called a 'success' in the light of the pursuit of the drug-free society. What is striking in this respect is that the surveys that are carried out every year among 9th grade school students show that increasing numbers declare that they want to try cannabis.

Estimations of the Number of Drug Addicts
There is an ongoing debate among scientists in Sweden about the number of drug addicts. Two case finding studies, carried out in 1979 and

1992, form the basis of these discussions. The debate is centred on the question of how the figures of these two case-findings studies should be interpreted and compared. Because of this ongoing debate, it is not possible to present here in an 'objective' way the expansion of the number of drug addicts in Sweden.

The case finding studies used the capture-recapture method to 'detect' heavy drug abusers. Different types of sources, such as social workers, the police, youth centres, etc., were asked to report drug users. The 1979 study was based on three reporting systems, the 1992 study on six. The first national case-finding study was carried out in 1979. Based on the capture-recapture method between 10,000 and 14,000 heavy drug abusers were found in Sweden (average: 12,000). Heavy drug abusers are defined here as "either injecting or using drugs in some other way daily or virtually every day".[16] This definition could be roughly compared to how some other countries label 'drug addicts'. As said before, in Sweden it is not so much heroin that was becoming the 'problem drug', but amphetamines. The population of heavy drug abusers basically consisted of amphetamine users, and only to a limited extent of heroin users and cannabis users. Approximately 90% of the heavy drug abusers were intravenous users.

The second case-finding study was carried out in 1992. The difference from the 1979 sample was that this time a regional sample was carried out, representing 45% of the population. The problem this can pose, concerns the comparability of the two studies. Since in 1992 a regional sample was made, it is a methodological question how these findings are adjusted and extrapolated to the national level to make a comparison with the 1979 study. The 1992 regional sample found approximately 19,500 drug users, who applied to the definition of 'heavy drug abuse', resulted in 9,000 people. Since not everyone is reported in the same municipality as where he or she is officially living, this number was corrected to 8,000. Since this figure referred to the regional sample of 45% of the population, the national number of heavy drug abusers in 1992 was estimated to be between 14,000 and 20,000, with an average of 17,000. Central stimulants (amphetamine) were the most commonly used drugs (82%), cannabis ranked second, whilst heroin came third (32%). As was the case in 1979, approximately 10% of the heavy drug abusers was not injecting.

Table 6.1 Age Distribution of the Number of Heavy Drug Abusers in 1979 and 1992

Age	1979		1992	
< 18	150	1%	50	0%
18 - 19	600	5%	200	1%
20 - 24	3,700	31%	1,450	9%
25 - 29	3,800	32%	3,650	21%
30 - 34	2,000	17%	4,250	25%
35 - 39	900	8%	3,800	22%
40 - 44	350	3%	2,050	12%
45 - 49	200	2%	950	6%
50 +	150	1%	550	3%
Total	12,000	100%	17,000	100%

Source: CAN (1997), p. 253.

The question now is how the increase of heavy drug abusers from 12,000 (10,000-14,000) in 1979 to 17,000 (14,000-20,000) in 1992 should be interpreted. In view of the goal of Swedish drug policy, to bring down drug use and drug addiction, this trend seems to run counter. However, the figures are interpreted as showing there were fewer first-time drug abusers in 1992 than in 1979. In *Drug Policy – The Swedish Experience*, one reads that the 1992 study suggests that "first time recruitment of young persons for severe drug abuse was at a very low level for the greater part of the 1980s".[17] In other words, one does no longer look at the prevalence, but now at the incidence, especially of young people. The argument then is, if one looks at the distribution into different age categories, the incidence among the younger age categories is lower than among older age categories. Hence, the higher number of heavy drug abusers in 1992 is interpreted as being partly an ageing group phenomenon. This would be supported by the fact that the average age increased from 27 in 1979 to 32 in 1992. Moreover, it is said that the age structure and the duration of drug abuse "suggest that most of the new recruitment occurred at the end of the 1970s and beginning of the 1980s, after which new recruitment appears to have fallen".[18] In short, Swedish drug policy would have been effective with respect to heavy drug abuse; not because the number has gone down, but because the incidence of young abusers (under 25) would have gone down.

Although this argument may look conclusive, several critical remarks can be made in about it. First of all, the same argument as mentioned before when the life time prevalence figures were discussed, may be valid here: to what extent is the applied drug policy of influence on the incidence and prevalence in use? As always when discussing trends in drug use, one should never exclude that if the incidence goes down, this is related to other (autonomous) processes other than the actual drug policy that was conducted. If it is true that the incidence of heavy drug abusers was lower in the 1980s than in the 1960s and 1970s, this may have resulted from the cultural fact that in the 1980s drugs were 'out', not only in Sweden but in most parts of the Western world. In this regard one should also point at another 'external' factor. In the appendix of the report on the 1992 study, Ole-Jorgen Skog writes that the recruitment in the younger age groups was indeed reduced, but he argues this was due to the Aids epidemic, rather than the effect of the restrictive drug policy.[19]

Secondly, the official figures show an increase from 12,000 heavy drug abusers in 1979 to 17,000 in 1992. The claim is that the incidence of heavy drug abusers went down during the 1980s. It is also claimed that the age structure and the duration of abuse suggest that most new recruitments occurred at the end of the 1970s and early 1980s.[20] If the latter is indeed the case, and bearing in mind both the estimation of 12,000 in 1979 and the increase of 5,000 heavy drug abuser in 13 years until 1992, this would imply the incidence of heavy drug abuse has been extremely substantial at the beginning of the 1980s.

A third aspect deserving a closer look concerns the drop-out rate. As was said, the increase from 12,000 to 17,000 heavy drug abusers is allegedly considered effective in the sense that the incidence went down, which happened especially among the younger age groups. However, this arguments only holds if the drop-out rate is not very high; the reason being that a higher drop-out rate would automatically imply a higher incidence (otherwise there could be no question of a 5,000 increase). In this case, the alleged drop-out rate is 3% a year. However, this drop-out rate is only based on mortality figures, in other words the heavy drug abusers that die.[21] The drop-out rate should also take into account the natural rate of people that stop using drugs (and stay alive). As a result, the real drop-out rate should be (much) higher. This however, also implies the incidence of heavy drug abusers between 1979 and 1992 was higher as well. Ole-Jorgen Skog calculated that about 40% of those who were heavy drug abusers in 1979 had left the population by the time of the 1992 study.[22] In a comprehensive and critical analysis of the Swedish prevalence figures Ted Goldberg has stated in this respect:

"If Skog comes close to the truth when he estimates that 40% of the 12,000 hard-core misusers in the 1979 study had left the population by 1992, and if UNO-92's[23] estimate of an increase of 5,000 hard-core misusers between the two studies is fairly accurate, Sweden has recruited approximately 10,000 new hard-core misusers in the 13-year period. Therefore there must have been a very significant recruitment of adolescents during the period 1979-1992. There is simply no other reasonable explanation".[24]

Goldberg also supports this thesis by other data. For example, he considers it unlikely that among the estimated 17,000 heavy drug abusers there were only 250 teenagers (see table 6.1). He points to the fact that the Maria Ungdom Youth Clinic, which recruits only from the Greater Stockholm Area, has contact with more than 500 drug consuming teenagers a year. When looked at the number of teenagers penalised from drug offences, this number rose from 585 in 1992 to 735 in 1994.[25] Although not every teenager in contact with the Maria Ungdom Youth Clinic, nor every penalised teenager belongs the heavy drug abusers category, Goldberg considers that these figures tend to support his point that the figure of the 1992 study is an underestimation.

In the appendix of a recent study by sociology professor Eckart Kühlhorn et. al. the data of the 1992 has been restudied.[26] Kühlhorn et. al. came to the conclusion that the estimation of 17,000 in 1992 is in fact an underestimation. Although not everyone subscribes to this conclusion, it may come as a surprise that Kühlhorn who is generally known as a supporter of the restrictive line, now questions the 1992 figure.

6.3 New Patterns of Drug Use

Besides an increase in both experimental drug use and more 'regular use' (last month prevalence) among teenagers as is seen by the available surveys, there are some other new trends in drug use as well. It was previously mentioned that for a few years heroin use has been on the increase, not only among (former) amphetamine users, but also among young people without a long drug career. It is especially the (smoked) brown heroin base, also known as brown sugar, Turkish heroin, or heroin No. 3, that is reported to be on the increase. Although this type of heroin is already easily available in other parts of Europe and probably is the most widely used substance among drug addicts, it is relatively new in Sweden. One reason is of course that, traditionally, most Swedish drug addicts took amphetamine; those taking heroin, were used to taking the (white) heroin No. 4.

Not many written sources report heroin smoking as being on the increase, the main reason being that no specific research has been done on this subject. In a police report it is stated that the habit of smoking heroin, reported for some years, "is no longer a tendency, but a clear trend".[27] Börje Olsson wrote that it is undeniable that both the use of cannabis and brown heroin is on the increase. The latter would be used by certain ethnic groups and socially disadvantaged young people.[28] In the latest CAN report issued in 1997 one reads there are reports that heroin smoking is on the rise, which is partly based on CAN's regional reporting system.[29] The rise in heroin use among young people can be derived from statistics of the social services.[30] Whereas amphetamine had always been more widespread than heroin use, for a few years now the number of heroin users has increased, and the two now balance one another out. If one looks at data showing the average age of drug users known to social services, the mean age of amphetamine users is going up; the mean age of heroin users on the other hand is not increasing at the same rate. If one looks at the lower age categories of drug users, one can observe heroin has overtaken amphetamine.[31] The needle exchange programme in Malmö in which 1,000 people a year take part, yields of a very rich databank. The available data clearly show the rise of heroin. If one looks at the younger people under 30, 75% were amphetamine users in 1992. Six years later, the picture has completely changed; 75% were using heroin as their main drug.

During the interviews and the several visits to underprivileged areas of the big Swedish cities, the increase in heroin smoking was a subject that was widely discussed. Both police sources and especially social workers working on the street level confirm the reporting of an increase in heroin smoking. This development occurs in particular in the underprivileged urban areas where several different immigration groups are living, some-times representing more than half, or practically the total population of certain neighbourhoods. Immigrants groups are also over-represented among the 'new' heroin use as it is observed. These factors probably ex-plain why it is often thought that this heroin use would in fact signify the 'import' into Sweden of traditional drug use of these population groups. In other words, it is alleged that some immigrant groups, especially from countries in the Middle East where traditional opium use exists, have continued their opiate use in Sweden. Because opium is not easily availa-ble, users would have shifted from opium to heroin in Sweden. The im-migrants groups would then have introduced heroin to other groups, like the indigenous Swedes.

However, this explanation of the increase in heroin use is too simple and short-sighted, and does not take into account other important possible explanations. One of the very few studies on this subject, is a study done by psychiatrist Riyadh al-Baldawi, working at the St. Görans Hospital in Stockholm, sheds a different light on the phenomenon. Around 10% of the total 400 to 500 patients Al-Baldawi sees every year belong to immigrants groups. In recent years there has been an increase in patients from the Africa, Latin America, and especially the Middle East. This situation led to dedicating a special study on 200 immigrant patients. His study showed that 72% of the immigrants of the studied group had started using drugs in Sweden, without having a background of traditional use.[32] Hence, most of these people had started taking drugs in Sweden; in a few cases use had begun in a third country. Although al-Baldawi's findings are only based on clinical experiences, implying that on the basis of these findings no gener-al statements can be made about substance abuse among immigrants in general, his data showed the relationship between the alleged traditional use and drug use in Sweden is far from certain.

Al-Baldawi categorises his patients into two groups: second generation immigrants and political refugees. The main reasons al-Baldawi sees for immigrants taking drugs are (besides self-medication in the case of psychiatric disorders) drugs as a weapon to defend or to escape from a crisis, and when it comes to younger people, to belong to the group and to find an identity.[33] The idea that people are using drugs to escape a 'crisis' is especially relevant since many of the patients are political refugees. The situations in which they find themselves are in many cases very difficult, not only when they are waiting in a refugee camp to hear what decision has been made about them, but also when they leave the camps to start living a 'normal' life in Swedish society.

The extent of the phenomenon is unknown. It may be that the issue of problematic drug use among immigrant groups is much bigger than is generally thought. There is certainly reason to believe that immigrant groups are reluctant to direct themselves to social and medical authorities. As al-Baldawi points out, many immigrants are suspicious of authorities and fear that seeking help from the social authorities will result in the police being notified and the loss of their residence permit.[34]

In drug research it is known that some people run a higher risk of developing particular patterns of drug use (like drug abuse) than others. Medical research has shown this vulnerability can have a psychological or psychiatric background. Sociology has made a contribution in the sense that these patterns of drug use may be associated with social problems, such as unemployment, the absence of future prospects, etc. For example, the fact that drug addicts are over-represented in certain deprived urban areas in the UK, France, and USA, seems related to the local, social conditions under which the inhabitants of these areas grow up.

Particular patterns of drug use can also be partly related to the problems immigrant groups are facing in the 'new' societies they live in. For example, in Amsterdam, the Surinamese population is very much over-represented among the population of drug addicts. Most of them arrived in the early 1970s in the Netherlands, just before the independence of Surinam in 1975. The many problems they were facing in adapting to the new society they were living in, contributed to the fact they started and continued using heroin, which was on the rise in the early 1970s. The same phenomenon can be observed in several other countries, especially if immigrant groups are living in difficult social circumstances without prospects.

On the basis of the fieldwork in deprived areas of Stockholm, Malmö, and Gothenburg, and the many conversations held with drug users and social workers, one gets the impression this phenomenon is also taking place in Sweden. Immigrants groups in general, and political refugees in particular, should, to some extent be regarded as 'risk groups'; having gone through hard times, they are now facing problems in the new society they are living in. However, this insight seems to have been somewhat neglected in Sweden, the main reason being that the emphasis was put on the availability of drugs as a factor explaining why people use drugs and have certain patterns of drug use. The fact that young people with an immigrant background are over-represented among problematic drug users in treatment centres, makes it clear the 'cause' might be of a different nature. For example, at the Maria Ungdom Youth Clinic in Stockholm, 40% of the 1200 clients in 1995 had an immigrant background; in the Hassela centres even 60% to 70% of the 'students' had an immigrant background.

Skärholmen
Skärholmen is a south eastern district of Stockholm. It has a population of 35,000 inhabitants, 30% of whom belong to immigrant groups. Most people live in high-rise apartments that were built in the 1960s as a part of the 'million programme', the goal being to build one million homes in a short period of time. Skärholmen cannot be designated as a real problem area. Neighbouring districts, in the municipality of Botkyrka, are much worse off with more immigrants and a higher unemployment rate. However, according to the social workers working in Skärholmen, the area is facing a growing drug problem. The drugs that are being used by young people are cannabis and heroin; the latter is sometimes smoked together with rohypnol. Other patterns of drug use are to mix beer and paracetamol, and to sniff lighter fuel and other solvents. In Skärholmen a few 'teenager gangs' can be found. Drug use has an important place in the lifestyle of these gangs of mixed ethnic background, but in which indige-

nous Swedes form a minority. Besides using drugs, these groups are also selling different kinds of drugs at the central market place, near to the subway station. However, in Skärholmen it is much more common to sell drugs from apartments, that are especially rented for this purpose.

Besides young people using drugs, social workers declare a few older 'heroin smoking groups' can be found, in the age group 25 to 40. Not much is known about these 'groups' since the heroin is used in 'social gatherings' in an apartment. These groups are not ethnically mixed; they are composed of either Arabs, or Latin Americans, many of whom are highly educated.

Botkyrka

Just outside the municipality of Stockholm and close to Skärholmen, one finds the municipality of Botkyrka. Generally the social problems in this municipality are (much) bigger, especially in the districts Alby, Fittja, Hallunda, and Norsborg. Most houses in Botkyrka were built in the 1960s as part of the 'million programme', especially in the northern part. In recent decades the population has grown substantially from 40,000 in 1970 to 70,000 in 1996. A large part of the population is under 30 years old, resulting in an unequal population distribution. Furthermore, the unemployment rate is high and immigrants form a large part of the population.

Botkyrka can be divided in two parts, a southern part consisting of the districts Storvreten, Tullinge, and Tumba; and a northern part where the districts Alby, Fittja, Hallunda, and Norsborg are found. Between the two parts there is, to some extent, an ethnic division: many Finnish immigrants live in the 'better' southern part, whilst the northern part is dominated by non-Nordic immigrants: Chileans, Lebanese, and especially Turks. Non-Nordic immigrants represent a large part of the population in these areas, varying from 40% in Halunda and Norsborg, to 70-80% in Alby and Fittja.

The general situation in Botkyrka seems to be worsening. Among the people there is an increasing feeling of frustration and tension. People do not freely go to the police anymore and the police are afraid to go into certain areas during the night, although one cannot yet speak of 'no go areas'. Despite these problems, the situation is not as bad as the popular press portrays it, or as the well-known hip hop group the *Latin Kings* it describes in their lyrics, talking about violence, guns, and drugs. Improvements are also taking place, especially with a housing policy directed towards having a more mixed population.

There are no recent figures concerning the drug problem in Botkyrka. The latest figures date from the 1992 case finding study, when 278 drug abusers were found (of a total of 19,500 for Sweden at large). The social workers are convinced that these 278 drug abusers detected in 1992 are an underestimation.[35] At the time (in 1992) the social services of Botkyrka were in the process of reorganisation, which led to a lower number of drug abusers to be reported than were actually known. Moreover, the 278 drug abusers of 1992 is certainly no longer applicable to today's situation since there is much more heroin use today than in 1992.

The drug problem can be found especially in the northern part of Botkyrka, where the unemployment is higher and many immigrants are living without real prospects. The majority of the new drug abusers known to the social services consists of youngsters under 25, many of whom have an immigrant background. The increase of heroin is very apparent in the activities of the social services. In the 1980s heroin was not very common in the case load of social workers who worked with drug addicts; heroin was the main drug in only one out of ten cases, with amphetamine and hash being more dominant. Today this balance has changed; around half of the drug addicts in contact with social workers is using heroin. Of those who get treatment, heroin is the dominant drug in the majority of the cases.

In the neighbourhoods which were visited with social workers, the drug problem became apparent.[36] For example, the Alby district has not much to offer to its population; for entertainment one has to go to Stockholm. Every night a group of 50-60 young people can be found 'hanging around' in Alby's small shopping centre. Drugs, especially heroin, are very present in this group. According to police figures, Alby should have around 50 heroin users. Social workers knowing the area and being able to 'trace' networks, state the real number should be 300 to 400. Many of the heroin users are immigrants with different kinds of problems, some of which are related to their past in their homelands. This is the case for example with the Lebanese who came to Sweden during the civil war.

Angered

The popular press, especially the tabloids, sometimes devote an article to the growing Swedish 'ghettos'. When this happens, certain districts of Stockholm, like for example Rinkeby and Tensta are usually the subject of the articles. One gets the impression this 'Stockholm bias' hides what is happening in other parts of Sweden, like in Gothenburg, the big working-class city in the west and Sweden's 'most segregated city'. Gothenburg has been mentioned earlier as having been an exceptional city in the sense that heroin use was absent for a long time; the typical drug addict here was consuming amphetamine. In the 1990s heroin was 'introduced'. As part of the fieldwork, a visit was paid to some of Gothenburg's suburbs.

Angered is a northern district of Gothenburg, with a population of 40,000, of which approximately 50% is immigrant. Angered is on the outskirts of Gothenburg, actually more outside than inside the city. To get to Angered one takes a tram that goes through a large uninhabited area first before reaching the buildings of the suburbs. The tram is sometimes (pejoratively) called the 'Garlic Express', probably because many of the passengers originate from countries where garlic is commonly used in the kitchen.

The two areas that were visited in Angered are Hammarkullen and Hjällbo. Most houses in these two areas belong to the 'million programme' of the late 1960s and early 1970s. Hammarkullen and Hjällbo are areas of Angered where a large groups of immigrants are concentrated, but the two differ substantially in the sense they are ethnically divided. Since the 1970s large groups of Latin American immigrants have lived in Hammarkullen, many of whom came to Sweden as political refugees. The immigrants originate from different countries: Argentina, Bolivia, Chile, and Peru. Hjällbo on the other hand, is populated by more recent immigrants, of whom a substantial portion arrived as political refugees. The inhabitants of Hjällbo originate from countries like Iran, Iraq, and Lebanon. In the 1990s many people have come from Somalia and the Balkan countries, like (former) Yugoslavians and Albanians (either from Albania or Kosovo), and Afghan children who have arrived without their parents. Very few of the original inhabitants of the 1970s still live in Hjällbo; most people have left, those who stayed are chiefly Turks and Yugoslavians. According to Elisabeth Karlsson, one of the fieldworkers who works with teenagers in the neighbourhoods, immigrants form around 90% of the population of Hjällbo. As a result, it is very rare to see white faces here, contrary to Hammarkullen where one can still find indigenous Swedes and Finnish immigrants. No precise unemployment figures have been found, but according to Elisabeth Karlsson the large majority of the people in Hjällbo are without work.

Young people (teenagers) form a large part of the population, but the neighbourhoods have nothing to offer them. A few years ago the city of Gothenburg had decided to cut down on the social services in these areas. As a result, the *Fritidsgård*, the community centre, is now only open a few days a week. The community centre in Hammarkullen is in a school canteen. The three fieldworkers (*Fältassistenter*) who are doing preventative work in the neighbourhoods (but have to cover a much wider area than just Hammarkullen and Hjällbo) are the people that are most familiar with the problems teenagers face in these deprived areas. The absence of any leisure facilities, the lack of any prospects for the future, and more generally, the fact of being excluded and not getting 'recognition', drives some young people into subcultures where 'respect' can be found. In such a situation 'respect' can easily turn into a hard and 'tough' attitude. The subculture that is developing seems to be influenced by the American subcultures of criminality, drugs, violence, and opposition to the police. Out of boredom and the desire for 'entertainment' it has happened several times that the police was called for the sole purpose of stoning the police car and 'fighting' the police. This has resulted in the situation where a police car will never come alone, but only with other cars or riot police. In Hammarkullen the relationship with the police has been particularly tense since 1994 when a Nazi meeting was held and the police 'protected' the Nazis. In the riots that broke out, many people were injured. Since many inhabitants in Hammarskullen are political refugees from Latin America, having had very bad experiences with the police and army, the relationship towards the police has deteriorated to an extremely low level, in some cases real 'hate'. The situation has deteriorated to such an extent that a police car cannot park any longer at the community centre without being damaged by local youths. In fact, one can talk about of the development of no-go-areas for the police.

In the railway station of Hammarkullen a group of teenagers (10-50) can regularly be found 'hanging around'. Many of these teenagers are developing deviant behaviour that consists of criminality, drug dealing and using drugs. All kinds of drugs are being used here, like hash, amphetamine, ecstasy, LSD, and to lesser extent (smoked) heroin. Drug dealing has become less visible, since it has moved from the street to apartments. Because of the fact that very few people are working with the teenagers in these areas, it is unclear how many teenagers are actually experimenting with drugs.

In the light of the difficult background of many of the teenagers, and the marginal situation they are living in, one can expect that experimenting with drugs can easily lead to patterns of drug use in which drugs will play a very dominant role. This is particularly true since many of the teenagers not only have a very fragile background, like for example the Afghan teenagers having experienced terrible things at an early age, nor are they now living is a very stable and secure environment. The absence of any real future prospects and the lack of any 'structures' may lead to the further development of alternative careers such as drug dealing.

If no real action is taken one can expect the worst in a few years time, when the teenagers have grown older and will serve as a role model for the younger ones. This can be reinforced by the fact that many feel excluded, both physically (far away in the suburbs outside Gothenburg) and socially (with very few possibilities for integration). One gets the impression that the authorities do not realise how serious the situation is and how it might deteriorate. This may lead to an even more aggravated and violent situation, resembling the experiences of France and the UK, where riots have taken place in highly segregated and deprived areas where young people (immigrants) grow up without hope.

6.4 Police Activities

It is impossible to judge a policy without taking into account its objectives. Since the focus of the police activities has shifted from the level of imports and 'catching big fish' to that of the drug users, the effectiveness of the police activities cannot be judged on the seized quantities of drugs. It was shown in section 5.3 that these figures are, by European standards, not very impressive. Of course, it should be said that this is largely due to Sweden's relatively small population (and thus, small potential market) and, more importantly, its peripheral location in Europe.

The task of the police is to enforce the law. Since the authorities have opted for a drug-free society, the Swedish house to be clean of drugs, and combatting drugs at a street level, thereby enabling the possibility of running a urine test to detect drug use, the police practice should be judged on these issues.

One can question several aspects of the urine tests that are being applied in Sweden. The reason behind the opportunity to force people to undergo a test of urine (or blood) is that this enables the detection of the criminal offence of drug use, without drug possession being a question. For example, it can now be verified if a person who denies having used drugs, speaks the truth. This is particularly relevant for young drug users; the urine test can detect drug use which makes an immediate intervention possible as the person can be directed to a social worker.

To begin with, the urine test has an ethical side. On the ground of suspicion that someone is under the influence of drugs, the suspect can be taken to a police station to undergo a test. The person does not have to cause disturbance, or make trouble or behave badly in any other way, since the reason for the police intervention is to detect any drug use. Besides questions related to the individual's freedom to use drugs if they cause no harm to anyone, this far-reaching measure can also be considered an infringement of people's rights in general, especially those who have not used drugs. This infringement was recognised by the government, but was considered justified in the light of the drug-free society. The then Minister of Justice declared in Parliament that "the interests of creating a drug-free society weighed so heavily that they justified the encroachment of an individual's integrity".[37]

Besides these ethical questions, one can also question whether the urine tests are efficient. The argument that urine tests also serve as a means to find drug dealers, suggesting drug users would say who is supplying them, cannot be taken seriously. If drug users give names, it is because of the tip-off money that is offered to them by the police. It has been shown that the amounts of money given to police informers can be considerable, especially for drug addicts eager to buy drugs. Moreover, one has to wonder if the urine tests make it really possible to detect 'new' drug users. Although new drug users have been found, this was basically the case in the period when the tests were introduced. Both drug users and drug dealers have adapted to the new situation and manage to stay out of the hands of the police, for example by not being too present at places kept under watch and guard by the police, like in Stockholm's drug scene *Plattan* and other well-known and visible drug scenes in the city centre. During the field-work that was done with one of the *Plattan* police teams, it appeared there were actually more police officers than drug addicts present. Of course this does not mean the number of drug addicts has dropped; they have simply moved elsewhere. An effect of the police presence here is that drug addicts have spread throughout the city. Those who have the opportunity, now make more use of other selling venues, such as apartments, or they buy from dealers equipped with a pager or mobile phone.

An effect of the police presence here has certainly been that the place has become 'cleaner'. In essence the goal to have the 'house clean of drugs' as was once stated by the late Olof Palme has been accomplished – at least at first sight. Therefore, in practice the police operations at street level, seem only to have led to a less visible 'drug situation', which in the eyes of most law-abiding citizens is also less threatening. Although the police operations certainly do not solve the Swedish drug problem, they may have contributed to a deeper desire as put forward by Arthur Gould. "Could it be [...] that social policies are characterised by a desire to 'keep the streets clean'? Is the desire to incarcerate alcoholics and drug addicts, in part, not simply a desire to care for or control them but a method by which they can be tidied away?"[38]

The original objective of the urine test was to detect young, new drug users, in other words new recruits. The Prosecutor General also recommended that the urine tests should be used for this purpose. As has been said, this was only the case in the beginning. The police soon applied the urine tests to the 'old' drug addicts who were already known to the police by and large. In practice this means that in many cases the urine tests are being used as a form of harassment. Another aspect of the urine test is that it is not applied everywhere or to the same extent. For example, in Gothenburg the police are more strict in doing urine tests than the Stockholm police. In some parts of Sweden the urine test is not performed at all.

As has been said before, the main effect of the special police actions has been that there are today less drug addicts and drug dealers concentrated in one area than before. This means of course a 'spread effect' has taken place. Hence, the police operations should be judged merely as symbolic, and as a method of assuring the general public than they have reduced the problem. Despite the almost continuous police presence at drug scenes like *Plattan*, drug dealers can be found at any time around *Plattan*. Just like the police the drug dealers seem to be working in shifts. Gambian street dealers have proved to be the 'die hards'. They usually club together in the central hall of the subway station. Due to the police presence and the constant possibility of being searched, they have adapted their strategy. A limited number (up to ten) heroin capsules is kept in the mouth, which can be swallowed if they are approached by a (plain-clothes) policeman. When swallowed the police cannot find any evidence of drug possession. If a police officer wants to arrest a drug dealer for selling, he has to see the transaction. Drug dealers and drug addicts have also made this more difficult. When a female drug addict approaches a drug dealer, the deal is often concluded by a 'kiss' by which the capsule is transferred. The constant presence of both the police and drug dealers and the way they interact, in one of Stockholm's main squares, reminds the observer of a cat-and-mouse game.

In section 5.3 it was also mentioned that the police also decided to target rave parties. The police raid on the 'Docklands' rave party in February 1996 was followed by a debate on the effectiveness of these 'razzias'. In an article in the Social Democratic newspaper *Aftonbladet*, written by Alec Carlberg, the chairman of RFHL, Margareta Olofsson, the chairman of the Freetime Council, and Gudrun Schyman, leader of the Left Party, all criticised the raid. The police did not intervene when a large Nazi meeting was held, but young people dancing at a party were thrown out, although the majority of them had not even taken drugs. In the following months 'Docklands' became a popular topic in the Swedish media, both on television, radio, and in the press. The serious daily newspaper *Dagens Nyheter* alone published fifty-nine articles on 'Docklands' and rave parties in a three-month period, eight of which appeared on the front page.[39] Esther van Fessem has shown how 'Docklands' was generally portrayed in the media, and how government institutions and pressure groups such as RNS treated the question. Even in the serious newspaper *Dagens Nyheter* one can see that the party visitors photographed in the paper are the ones dressed most extravagantly, and when some of them do not use drugs, they are presented as untypical cases.[40] Although it was never proved that many party visitors were consuming drugs, the 'Docklands' and drugs were clearly connected to each other. This was reinforced by the fact that the party organisers were associated with the liberal organisation *Freedom Front*, which is opposed to strong State interference in general. In this respect the phenomenon was perceived by some as a return to the 'liberal' late 1960s, and in fact a threat to the traditional values. It was alleged the *Freedom Front* also had liberal ideas on drugs. Eventually the court decided that the rave parties could continue, as there was no evidence they were promoting drug use.

The bias the police puts on rave parties and visible drug scenes in the city centres, for which many officers are being deployed, is in great contrast to what happens in some of the main cities' suburbs or 'ghettos', as described in section 6.3. In these areas some young people are experimenting with all kinds of drugs, which should be regarded as a far greater risk than the teenagers who take drugs at rave parties.

Those who are taking drugs at rave parties, are usually young people from the 'middle class'. Since most can be considered 'normal' young people without indications of being exceptionally vulnerable, it is to be expected that of those who consume drugs, only a (small) minority will, in the long run, develop problematic drug use. Even if some will encounter the negative effects of drugs or observe this in their surroundings, the probable effect will be that many people stop using drugs, or otherwise continue using but in a more moderate way. The self-regulating mechanisms that occur within groups cannot be underestimated.

However, the 'new' drug users in the suburban areas of the big cities, especially those living in the 'one million' housing schemes, are a completely different group from the 'middle class ravers'. First of all, the new drug users as they were described in section 6.3 live in 'working' or lower class areas with (very) high unemployment rates, resulting in many young people having few future prospects or no prospects at all. Hence, young people living in these areas, do not grow up in the same somewhat 'protected' surroundings as do their middle class peer groups. The unemployment rate in these areas can be over 50%; some neighbourhoods that have been visited, like for example Hjällbo in the north of Gothenburg, have an unemployment rate that is far higher.

Another characteristic of these suburban areas is that a large part of the population belongs to immigrant groups, many of whom who have a problematic background, especially the political refugees. The problematic background of fragile young people in the deprived areas that are experimenting with drugs, a situation that should be judged as relatively 'risky', places the priority the police has put on fighting drug use among middle class ravers in a strange light. The real potential drug problem is not to be found here, but among the young people in the suburbs.

However, the problems in the deprived suburbs are only known to a very limited extent. Few social workers, fieldworkers, and police officers are working in these areas. For example, the Gothenburg police have invested in its fight against drug use at weekend parties, while the city of Gothenburg has cut down substantially in its fieldworkers. Whereas ten years ago, Gothenburg had 40 fieldworkers, today only 15 are left.

6.5 The Treatment System

Drug Treatment Programmes

One of the central elements of Swedish drug policy consists of the treatment and rehabilitation of (problematic) drug users. As was said before, the aim is not to punish drug users but to help them to get off drugs. For this purpose the police and social workers work together to find drug users so that they can be offered treatment. The urine tests serve the same goal; when someone is taken to the police station for a urine test and found positive, the person is referred to the social workers who decide what kind of treatment or help can best be offered. In *Drug Policy – The Swedish Experience* one reads that "a drug-free society is a vision express-ing optimism and a positive view of humanity; the onslaught of drugs *can* be restrained, and drug abusers *can* be rehabilitated".[41]

The principle that it is not the intention of the drug policy to punish drug users should be judged positively. However, it is questionable if it is indeed possible to really rehabilitate drug addicts. International studies show that, in the long run, the results of drug treatments are generally poor. A frequently-occurring problem with the statistics from treatment centres is that is unclear as to what exactly they refer. In the first place one has to know if there were any admission criteria. If a selection takes place at the 'gate' of the treatment centre, this influences the end results. Secondly, do the abstinence figures refer to all clients who started the pro-gramme or only to the clients who managed to finish it? If the latter is the case, if the drop-out rate is excluded, one automatically has a second selection effect. Those who completed the treatment were the most moti-vated clients. A third aspect which should be looked at when discussing the efficacy of treatment is at what point in time does one sample. Does the success rate of a treatment programme refer to the end of the pro-gramme, or is this success rate measured at some time after the program-me is finished and the (former) drug addict is back in society? This last question is relevant since kicking off the habit is for most drug addicts not the real problem. The real problem is to stay drug-free. To really know the success rate of a programme one has to look, for example, six or twelve months after the programme is finished. To have a real idea of the effect, one even has to look two years later. However, this is not often the case, not only in Sweden, but internationally.

Although huge sums of money have been invested in treatment pro-grammes in Sweden, few have been evaluated. It also happens that the evaluation was not properly executed, for example because the selection effects were not taken into account, because the treatment institution itself carried out the evaluation instead of an independent researcher, or because a control group was absent. All these factors can make it difficult to make statements about the effects of drug treatment. As will be shown, in the long run the results of treatment programmes in Sweden do not differ substantially from what happens internationally. It should be said that generally these outcomes are relatively poor.[42]

Hassela states their programmes have very good results. It is stated that 60-80% of those who have entered the programmes (since 1969) has successfully finished the treatment and now "live a good life".[43] However, these extremely high figures as compared to the general outcomes of drug treatment are much doubted by people working in drug treatment. As will be shown in the overview that follows, Hassela's extraordinary results should be questioned. Even if Hassela has relatively good scores with regard to drug treatment, one should realise Hassela has admission criteria, which already leads to a selection of those who participate in the Hassela programmes. One of the criteria to enter a Hassela programme is that the 'student' does not have any psychological problems or psychiatric disorders; criteria that already exclude a substantial part of the problematic drug users. Furthermore, Hassela works only with young people from the age of 13 to 21 who (logically) do not have a long career of problematic drug use. As a consequence they are easier to rehabilitate than 'old' drug addicts with a long addiction career, for whom drugs have become an integral part of daily life.

The lack of sound, scientific evaluations in drug treatment not only applies to the Hassela programmes, but to the drug treatment programmes in general. Lars Oscarsson of the School of Social Work of Stockholm University, who together with his colleague Anders Bergmark is considered to be the specialist in the evaluation of treatment programmes, states that as a general rule very few drug treatment programmes in Sweden have been evaluated.[44] One of the few overviews that exist in Sweden of the evaluations of treatment programmes, is written by Anders Bergmark and Lars Oscarsson.[45]

Bergmark and Oscarsson begin their overview by saying that most Swedish studies on treatment of the 1970s have, as a result of the poor methodology not as much a scientific, but merely a historical interest. There are, however, two studies that should be mentioned: a study done in the Långbro hospital in Stockholm in which 226 clients were tracked for a period of four years, from 1969 to 1974; in another study carried out by St. Lars hospital in Lund 562 clients were followed in the period 1970-1978. The differences in outcome between the two studies are considerable: in the Stockholm study 50% was abstinent, whilst in the Lund study only 12% were. The similarities between the two studies are that the social economic problems of the clients decreases during and after the treatment, even in the cases where the clients do not stop using drugs. Another study in Lund in the period 1971-81 had shown the same results. Finally, what the (three) studies have in common is that opiate users in treatment display worse results than users of central stimulants (amphetamine).

Methadone programmes in Sweden have shown positive results. From a study carried out from October 1990 to March 1991 it seems that those who are in a methadone programme generally are in a better 'social situation' during the treatment period than those who are not. An example is that 47% of the methadone clients had injected drugs (heroin), as compared with 90% of those who were not in the programme. Another study by Grönbladh et. al. shows the degree to which mortality can decrease if opiate users are given methadone maintenance treatment.[46] It is relevant to note in this regard that this study has been used in several countries as 'proof' of the positive aspects of methadone treatment. The study of Grönbladh et. al. shows the death rate of the patients undergoing methadone treatment was 1.4% a year, as compared to 7.2% in the control group. It may come as a surprise that the argument of a much lower mortality resulting from methadone programmes as this Swedish study clearly shows, has not been used to introduce methadone programmes on a larger scale in Sweden; although methadone programmes have been introduced or increased in other countries on the basis of this study. The main reason is probably the general reluctance in Sweden regarding legal prescription programmes, which can be explained by the experiences of the experiment of 1965 to 1967 (see section 3.3).

With respect to the Hassela treatment programmes in which young drug users are placed in compulsory care, that were evaluated in the late 1970s, Bergmark and Oscarsson noted that the results of these studies have been used as an argument to show that compulsory treatment can be effective. However, the control design of these studies was insufficient. Bergmark and Oscarsson do not go into the details of the Hassela programmes, but critically conclude that the positive results of their programmes only have a hypothetical, and not an empirical basis.

The first attempt to make a comparative study of different treatment programmes was the 'Swedate project'.[47] This study included 22 different treatment programmes, of which seven programmes were for young people, who formed 18% of the clients. Most of the adults (mean age 28) took part in treatment on a voluntary basis, the young people (mean age 18) underwent compulsory treatment. From the one-year follow-up of 436 clients, 51% was abstinent of (illicit) drugs for the last six months, and 36% was abstinent for the last twelve months. In the six month follow-up, 37% of the clients appeared to be completely 'drug-free', that is including alcohol, medicines, and solvents. If the criteria for a successful outcome assessment, besides the cessation of drug use, includes criminal behaviour and some kind of institutional care, the 'success rate' drops to 22%. Accompanying other studies, it would seem from the Swedate project that amphetamine users show better results than the heroin users.

If one looks at the 22 different treatment institutions, the success rate varies from 0% to 67%. However, Bergmark and Oscarsson note these differences should be interpreted with caution, since there was no control design. Furthermore, some institutions seem to have the 'talent' to select clients that fit best into their programmes.

From data of the social services in Stockholm over the period October 1990-March 1990 it appears that of the 104 adult clients that followed drug treatment on a voluntary basis, 39% was abstinent between six and twelve months after ending the treatment. If (other) social economic criteria is looked at, an improvement was also observed. On the other hand, it appeared that further treatment in other institutions was very common. A less positive outcome was observed in a study conducted in 1990 in the cities of Kumla and Karlskoga. Of the 80 clients 20% used only illicit drugs, and 40% used both licit and illicit drugs. From the study it results that six months after treatment 29% had improved their 'abuse situation', and 19% their social situation.

A Stockholm study tracked 176 clients for four years, from 1987 to 1990. After four years 15% of the clients were abstinent. Furthermore it appeared that 22% had improved their social situation with regard to housing, and 10% were able to 'support themselves'.

In conclusion we can say that the (few) programmes that have been evaluated, show that in the long run the drug treatment programmes in Sweden that are focused on total abstinence are not very 'effective'. In the six month follow-ups it appears that roughly one third of the clients are drug-free.[48] The absence of control groups however, makes it difficult to make any sound statements about the efficacy of drug treatment as compared to the maturing out. For example, except for the well-known methadone study of Grönbladh,[49] no study has been found in which a treatment cohort was compared with a control group. Analogous to international evaluations, it appears that programmes with a longer duration generally have a better score than short-term treatment. However, the selection effect (those who stay longer, are more motivated) should not be underestimated here.

The impression that is sometimes given of the Swedish treatment programmes that it is 'really possible' to get drug addicts drug-free and rehabilitated back into society, is not founded on the available material. It should be noted as well that the idea that 'every' drug addict that is referred by the social workers and the police, is put into treatment, is not correct either. This was only to some extent true in the second half of the 1980s when Aids and HIV were spreading and the objective was to reach all intravenous drug users to stop the further spread of the epidemic. Apart from this period, it has never been the case that every 'detected' drug user was treated and socially rehabilitated.

The official aim is to rehabilitate drug addicts and a lot of effort and financial means are allocated to achieve this; much more than in many other European countries. However, despite all these good intentions, the reality is that the effectiveness of these very expensive programmes is relatively low. In the long run, the Swedish drug treatment programmes do not show better results than what is found internationally.[50] To put it in simple terms: a lot of input results in little output. In their dissertation on drug treatment (from 1988), Bergmark & Oscarsson wrote that in the official descriptions of the treatment system the emphasis is mainly put on the 'treatment chain' and a general expansion of its parts.

"This expansion would be rational and motivated if the treatment methods were known to be effective. But the situation is the opposite – there is almost no evidence of effective treatment methods for drug abuse. But the government discourse proceeds as if such knowledge and such methods were at hand [...]. In our opinion, descriptions of an existing body of rational knowledge within the drug abuse treatment system are not based on facts. Formulations in governmental texts [...] is a form of 'necessary' wishful thinking. It is necessary in the sense without it the efforts and resources spent on expanding the treatment system would make no sense."[51]

The low effectiveness of the very expensive treatment was not really considered a problem during the 1980s since the economy was in good shape. There was enough money available to finance in-patient treatment programmes that could easily last two years. The fact that society offered treatment and rehabilitation to drug addicts was considered as something very positive by most people, the politicians in particular. The fact that the effectiveness was not so high, seemed to be less important.

The economically difficult situation of the 1990s has changed the situation dramatically. First of all, rehabilitation has become increasingly difficult since there is not much to 'offer' anymore to a drug addict leaving a drug-free clinic. In the light of the high unemployment rate, it is very difficult for former drug addicts to find jobs; employers would prefer people without a drug history. Furthermore, the difficult position of the Swedish economy has resulted in substantial budget cuts which have affected the treatment sector. This means that the extensive treatment system of the Swedish drug policy as it is often presented – to put drug addicts in a clinic for one to two years – in fact refers to the 1980s, and is no longer applicable to the 1990s. In this climate of the declining welfare state and budget cuts in the money that is available for treatment, many institutions have to compete with each other.

This problem became very clear during discussions at some treatment centres that were visited. The fact is that they have to earn the money for the services they offer, they have to sell and market their services, especially to the municipal social services that are responsible for the funding.

Treatment institutions need drug users or addicts simply to survive. In some cases this leads to a situation in which the scale of the drug problem can be exaggerated. During the many discussions that were held on this subject, it became clear the treatment sector in itself not only has a strong lobby only because of its size; the situation goes further: the several institutions now even have to lobby if they want to survive and not sack employees. Hence, this can result in a situation that, for example, parents are invited to visit a treatment centre because there are indications that their son or daughter is using drugs. At the treatment centre this will be 'made' a problem, even if the parents are not too worried about it, for example in the case of cannabis use. At the Maria Ungdom Youth Clinic in such a case, they will try to convince the parents there *is* question of a (family) problem if the teenager is using drugs. Different kinds of arguments are used for this purpose, such as saying that drug use is illegal and immoral; that it can lead to problems within the family and with friends; and that taking drugs means, in fact, contributing to the mechanisms of the global drug economy, going as far as to mention the Golden Triangle and Columbia, since the dealers (it is alleged) are often drug addicts.[52]

Because of the severe budget cuts and the fear of even more economising measures, the (immense) treatment sector has become one of the strongest lobbying groups for maintaining a restrictive drug policy. In 1995 Henrik Tham wrote about this:

"Given the fear of losing their jobs, in a situation where the public sector is being reduced generally, the treatment personnel may be expected to unite in the demand for unchanged resources and a restrictive drug policy. Tougher laws would be seen as a means of reaching more drug abusers. The Swedish Psychological Association for example, supported the introduction of imprisonment in the punishment scale for the consumption of drugs since that would facilitate (compulsory) treatment. In an appeal in the press for 'a more restrictive and more humane drug policy', earlier lines of contention between right and left and between those opposed to and those in favour of compulsory treatment had become blurred".[53]

Compulsory Drug Treatment

In their overview of the evaluations of drug treatment programmes Bergmark and Oscarsson have also looked at the compulsory treatment (LVM).[54] The general duration of compulsory treatment is six months. As was described in section 5.5, compulsory treatment is used in rare cases, if a person is a direct danger to himself or to others. The purpose of this short-term intervention (compulsory treatment) is "to overcome a 'life-threatening situation and motivate the individual for continuing care on a voluntary basis".[55] Compulsory treatment has never been evaluated scientifically with control groups, so that it is difficult to say something about the real effects.[56] On the other hand, the available material enables to make some general statements to be made.

It may come as no surprise that the results of compulsory treatment are poorer than those of voluntary treatment. From a 1987 study it is shown that after a one-year follow-up only 3-4% were abstinent. Moreover, their social situation had deteriorated. If one looks at in how many cases compulsory treatment is followed by voluntary treatment (the main aim), this was 15% in 1990 and 18% in 1991. The negative picture is confirmed by other studies. For example, from a Stockholm study conducted from October 1989 to March 1990 among 57 drug users that were placed in compulsory treatment, 7% was abstinent in the six and twelve month follow-ups. Moreover, the follow-up showed 25% had their own housing, 2% were able to support themselves, 42% underwent another compulsory treatment in the same period, and for 28% the compulsory treatment was followed by voluntary treatment.

A more recent follow-up study (1992) was carried out among 102 people having undergone compulsory treatment. After six months 9% was abstinent, 18% had reduced abuse, 28% had gone to voluntary treatment, and 13% underwent compulsory treatment again. The socio-economic situation had hardly improved during the follow-up. It also appeared in the six month follow-up that 7% of the clients had died.[57]

With regard to this high mortality rate, Bergmark and Oscarsson note that the studies on clients undergoing compulsory treatment seem to indicate the mortality among this group is (even) higher than the mortality of clients in voluntary treatment. Bergmark and Oscarsson draw the conclusion there are no studies showing that compulsory treatment has a 'life-saving' effect, although this should be one of the main reasons to put someone in this type of treatment. As a matter of fact, there are only studies that cast doubt on the 'life-saving' effects of compulsory treatment.

6.6 Mortality and Morbidity

Generally speaking, the prevalence of Aids and HIV is relatively low in Sweden, both with regard to the general population and the population of drug users. One reason for this seems to be the general public health policy that has been conducted since the virus was identified in Sweden. As was described in section 5.4, after 1985 substantial sums of money were allocated for the purpose of finding all intravenous drug users and to offer treatment, as the government considered them a key group that could spread the infection. Of course, this massive operation led to an awakening to the contagious risks of the HIV virus. As a result, most people, including drug addicts were (well) informed about the risks.

Not only did the authorities introduce these special measures for drug addicts, this was also true for another so-called risk group, homosexuals. They also put restrictions on homosexual behaviour, by passing the Sauna Clubs Act in 1987 and the Contagious Disease Act in (1989). The Sauna Clubs Act prohibits clubs (saunas) or other places where casual sexual encounters are encouraged.[58] The Contagious Disease Act was passed with the intention to prevent the further spread of HIV (and other contagious diseases or viruses).

Finally, Sweden's geographical location on the periphery of Europe, probably has also been an influential factor. One can suppose HIV to be more prevalent and to spread more easily in (international) meeting places as compared to more static, peripheral places and regions. Hence, since Sweden is not a (international) meeting place for any of the so-called risks groups (intravenous drug users, homosexuals), one can allege that HIV does not spread very fast.

Despite all these efforts it may come as a surprise that the prevalence of HIV and Aids in Sweden is relatively low among drug addicts, taking into consideration that most drug addicts are intravenous users and Swedish health authorities have never introduced large-scale needle exchange programmes. There is only two needle exchange programme in the south of Sweden, in the cities of Lund and Malmö. In Stockholm and Gothenburg on the other hand there are no needle exchange programmes at all. Hence, the question that arises is how can this be possible.

It is difficult to have a complete answer to this question, since there may be several explanations. One reason why HIV has not spread as rapidly as expected, was the simple fact that most intravenous drug addicts use amphetamine, and amphetamine users share needles to a much lesser extent than heroin addicts do. One can see this confirmed by the fact that that HIV is much more widespread among heroin users.

In the light of the increase of heroin use it is inevitable that more needles will be shared in the future. The mode of administration of heroin use may still be predominantly smoking (chasing the dragon), but is already reported that, at a certain stage, smokers switch to injecting, the simple reason being that smoking has become to expensive. Since heroin has a high tolerance, a daily heroin smoker will gradually need a larger quantity to reach the same desired effect. Another reason to switch to intravenous use, is because this mode of administration is more efficient; the reason being that with smoking, a part of the heroin literally goes up in the air. Given the high prices for heroin, it is very likely that in the (near) future more heroin will be used intravenously.

Mortality

It is always difficult to determine (and compare) the number of deaths caused by an overdose of drugs, or the exact number of drug-related deaths, the main reason being that different definitions are used in this respect. It should be noted that only a minority of the deaths in Sweden are followed by an autopsy; in 1975 around 50% of the deaths were followed by autopsy, in 1994 this was 20%. Whatever may be the problems with these figures, especially if one wants to compare them to other countries, one can conclude the mortality of drug addicts in Sweden is high.

Earlier some figures were briefly presented with regard to the mortality rate of drug addicts. Bergmark & Oscarsson first noted that in absolute numbers the number of drug-related deaths is not very high if compared with other risk behaviour (the use of alcohol, tobacco, and medicines, and traffic).[59] They state that in absolute numbers the mortality of drug addicts is at its peak at 200 to 300 a year. On the other hand, the mortality rate (on a yearly basis) that is observed among 'drug abusers' varies from 1-3% a year, meaning 2-5 times the normal mortality. Other figures one sees in this respect is that the mortality figure of drug addicts is approximately 3% a year. This percentage would be based on the yearly mortality figures among drug addicts, from 1.5-2.0% for amphetamine addicts to 4% for heroin addicts.[60] Hence, the mortality among intravenous heroin users is twice as high as among intravenous amphetamine users. The higher mortality of heroin users also appears from data of the Department of Forensic Medicine in Stockholm. Of the 19,500 deaths that were investigated in the period 1986-1993, 658 were proved to be drug-related. Of these 658 drug-related deaths, in 417 cases (63%) opiates were found in the blood. In 147 cases (22%) amphetamine was found in the blood or urine.[61] The following table 6.2 shows the number of drug-related deaths over the last ten years in Sweden.

Table 6.2 Number of Drug-Related Deaths in Sweden

1985	1986	1987	1988	1989	1990	1991	1992	1993	1994	1995
150	138	141	125	113	143	147	175	181	205	194

Source: CAN (1997), p. 284.

Note: The numbers here refer to: deaths with drug addiction (ICD 304) or poisoning by narcotic substances (ICD 965.0, 968.5, 969.6 and 969.7) as underlying or contributing cause of death.

Bergmark & Oscarsson note that drug user groups show different mortality rates. The mortality rate is the highest (12%) among clients that are undergoing compulsory treatment, which is 60 to 70 times higher than the mortality in the general population if the same age categories are looked at.[62] The highlighted factors that influence higher mortality figures are opiate use, combination with alcohol use, and psychiatric disorders.

It is hard to find complete explanations to this high mortality rate. One possible factor was mentioned by unofficial sources (policemen, social workers, drug addicts) that were interviewed. They all mentioned a high level of frustration and fury among clients that have undergone compulsory treatment, which would lead to a 'suicidal pattern of drug use'. Another factor might simply be the very skewed sample of drug addicts in general that is represented by the group of compulsory care clients.

Table 6.2 shows that, in general, the number of drug related deaths in Sweden has increased over the last few years. With regard to the increase in drug-related deaths, it is often thought this is related to the fact that drug addicts are getting older. Since the incidence is (alleged to be) relatively low, the mean age of drug addicts is increasing. With the increase in age of the population, drug addicts in general would become more 'vulnerable' and thus have a lower life expectancy. In the latest CAN report one reads about this: "The observed increases can largely be due to the fact that more drug addicts are becoming older and more infirm. Regarding drug-related deaths, it can also be noted that although the average at death is gradually increasing, there has been no discernible decrease in the death rate among drug abusers under 30." (see table 6.3).[63]

Table 6.3 Number of Drug Related Deaths in Sweden in Different Age Categories

Age Group	1990	1991	1992	1993	1994	1995
-19	1	2	1	2	4	1
20-29	44	32	30	30	39	36
30-39	49	61	73	76	80	64
40-49	28	27	36	44	47	58
50 -	21	25	35	29	35	35
Total	143	147	175	181	205	194

Source: CAN (1997), p. 284.

Mortality rates among drug addicts are not a commonly discussed subject in Sweden; these figure are seen as far less important than other figures. As a matter of fact, the drug-free society does not attribute a lot of importance in reducing this mortality figure; as a much more important indicator for measuring the 'success' of the applied policy is the prevalence and incidence of drug use. Cynics say that the high mortality rate can serve as an 'example' or 'preventive measure' of how dangerous drugs are. In any case, the high mortality rate is one of the reasons why the numbers of drug addicts are not increasing much. In the same cynical vein one could say the heroin addicts are the ones who pay the price for the drug-free society and the restrictive policy that results from it.

Another reason why mortality among drug addicts is not greatly considered as a public health problem is that the number of deaths caused by alcohol poisoning is actually higher (see table 6.4). If the number of deaths from other alcohol-related diagnosis are added to these figures, the alcohol-related mortality rate rises to almost 2,000 a year.[64]

Table 6.4 Alcohol-Related Mortality: Alcohol Poisoning (ICD 980)

	1990	*1991*	*1992*	*1993*	*1994*	*1995*
Underlying cause of deat	163	175	141	136	129	122
Contributory case of de	238	260	228	224	208	250
Total	401	435	369	360	337	372

Source: CAN (1997), p. 227.

Morbidity

In January 1996 a total number of 1,324 Aids cases were known in Sweden. In 142 cases (11%) this was related to intravenous drug use. At this same date the cumulative number of reported HIV cases totalled 4,207. Of these 4,207 cases, 707 (17%) were related to intravenous drug use.[65] In the following table one finds the cumulative number of both reported HIV positive persons and Aids cases.

There is no data on the number of IV users that have Aids or HIV. Since it is known that heroin users share needles to a higher degree than amphetamine users, one can suppose both HIV and Aids to be more prevalent among intravenous heroin users than among intravenous amphetamine

Table 6.5 Reported HIV Positive Persons and Aids Cases (Cumulative Numbers)

	1990	*1991*	*1992*	*1993*	*1994*	*1995*	*1996*
HIV	2,641	2,969	3,319	3,702	3,958	4,207	4,425
iv related	22%	20%	19%	18%	17%	17%	16%
Aids	500	637	763	940	1,128	1,324	1,477
iv related	3%	6%	7%	9%	10%	11%	11%

Source: CAN (1997), pp. 281-282.

users. This is confirmed by figures of the Remand Prison in Stockholm in the period 1987-1995 where 20% of the intravenous heroin users were HIV positive, as opposed to 'only' 5% for intravenous amphetamine users.[66] In 1990, 50% of the clients of the Stockholm methadone programme were HIV infected, but this programme gives priority to HIV positive opiate users.[67]

In Stockholm the prevalence of HIV among intravenous drug users is much higher than in Malmö, the city where heroin use is also quite widespread. The reason for this is, probably, the needle exchange programme in Malmö. Because of the needle exchange programme and the other (social and medical) services that are here, many or most of the intravenous drug users are reached. This gives one a very clear idea of the spread of the epidemic. In the needle exchange programme in Malmö, where there are files on 2,800 people and approximately 1,000 people a year exchange needles, there are only eight people known to be HIV positive. The last time an intravenous drug user was infected in Malmö was in 1989.[68]

If one looks at the geographical distribution of clinically reported HIV cases, the possible impact of the needle exchange programme becomes apparent. Whereas in Greater Stockholm 551 intravenous drug users are clinically reported to be HIV positive, there are only 38 in Greater Malmö.[69]

No precise figures are available with regard to the number of intravenous drug users that are infected with hepatitis B or C. There is though, data on the number of reported HIV cases, and which cases were related to intravenous drug use (see table 6.5).

Table 6.6 Reported Cases of Hepatitis B and Hepatitis C

	1990	*1991*	*1992*	*1993*	*1994*	*1995*	*1996*
Hepatitis B	258	255	204	211	259	294	185
iv related	35%	37%	32%	41%	53%	51%	48%
Hepatitis C	447	2,350	4,463	4,023	3,725	2,872	2,613
iv related	62%	67%	72%	68%	68%	64%	64%
Total	827	2,750	4,953	4,251	3,984	3,166	2,798

Source: CAN (1997), p. 280.

Note: The sharp rise in reported Hepatitis C since 1991 is explained by the fact that hepatitis C was first diagnosed in 1990.

6.7 The Debate on Swedish Drug Policy

Generally speaking there is a large consensus in Sweden on the unaccept-ability of drugs. In 1977 the goal of the drug-free society was adopted by a large majority in Parliament. Today there is still a cross-party consensus that the restrictive drug policy is necessary to keep the drug problem in Sweden within acceptable proportions. Moreover, it is thought that the restrictive policy has resulted in a drug problem that is smaller in magnitude than is the case in many other Western countries.

The role of public opinion is central to understanding the attitude of the different political parties. Opinion polls show that a large majority of the people subscribe to a restrictive drug policy. The same polls indicate that drugs are perceived as one of society's main social problems. The moral panic surrounding drugs is such, that no political party dares to speak out against any measures that may appear to move in the direction of a more liberal drug policy. Supporting the restrictive policy, or even asking for more restrictive measures to curb the increase in the drug prob-lem are essential for a political party to win votes. Saying the contrary, to back a more liberal approach, is not an option for a political party and would almost mean its political death. It has already been pointed out that anti-drug pressure groups have been the driving forces behind influencing public opinion, and through them the political parties. It has also been shown that besides the social movements, the media have also contributed to the drug scare that exists today and the defining of drugs as a major social problem.

The situation that has arisen seems an almost 'uncontrollable' one, in which the original objective, namely keeping the drug problem small, has been surpassed. The concept of the drug-free society has come to represent more than just 'to get rid of drugs'; it has become a national project in the sense that it has come to symbolise the protection of what is typically Swedish. As Tham has pointed out, the struggle against drugs is so strong and widespread that it has come to serve as the tool to strengthen a threatened national identity.[70] Previously, Tham, Nils Christie and Kettil Bruun have made similar analyses. Their thesis is that within Nordic societies drugs are highly appropriate enemies, in the sense that they have been defined as the ideal 'social problem', in other words a scapegoat on which other social problems can be blamed.[71] Of course, a necessary precondition for this situation to exist is that the 'target' has gained a special status: "The moral panic raging over certain drugs would not have been conceived of without the image that has been built up around certain drugs as representing the most overwhelming danger for our societies in general and for our youth population in particular".[72]

Since the fight against drugs has been given this status as a national project, meaning that the drug-free society now serves a higher goal than only to keep the drug problem within acceptable boundaries, the basic tenets of the restrictive drug policy are no longer questioned. As a matter of fact, is has become almost impossible to have a serious, rational debate on drugs and the applied drug policy in Sweden. For example, speaking in a dispassionate way about drugs is not possible; the official dogma requires it is only possible to speak in very negative terms about drugs. Saying for example, that the health hazards of some illicit drugs like cannabis are not very serious, or saying that some people use drugs simply for pleasure is, in the context, entirely 'not done' and actually impossible. Any insinuation may result in being called a 'drug liberal', a qualification which is the most powerful weapon one can use in a drug discussion to paralyse the opponent.[73] The whole situation leads the British Sweden-watcher Arthur Gould, who specialises in social policy and is not a drugs policy expert, to astonishment:

> "The restrictive discourse that has gripped the official Swedish mentality has taken on a paranoid dimension. What began as the idea of one association and its guru, Nils Bejerot, has become the dogmatic ideology of the whole political system. What started as a reasoned alternative to liberal ideas has become the basis for fanatic intolerance, so much that the academics and administrators who question, let alone, criticise, the official line, are dismissed as 'traitors' or 'capitulators'."[74]

The American, Ted Goldberg, who has lived in Sweden for three decades, made a similar remark: "In Sweden, anyone who questions the Swedish model runs the risk of personal attack. Critics are threatened, scorned, risk losing their job, etc. Sometimes the attacks are extended to a critic's family".[75] The way the Swedish drug policy model is being praised and defended in Sweden, has gained a near religious dimension. As Gould point out, policies of legalisation and decriminalisation which in other countries can be discussed, are attacked with "McCarthyite intolerance".[76] In essence, the drug policy debates in Sweden should be seen in black and white terms: if you're not with us, you're against us.

During the many discussions with people working in the field of drugs in Sweden the dogmatic character of the situation became very apparent. Under the current circumstances it is impossible to criticise or question even some aspects of the official line. In private, policy makers and civil servants will confess not to subscribe to the Swedish 'success' in pursuing the drug-free society. Others will point out the other side of the picture, for example the increasingly repressive measures that are taken in the name of the drug-free society. Moreover, some people that have been interviewed, admitted knowing that cannabis is not as dangerous as it is officially stated. It is however, impossible to make one of these remarks or criticisms in public. In that respect, the internal 'controlling mechanisms' of the official drug policy dogma are an important explanation for the broad consensus on the drug policy as it come across externally.

For scientists, the situation is a delicate and difficult one to work in. For example, by only questioning some aspects of the Swedish drug policy model and its alleged success, a scientist can run the risk of being (fiercely) attacked, either by popular movements or by government officials. Without having any interest in taking these standpoints but just having the desire to carry out serious and rational research, a scientist can be accused of irresponsible behaviour or even treason. Gould mentions two leading researchers who dared to suggest that the link between a restrictive policy and the small size of a country's drug problem was not proven, a prominent civil servant castigated their work as "deficient, misleading, and speculative".77 In the long run, a critical stance can have repercussions. Since the label 'drug liberal' is sufficient to render a critic powerless, someone who has acquired this stigma, is placed in a somewhat marginalised position. This can lead to a peripheral position or even exclusion from government committees and other posts, and some kind of marginalisation with regard to the decision makers, government officials, and fund suppliers.

In this climate, scientists have to make a choice. One can chose the uneasy road by staying loyal to one's academic convictions. One is almost certain that this attitude will not lead to prestige, and it may imply risks for one's future career if one criticises 'too' severely. To make this choice, one needs to be either brave or one needs to be in a comfortable position already, like having a stable, unassailable professorship that is independent from government funding. A second, much more easy and rewarding option for a scientist is to toe the official line and to do research that is more or less in line with official policy. This option definitely leads to much more prestige and one is more likely asked to become a member of commissions and boards, and to make presentations at meetings. In line with the honour one gets in fighting the 'social problem drugs', as described by Nils Christie & Kettil Bruun in *Den gode fiende* (The Ideal Enemy), scientific research into the dangers of drugs, or research showing the positive effect of law enforcement measures on the development of drug use, are typical subjects by which one can earn credit and enjoy prestige. Finally, the third possibility scientists have is to chose another field to work in, a field that is not so politicised or politically sensitive, and affected by ideologies; in other words, a field that enables one to have open, rational, and critical discussions, and a job where one does not run the risk of being personally attacked for the professional position one takes.

On the surface there exists in Sweden a large consensus on the restrictive drug policy. The only voices that sometimes oppose the official line, are foreign commentators, the client-organisation RFHL and some scientists, especially criminologists. The fact that it is especially criminologists that make comments in this respect, is because a parallel can be made with criminality. Since criminality will always exist and can never be completely eliminated, the question criminologists pose is how much effort can a society invest in fighting crime, without infringing basic civil rights and sliding towards a totalitarian system.

The pursuit of a drug-free society has developed in such a way that the goal seems to justify almost all means. Not only are, in a very paternalistic way, drug-scare messages being employed to prevent people from taking drugs, more importantly the State now has the ability to intervene strongly into the private lives of its citizens, as is indicated by the urine tests that are applied to people who are suspected of being under the influence of drugs. Although there are exceptions, few people ask the question what is the price that has to be paid for this policy.

A possible reason can be that, to a certain extent, Swedes are 'familiar' with the fact that the Swedish State intervenes in the private lives of people. In the Swedish welfare state model, an important role is attributed to the State as a 'social engineer', making sure the large majority of the people can live a decent life. In some cases, far-reaching measures are considered necessary for the sake of the public good. For example, HIV-positives or people having Aids can be incarcerated in special sections of hospitals if their behaviour is considered to present a 'risk' to society. In international circles of people working in the field of Aids, Sweden is often criticised and attacked for its policy in this regard. In Sweden however, one does not hear these criticisms very much. One possible reason is that Sweden does not have a strong tradition of liberalism. As Tham points out, "this relative absence of a strong civil liberty tradition might be deemed a more general trademark of Sweden, which has a long tradition of a strong State".[78] During the 19th century when liberalism developed in

Europe's cities, Sweden was a poor and basically agrarian society without a strong urban culture. The absence of a strong urban culture also explains why an urban liberal culture did not develop.

Since Sweden has become member of the EU, it has quickly gained a reputation being one of the leading countries opposed to any drug liberalisation initiatives. The way this is done by Swedes, for example in EU meetings in Brussels and the European Parliament, sometimes leaves a strange impression on other nationals. This holds true not only for government officials and politicians, but even more for militants like Torgny Pettersson who is working both for European Cities against Drugs (ECAD) and the Hassela Nordic Network (HNN).

When the Swedish drug policy is criticised by foreigners, something very 'deep' and fundamental seems to be being touched. Whereas Swedes are usually rational and calm, when drugs are discussed, rationality seems very distant and emotions get the upper hand, which in the Swedish context and in the light of their debating culture is very unusual. A foreigner criticising Swedish drug policy can trigger violent reactions. One gets the impression this criticism is interpreted as an attack on something profound and very Swedish, which almost automatically leads to a nationalistic sense of oneness. Possible explanations for these kind of reactions can be found in what was mentioned previously, namely the broader, symbolic function the drug policy has within Swedish society, as shown by Tham, and before him by Christie & Bruun.[79]

In this respect one should also take into consideration the magnitude of the Swedish drug education programmes and their impact. The massive drug education programmes start in the primary schools and regularly recur throughout the school curriculum. Without exaggeration, this opinion forming could be described as a process of indoctrination. Considering the magnitude of these programmes, the contents of them have gradually become something so indisputable and conclusive that one incorporates them into one's own value system. Because the ideas have become part of one's inner life, there is hardly any possibility of putting things into perspective or looking upon them in a rational fashion. Attacking or questioning these basic tenets, can then trigger violent reactions. In this perspective, a comparison can be made with democracy. Most people in Western societies do not question the concept of democracy since the virtues of the political model have been so internalised one no longer questions its principles; it is something one simply takes for granted. Questioning the concept of democracy, can lead to reactions that are similar to criticism of Swedish drug policy.

6.8 The Future of Swedish Drug Policy

Before discussing the possible future of Swedish drug policy, one should first point out the fact that, in recent years, many changes have already occurred. For example, as was discussed in chapter five the Swedish treatment system that is often described, namely offering a drug addict a long, two year's stay in an in-patient treatment home, today no longer exists. The main reason for this is the economic crisis and, resulting from that, the cutbacks in the treatment budget. Since the municipal social services have become responsible for the money that is spent on treatment, one observes a parallel shift to lesser treatment and shorter treatment programmes. The overall background of these developments are the poor results of very expensive drug treatment programmes.

What is changing in recent years as well, at least among specialists, is the way one looks upon the possible 'causes' of problematic drug use. For a long time the dominant views emphasised the substances themselves and their availability as explanatory factors as to why people use or abuse drugs. Of the three basic elements that Zinberg considered central to an understanding of how a substance is being used, namely drug, set, and setting, the Swedish drug policy paradigm focused almost entirely on one determining factor: drugs.[80] This bias has resulted in narrow views on both drugs and the backgrounds of (problematic) drug use. For example, the fact that a large number of drug addicts have psychiatric problems has for a long time been a highly neglected topic in Sweden. When a drug addict left treatment, one would ask "so, is he normal again now?". The specialist's answer would then be positive, since the person was drug-free. It is only in recent years, that the difficult psychiatric background of problematic drug use as an explanatory or contributory factor has been acknowledged in Sweden. Among specialists it is now becoming more accepted that a drug addict may have personality disturbances, which can explain why this person has developed specific patterns of drug use, instead of pointing solely at the properties of the substance.

On the other hand, what is still lacking in the drug policy debates in Sweden, is a sociological insight into the development of certain patterns of drug use. First of all, the descriptions of the deprived suburbs where 'new' types of drug use are developing, are indications that there may be other explanations of drug use other than just the availability of drugs. Growing up in an physically unpleasant environment that has few possibilities of amusements and distractions to offer, and a social environment that is characterised by a high unemployment rate and few future prospects, can make someone more vulnerable to drug abuse. The situation becomes even more precarious if this is accompanied by large numbers of immigrants living together. The fact is that, for several reasons, both the first and second generation immigrant groups have difficulties in adapting to, and being accepted by the (new) society they live in. These difficulties are even more present if it concerns political refugees who have endured terrible experiences in their homeland. All these factors can contribute in leading someone into specific patterns of drug use. The experiences of other countries with longer 'records' of underprivileged and segregated urban areas and the manifestation of these patterns of drug use, may indicate the problematic drug use Sweden still has in prospect. The reason why these social risk factors for the development of drug abuse seem to be underestimated in Sweden, can partly be found in the fact that Sweden was never confronted with social problems of this scale until recently. Sweden may have served as a model country in several areas for other countries, it now can learn from other countries how to deal with almost uncontrollable social problems such as segregated suburbs with high unemployment rates. The firm belief in the social engineering capacities of the welfare State, may have been a hindrance in acknowledging that some social problems are almost insoluble.

A second sociological insight that is lacking in Sweden, concerns the relationship between the patterns of drug use that are observed and the way society looks upon drug use in general. Since drug use is considered as extremely deviant behaviour, the result will be that most ordinary people will not try drugs on a regular basis. On the other hand, many of those who do continue taking drugs regularly, are precisely the ones who were already deviant, for example by belonging to a marginal subculture, or by having psychological problems or a psychiatric disorder. Hence, just because of the very deviant status of drug use, one will see a self-fulfilling prophecy: most of the people who cross the line are people who were already deviant. This situation of already deviant people behaving unacceptably, implies that the possibilities to see a 'normal' or moderate consumption patterns developing are almost automatically excluded. What is more likely under these circumstances, is that one will see a confirmation of the stepping stone hypothesis. Since one is always told that (regular) cannabis use will lead to the use of harder drugs, one should not be surprised if some of those who crossed the line and conduct deviant behaviour (by using cannabis), will eventually indeed use amphetamine or heroin.

What should be added to this is that most knowledge on drug use in Sweden is based on clinical experiences. The two factors combined might explain the terrible 'consequences' of drug use one can find in Sweden. For example, the typical client profile of a cannabis user in treatment as is shown by Lundqvist (see section 4.4) clearly indicates these clients can not really considered as normal, mentally healthy people.[81]

Another area where changes are happening, concerns the drug prevention programmes in Sweden. In many respects, drug prevention information in Sweden resembles American material. Both put the emphasis on the dangers of the drugs, with the intention to scare teenagers into not trying any drugs. However, several indicators show that the drug-scare messages in Sweden do not have the desired effect anymore. The number of young people experimenting with drugs has increased considerably in the 1990s, and more teenagers now declare that they want to try drugs. Besides that, there also is an increase in heroin smoking.

In a matter of speaking, one can say drug scare messages that emphasise or exaggerate the dangers of drugs, are efficient as long as (very) few people try these drugs. This can be illustrated by what a government official confessed in private: "I know cannabis is not as dangerous as it is presented in the campaigns, but if the people believe it, that isn't too bad". If however, more people experiment with these drugs, the drug scare message is surpassed by reality and loses credibility. If the effects and dangers of cannabis use as they are described in the campaigns, do not happen to the people who try cannabis, and, consequently, are not observed by even more people knowing those who tried, one is obliged to change the campaigns into a more sound and scientific-based information campaigns. The need to change the content and nature of prevention is even more serious in the light of the increase in heroin smoking.

Since cannabis generally is the illicit drug young people encounter first, the emphasis of the information campaigns has been put on the dangers of cannabis, as a way to prevent people from starting a drug use career. The effect of this 'cannabis bias' is people are not always well informed about the 'real' risks of the different drugs and the many differences that exist between different illicit drugs. The message generally is that all drugs are bad and are associated with many health hazards. For example, from the information spread by the police – playing a very active role in this respect – one cannot always assume that heroin has more dependence-creating properties than cannabis.[82] In suburban neighbourhoods social workers have been interviewed who, during their work, were faced with young people experimenting with smoking heroin. During the conversations it became clear that the social workers were not aware of the fact that smoking heroin on a daily basis over a longer period, will very likely lead to physical dependence. Although they had been educated about drugs by a police drug expert, they were of the opinion that as long as one does not inject, dependence cannot occur. What had contributed to the social workers' beliefs, was that the young heroin smokers they knew, did not look like 'typical' heroin addicts.

In the light of these developments, it is surprising that the authorities are still trying to use their traditional drug-scare methods. For example, in 1994 the National Institute of Public Health started the Black on White campaign to prevent the use of hash. On the front page of the information booklets was written: "Nobody has died from hash, or....?". The Swedish policy has recently copied the American Dare (to say no) Programme, which was adapted to the Swedish situation. In this prevention pro-gramme police officers educate school children on drugs. This very expensive drug prevention programme was evaluated in the United States and it was shown that the prevalence of drug use among school students having participated in the programme was actually higher than among those who did not participate. An evaluation of the Swedish Våga (Dare) programme that was done after one month, showed similar results.[83]

On the other hand, there are also indications that there is indeed a development taking place towards a more rational and scientifically based drug information campaign. As mentioned previously, the most obvious drug-scare elements that were not founded on a scientific basis, have been removed from the *Hash Book*, the book that is send to all parents of 8th grade school students. During a speech held in June 1997 in Gothenburg, the Minister of Social Affairs, Margot Wallström declared that we have to live in the present and that young people do not listen to unscientific and moralistic messages any longer.

The fact that, apparently, the drug information campaigns do no longer have the desired effect, may be partly attributed to the changing attitude towards 'the State'. In chapter two Swedes' attitude in this respect was shown to be usually a positive one, resulting in a attitude that can be somewhat trustworthy and even 'naive'. However, due to the widening gap between the people and the politicians (many of whom used to have their roots in the working class), and some political corruption affairs and scandals, the people's attitude to the State and system seems to have changed to a more critical stance. This also means people no longer automatically accept what they are told. Of course, the messages also lose credibility because of the increased exposure to what is happening in other countries where governments have more differentiated ideas about drugs.

An important question with regard to drug use is to what extent it can be influenced by drug policy. Of course, governments and government institutions will say there is a clear relationship, but comparative prevalence studies suggest this influence of policy on drug use is minor. It is interesting to note that as long as the trend is positive (i.e. drug use is decreasing), authorities tend to react as if this is this result of the applied policy. If on the other hand, the trend is negative (drug use is increasing), a possible reaction is that the policy was insufficient and should be reinforced. Another reaction can be that one seeks other, external causes to explain the increase in drug use. The latter seems applicable to the situation in Sweden. The availability of cheaper heroin is attributed to foreign importers and the opening of the borders with 'Europe'; the increase in heroin smoking is said to have been introduced by immigrants; and more generally, the social problems Swedes undergoes, are in many cases attributed to 'Europe'.

It is true that Sweden has become part of Europe, and not only in the sense that it has joined the European Union. Already in the run-up to EU membership in 1995, Sweden was becoming more and more part of Europe and the world, in several respects. In the early 1990s when the country was faced with economic difficulties, the Swedish economy had to be competitive with other economies. Sweden was also becoming part of Europe in the sense that social problems can not always be completely solved. Several examples can be mentioned, from unemployment to social and ethnic segregation, resulting in the rise of 'ghettos'. Finally, Sweden is also becoming part of Europe and the world in the sense that foreign ideas and cultures are influencing Swedish culture. The latter aspect is very relevant with respect to the trends in drug use.

Comparative studies on the prevalence of drug use indicate that the evolution of drug use is not so much influenced by drug policy, but much more by the international cultural trends of popular music, youth culture, etc. Of course, Sweden has never been excluded from these trends, but one can suggest that due to Sweden's peripheral position and its somewhat provincial culture, international trends have not had the same impact in Sweden as in other, more urbanised European countries. However, with the increasing internationalisation and mondialisation of the 1980s and especially the 1990s, local specificities are becoming less determining factors. "The population of Sweden has become less 'provincial' due to immigration, a more open economy, foreign travel, and television, all of which have undoubtedly expanded our horizons."[84]

This increased exposure implies that Sweden is increasingly influenced by international cultural trends, norms and lifestyles. It has been already shown that a new pattern of alcohol use is developing in Sweden: European drinking. One of the reasons is of course that Swedes are travelling more than before which means they encounter other (enjoyable) patterns of alcohol use and find out that drunkenness is much less socially acceptable than in Sweden. Sweden is also becoming more European in the sense that alcohol has become more widely available in recent years. When it comes to drugs, it is inevitable that international trends will also affect Sweden. In other words, European consumption patterns will (eventually) also be found in Sweden. The consequence of increased international exposure, especially of young people, will be that the drug-scare messages will lose credibility. Young people who are travelling will meet other young people using cannabis without the 'expected' terrible consequences manifesting themselves. To remain credible to its citizens and to anticipate the new trends in drugs use, the authorities have not much choice but to make its drug education programmes more realistic.

6.9 Conclusion

The Swedish drug policy is generally presented as being successful. Since the government's objective is to reach a drug-free society, one usually refers to prevalence figures that would indicate the prevalence of experimental drug use has decreased since a restrictive policy was introduced around 1980. In section 6.2 the prevalence figures have been discussed and critically analysed. The available prevalence figures indeed tend to indicate the prevalence figures went down during the 1970s and 1980s, but the limitation of this data is that it only refers to 15-16 year-old school students and 18 year old military conscripts. Looking at prevalence figures of other countries, one can suggest data only of these young age categories, is insufficient to comment on the development in the prevalence of drug use in general. Moreover, the major decrease in experimental drug use as shown by the Swedish data, did not take place during the 1980s when the concept of the drug-free society was introduced, but in the decade before, when the policy was less restrictive. Hence, the alleged relation between the restrictive drug policy and the decrease in experimental drug use is far from clear. This becomes even more apparent if the rising prevalence figures in the

1990s are taken in consideration. Both experimental drug use and last month use have grown considerably over the last few years, although there has been no question of any relaxation of the drug policy. On the contrary, the increase in drug use has occurred in a period where in practice the drug policy gained a gradually more repressive character.

In Sweden a lot of importance is attributed to the incidence and prevalence of drug use. The reason for this is that the scientific model on which the alcohol policy is based, the total consumption model, is supposed to be valid for drugs as well. The total consumption model suggests that the more people drink alcohol, the greater the number of problematic alcohol users and the greater the total damage caused by alcohol will be. As a consequence, policy should focus on limiting total alcohol consumption. When adapted to the field of drugs, it is alleged that the fewer people try drugs, the lower the number of drug addicts there will be. The latter model is supported by the theories of Nils Bejerot, the 'guru' of Swedish drug policy, according to whom (almost) anyone who continues to take drugs, will sooner or later become dependant.

However, the fact is that these theoretical assumptions are not supported by empirical evidence. The statistics show that although experimental drug use has declined during the 1970s and 1980s, the number of heavy drug abusers (drug addicts) has not. In 1979 the number of heavy drug abusers was estimated at 12,000, in 1992 this number was estimated at 17,000. In section 6.2 it was discussed that these two figures are, still today, debated for various reasons. One argument is about the question of whether these figures are valid (some say the number of drug addicts should be higher), but what is even more debated is whether the increase from 12,000 to 17,000 heavy drug abusers can be called 'successful'. The official explanation, supposing that despite this increase, the number of new recruits has gone down thanks to the more restrictive policy, is not very conclusive. Therefore, the conclusion should be that either the figures are incorrect, or the theories on the development on drug use are.

Although no sound figures are available on the number of drug addicts after 1992, several indicators show heroin use is on the increase. Both the fieldwork in suburban areas and interviews that were conducted with police officers and especially social workers, indicate an increasing number of young people are smoking heroin, especially in the deprived neigh-bourhoods where young people grow up without many future prospects. Many of the neighbourhoods where this development is taking place are characterised by a (very) high unemployment rate and a (very) large per-centage of immigrants. The assumption that the increase in heroin use is the result of traditional opiate use that is 'imported' to Sweden, is only one part of the explanation that neglects other important factors. For example, in many Swedish drug policy debates the relationship between young people growing up in problematic social circumstances and their vulnerability to abuse drugs, seems to be very underestimated.

This situation places the activities of the police, focusing on visible drug scenes and rave parties in a somewhat strange light. The potential problematic drug users do not seem to be found here, but among the drug using population in the deprived suburban areas. Moreover, the urine tests that were originally meant as a way to find previously unknown drug users, only had the desired effect in the introduction period. Most of the (alleged) drug users undergoing the test are actually drug users who were already known to the authorities. Considering the fact that due to the po-lice presence at certain drug scenes, drug users have 'spread out', and the fact that the urine tests are not performed in all parts of the country, one could wonder if the six million kronor that the urine tests cost on a year-ly basis are being spent in an efficient way. Besides that, the urine tests touch a very basic ethical question as to whether they are not an infringe-ment of civil rights.

The treatment programmes were also discussed in this chapter. Despite the extensiveness of the treatment system, few treatment programmes have been evaluated in a scientific way. However, the available evaluations show that the programmes do not seem to be very effective; at least to a lesser extent than is sometimes presented. This may come as no surprise, since international data on evaluations of drug treatment programmes show similar, relatively poor results. The evaluations of compulsory treat-ment programmes do not give a positive picture. As a matter of fact, there are no indications that they have a life-saving effect, although this is only one of the main reasons to put someone into compulsory treatment.

The mortality figures among drug addicts in Sweden are high. Intravenous amphetamine users have a yearly mortality of 1.5-2.0%, whilst the figure for intravenous heroin users is twice as high. The mortality rate is particularly high among drug users who have undergone compulsory treatment. The prevalence of HIV, on the other hand, is not as high as one would expect, considering there are only needle exchange programmes in the south of Sweden. An important reason for the low prevalence of HIV seems to be related to the fact that most intravenous drug users in Sweden use amphetamine, who share needles to a much lesser extent than heroin users.

At first sight there exists in Sweden a very large consensus on the correctness of the drug policy that is applied. Opinion polls show the restrictive policy is supported by a large majority of the people. Moreover, most people believe it is because of the restrictive drug policy that Sweden has a relatively small drug problem. There is, however, an exception in the sense that scientists, especially criminologists, do have serious doubts about the price to be paid in the name of a drug-free society. But the position of critics is precarious, as it comes down to questioning the ways in which the drug-free society is being pursued. Questioning this can be sufficient to be labelled a drug liberal, which in the public debate, means one has lost one's credibility. In essence, this situation is very black and white: "if you're not with us, you're against us".

In the light of the increase of both experimental drug use and the increase in heroin use, it seems that the traditional drug-scare messages no longer have the desired effect. In the light of increased mondialisation and exposure to other cultural trends, by which young people especially are influenced, this comes as no surprise. One can see the latter confirmed by the fact that with regard to alcohol, other, more European consumption patterns are already developing. In the light of these developments, it is inevitable the drug prevention material and the drug policy at large will be changed into a more realistic format that is more suitable to tackle the drug problems that are currently arising.

Notes

Foreword

1 See the magnificent comparison about drug control systems in France and the Netherlands by the Belgian authors Isabelle Stengers and Olivier Ralet (1991), *Drogues, le defi hollandais.*

1 Relevance and Methodology

1 See interview in *Svenska Dagbladet*, 6 November 1995.
2 Martin Grapendaal et. al. (1995), *A World of Opportunities. Lifestyle and Economic Behaviour of Heroin Addicts in Amsterdam*, p. 4.
3 Ibid. p. 7.

2 Understanding Sweden

1 Ironically, at Christmas 1996 a 'terrorist group', later turning out to be one man, threatened to place bombs as it demanded the return of the welfare state.
2 Åke Daun (1996), *Swedish Mentality*, p. 2.
3 Ibid., p. 22.
4 In the late 1980s two-third of the marriages took place in church.
5 Åke Daun (1996), op. cit. p. 58.
6 Ibid., p. 107.
7 Arthur Gould (1993), *Capitalist Welfare States. A comparison of Japan, Britain & Sweden*, p. 177.
8 Åke Daun (1996), op. cit. p. 107.
9 Hans-Ingvar Johnsson (1995), *Spotlight on Sweden*, p. 125.
10 Ibid. p. 21.

11 Several explanations are given for this: the social democratic policy that took roots in the 1930s, the fact that Sweden left the gold standard in 1931 which led to a devaluation and, consequently, an export increase, and the economic ties with Britain. See: Hans-Ingvar Johnsson (1995), op. cit. p. 127.

12 Arthur Gould (1993), *Capitalist Welfare States. A comparison of Japan, Britain & Sweden*, p. 166.

13 Hans-Ingvar Johnsson (1995), op. cit. p. 125.

14 Dennis Lachman et. al. (1995), *Challenges to the Swedish Welfare State*, p. 1.

15 Ibid. p. 134.

16 Tim Tilton (1991), *The Political Theory of Swedish Social Democracy*, pp. 2-3.

17 Ibid. p. 4.

18 Filip Wijkström (1996), *Movements, Members and Volunteers in Sweden*, p. 8.

19 Quoted in Filip Wijkström (1996), op. cit. p. 3.

20 Peter Antman quoted in Filip Wijkström (1996), op. cit. p. 3.

21 Filip Wijkström (1996), op. cit. p. 8.

22 Hans-Ingvar Johnsson (1995), op. cit. p. 60.

23 Filip Wijkström (1996), op. cit. p. 4.

24 Hans-Ingvar Johnsson (1995), op. cit. p. 60

25 In Swedish CAN stands for *Centralförbundet för alkohol- och narkotik-aupplysning.*

26 Filip Wijkström (1996), op. cit. p. 6.

27 Ibid. p. 7.

28 Ibid.

3 THE SWEDISH DRUG EXPERIENCE

1 CAN & National Institute of Public Health (1993), *Trends in Alcohol and Drug Use in Sweden*, p. 55.

2 Ibid. p. 54.

3 Ibid.

4 Ibid. p. 57.

5 See for example: National Institute of Public Health (1995a), *Drug Policy. The Swedish Experience*, p. 5.

6 According to G.H.A. van Brussel & G.K.T. van der Giessen (1996), *Sweden and the Drugs Problem Seen Through Dutch Eyes.*

7 Leonard Goldberg (1968a), 'Drug abuse in Sweden', p. 3.

8 Börje Olsson (1995), 'Utilization et abus de narcotiques et de drogues illégales en Suède', p. 172. See also G.H.A. van Brussel & G.K.T. van der Giessen (1996), op. cit. p. 12.

9 Börje Olsson (1995), op. cit. p. 172.

10 Leonard Goldberg (1968a), op. cit. p. 3.

11 Ibid. p. 4.

12 Ibid.

13 Leonard Goldberg (1968b), 'Drug abuse in Sweden (II)', p. 20.

14 Leonard Goldberg (1968a), op. cit. p. 4.

15 Leonard Goldberg (1968b), op. cit. p. 21.

16 Börje Olsson (1995), op. cit. p. 172.

17 On the other hand, the legal prescription experiment (as described in 3.3) led to an increase in legal sales. The increase to 5.9 million doses in 1966 (see table 3.2) should be attributed to this.

18 Börje Olsson (1995), op. cit. p. 173.

19 Nils Bejerot (1975), *Drug Abuse and Drug Policy*, p. 21.

20 Leif Lenke & Börje Olsson (1996b), *Legal Drugs - The Swedish Legalizing Experiment of 1965-1967 in Retrospect*, p. 3.

21 Ibid p. 4. According to Nils Bejerot (1975, p. 23) these quantities have been prescribed to an average of 83 patients.

22 Nils Bejerot (1975), *Drug Abuse and Drug Policy*, p. 21.

23 Ibid. p. 214.

24 Ibid. p. 22.

25 Ibid. p. 214.

26 See section 6.3 (results) for a brief overview of Bejerot's findings. See Nils Bejerot (1975), op. cit. pp. 218-224.

27 As became clear during the many interviews and conversations that have been held in October and December 1996.

28 See chapter 'Is Swedish Drug Policy Successful?' in: National Institute of Public Health (1995a), op. cit. p. 31.

29 Leif Lenke & Börje Olsson (1996b), op. cit. p. 5.

30 Ibid. p. 5.

31 See e.g. National Institute of Public Health (1995a), op. cit. p. 8.

32 Leif Lenke & Börje Olsson (1996b), op. cit. p. 6.

33 Cited in Lenke & Olsson (1995), *Constructing a Drug-Free Society – Swedish Drug Policy in Perspective* op. cit. p. 3.

34 Leif Lenke & Börje Olsson (1995), op. cit. p. 3.

35 Ibid. p. 4.

36 CAN & National Institute of Public Health (1993), op. cit. p. 57.

37 Börje Olsson (1995), op. cit. p. 173.

38 This outline of the comparison between licit and illicit drug is taken from Mikalel Nilsson (1995), 'La législation suédoise relative à la drogue', p. 162.

39 For example, 1964 is referred to as the basis for the present drug legislation in Pekka Hakkarainen et. al. (1996), *Discussing Drugs and Control Policy*, p. 26. The National Institute of Public Health (1995a), *Drug Policy*, pp. 9-10, considers 1977 a turning point, while Mikalel Nilsson (1995) chooses for the year 1968 in *La législation suédoise relative à la drogue* (p. 159).

40 In practice however, there is a difference between soft and hard drugs: cannabis possession is treated less severely than e.g. possession of heroin or amphetamine. See: Mikalel Nilsson (1995), op. cit. p. 160.

41 See Mikalel Nilsson (1995), op. cit. p. 164.

42 National Institute of Public Health (1995a), op. cit. p. 9.

43 Leif Lenke & Börje Olsson (1995), op. cit. p. 5.

44 Ibid. p. 5.

45 Mikalel Nilsson (1995), op. cit. p. 165.

46 National Institute of Public Health (1995a), op. cit. p. 8.

47 Ibid. p. 9.

48 National Institute of Public Health (1995a), op. cit. p. 9. See also Henrik Tham (1996b), *Sweden: the Case for a Restrictive Drug Policy*, p. 1.

49 National Institute of Public Health (1995a), op. cit. p. 9.

50 Leif Lenke & Börje Olsson (1995), op. cit. p. 5.

51 Ibid.

52 National Institute of Public Health (1995a), op. cit. p. 14.

53 For these data see: CAN & National Institute of Public Health (1993), op. cit. or see Mikalel Olsson (1995), op. cit.

54 See for example National Institute of Public Health (1995a), op. cit. p. 13.

55 See for example Lana Harrison et. al. (1996), *Cannabis Use in the United States: Implications for Policy.*

56 National Institute of Public Health (1995a), op. cit. pp. 9-10.

57 Leif Lenke & Börje Olsson (1995), op. cit. p. 5.

58 Ibid.

59 National Institute of Public Health (1995a), op. cit. p. 10.

60 Dolf Tops (1996), *Zweden en het Nederlandse drugbeleid*, p. 15.

61 National Institute of Public Health (1995a), op. cit. p. 10.

62 The degree of ruthless can e.g. depend on the substance, if drugs are being sold to minors, and if the dealer is using drugs himself or only to selling for economic gain.

63 Arthur Gould (1989), 'Cleaning the People's Home: recent developments in Sweden's addiction policy', p. 732.

64 Ibid. p. 735.

65 Mikalel Nilsson (1995), op. cit. p. 166.

66 Ibid.

67 Arthur Gould (1989) op. cit. p. 733.

68 Arthur Gould (1994), 'Pollution rituals in Sweden: the pursuit of a drug-free society', p. 86.

69 Ibid.

4 UNDERSTANDING SWEDISH DRUG POLICY

1 Leif Lenke (1991), *The Significance of Distilled Beverages. Reflections on the Formation of Drinking Cultures and Anti-Drug Movements*, p. 5.

2 National Institute of Public Health (1995b), *Swedish Alcohol Policy. Background and present situation*, p. 37.

3 Ministry of Health and Social Affairs (1993), *The Swedish Alcohol Policy. Caring About People's Health*, p. 4.

4 See the section 'The Influence of Climate on Mood' by Åke Daun (1996), pp. 163-165.

5 Åke Daun (1996), op. cit. p. 112. Daun's chapter *Feelings* is very interesting in this respect.

6 Ibid. p. 51.

7 Ministry of Health and Social Affairs (1993), *The Swedish Alcohol Policy. Caring About People's Health*, p. 1. This brochure gives a brief overview of the basics of Swedish alcohol policy.

8 Harry G. Levine (1992), 'Temperance cultures: concerns about alcohol problems in Nordic and English-speaking cultures', p. 16.

9 Ibid. pp. 16-17.

10 Ibid. p. 20.

11 Ibid. p. 26.

12 Tom Nillson, 'The Current Alcohol Situation in Sweden' in: Timo Kortteinen (ed.) (1989), op. cit. p. 311.

13 Swedish Institute, Fact Sheets on Sweden. *Alcohol and Narcotics in Sweden.*

14 Tom Nillson, 'The Current Alcohol Situation in Sweden' in: Timo Kortteinen (ed.) (1989), op. cit. p. 311.

15 K. Bruun & P. Frånberg (eds.), 'The Swedish Schnapps. A History of Booze, Bratt and Bureaucracy' in: Timo Kortteinen (ed.) (1989), op. cit. p. 284.

16 Ministry of Health and Social Affairs (1993), *The Swedish Alcohol Policy,* p. 6.

17 Tom Nillson, 'The Current Alcohol Situation in Sweden' in: Timo Kortteinen (ed.) (1989), op. cit. p. 312.

18 Ibid.

19 For the trend in the total registered alcohol consumption see the graph in: National Institute of Public Health (1995b), *Swedish Alcohol Policy. Background and Present Situation,* p. 14.

20 Ibid. p. 36. It should be noted that the unregistered alcohol consumption is mainly comprised of legal imports.

21 Preliminary results of a research by Eckart Kühlhorn, sociology professor at Stockholm University, interviewed in October 1996.

22 National Institute of Public Health (1995b), op. cit. p. 19.

23 K. Bruun et. al. (1975), *Alcohol Control Policies in a Public Health Perspective.*

24 National Institute of Public Health (1995b), op. cit. p. 8. For a more recent publication on the total consumption model, see: Griffith Edwards et. al. (1994), *Alcohol and the Public Good.*

25 H.D. Holder et. al. (1993), *Assessment of consequences resulting from the elimination of the Swedish alcohol retailing monopoly (Systembolaget).*

26 National Institute of Public Health (1995b), op. cit. p. 41.

27 Information Department (1996), *Systembolaget and the European Union,* p. 4.

28 For a more detailed description (in Dutch) of these Popular Movements, see Dolf Tops (1996), op. cit.

29 Interview Mia Sundelin, Hassela Solidaritet, (Stockholm, December 1996).

30 See also section 6.6 (*The Treatment System*).

31 Torgny Peterson (1993), brochure *Hassela Solidarity Sweden*, pp. 4 and 9.

32 Dolf Tops (1996), op. cit. p. 37. In RNS Magazine *Narkotikafrågan* nr. 2 (1988) Nils Bejerot outlines the RNS principles.

33 Interview with Per Johansson, RNS (Stockholm, October 1996).

34 Dolf Tops (1996), op. cit. p. 17. See also Arthur Gould (1989), op. cit. p. 732.

35 Henrik Tham (1995a), 'Drug control as a national project: the case of Sweden', pp. 117-118.

36 Leif Lenke & Börje Olsson (1995), op. cit. p. 4.

37 Lenke & Olsson (1996a), 'Sweden: Zero Tolerance Wins the Argument?', p. 111.

38 Ibid.

39 Dolf Tops (1996), op. cit. p. 40.

40 Ibid.

41 Interview Åke Setréus, ECAD (Stockholm, December 1996).

42 *Narkotikafrågan*, No. 5-6, 1996.

43 Interviews with Ola Sigvardsson of the newspaper Dagens Nyheter (Stockholm, October 1996), and Per Johansson of RNS (Stockholm, October 1996).

44 See his dissertation: Nils Bejerot (1975), op. cit. See also: Nils Bejerot (1988), *The Swedish Addiction Epidemic in Global Perspective* gives a good (short) overview of his concept.

45 Nils Bejerot (1975), op. cit. p. 24.

46 Ibid. p. 25. On the other hand, Bejerot considers the availability of little importance if an epidemic has not arisen.

47 For a shorter overview, see Nils Bejerot (1988), op. cit.

48 Ibid. p. 8.

49 Ibid. p. 10.

50 Gabriel Nahas (1990), *Keep off the Grass*, Preface.

51 Ibid.

52 In 1996 the life time prevalence of solvents was 11%; for cannabis this was 8%. Source: CAN.

53 Jovan Rajs (1994), *Narcotic-Related Deaths in Stockholm 1986-1993*, p. 1.

54 Interview Gunilla Olofsson and Bengt Forsman at Maria Ungdomsenhet (Stockholm, December 1996).

55 Taken from the drug information brochure issued by the police: National Police Board, Carnegie Institute, & Swedish Narcotics Police Association (1990), *Narkotika. Illustrerad information*, p. 9.

56 Ibid.

57 Reference.

58 Richard Smith, 'The war on drugs. Prohibition isn't working. Some legalisation will help', editorial *British Medical Journal*, Vol. 311, Dec 23-30, 1995; *The Lancet*, editorial, 'Deglamorising cannabis', Vol 346, November 11, 1995.

59 Patricia & Jacob Cohen (1984), 'The Clinician's Illusion', in: *Arch Gen Psychiatry* 41: pp. 1178-1182.

60 Thomas Lundqvist (1995), *Cognitive Dysfunctions in Chronic Cannabis Users Observed During Treatment. A integrative Approach.*

61 Ibid. p. 134.

62 Peter Cohen (1995), *Cannabis Users in Amsterdam.*

63 See for example: Vera Rubin & Lambros Comitas (1975*), Ganja in Jamaica*; Costas Stefanis et. al. (eds.) (1977), *Hashish. Studies on Long-Term Use*, Jack M. Fletcher et. al. (1996), 'Cognitive Correlates of Long-term Cannabis Use in Costa Rican Men', Dieter Kleiber et. al. (1996), *Long-term Effects of Cannabis Use.* See also Lester Grinspoon (1994), *Marihuana Reconsidered.*

64 It is not rare in Sweden and Denmark that a person smokes a joint or pipe containing one gram of hash.

65 According to social workers that were met at the youth Treatment Centre *Mini-Maria* in Gothenburg (October 1996).

66 Henrik Tham (1995a), op. cit. p. 114.

67 Ibid.

68 Interview with Ola Sigvardsson of the newspaper Dagens Nyheter (Stockholm, October 1996).

69 Interview with Ola Sigvardsson of the newspaper Dagens Nyheter (Stockholm, October 1996).

70 Anders Bergmark & Lars Oscarsson (1988), *Drug Abuse and Treatment.* p. 61.

71 Ibid. p. 63.

72 Henrik Tham (1995b), 'From Treatment to Just Deserts in a Changing Welfare State', p. 106.

73 So declared Swedish Member of the European Parliament Malou Lindholm

during a debate on European drug policies organised by the Green Group. (Amsterdam, June 4, 1997).

74 The original Norwegian publication was translated into German. See: Nils Christie & Kettil Bruun (1991), *Der nützliche Feind.*

75 Anders Bergmark & Lars Oscarsson (1988), op. cit. p. 168.

76 Ibid.

77 Henrik Tham (1995a), op. cit. p. 113.

78 Ibid. p. 117.

79 A clear example of this was when I was discussing the smoking of heroin (chasing the dragon) with a social worker in one of Stockholm's suburbs. According to him smoking heroin was very dangerous to the drug user's health as it would destroy many organs. When I replied heroin in itself was not very toxic, he reacted 'O, you are very liberal!'.

80 RNS sometimes goes as far as accusing rock groups to advocate drug use, which would typify a permissiveness reminiscent of Nazi Germany with its cabaret shows. Furthermore, RNS points at the danger of liberalism, by making a comparison between the deterioration of Sweden and the liberal Weimar Republic. See: Henrik Tham (1995a), op. cit. p. 117.

81 Ibid. p. 117.

82 Ibid. p. 119.

83 Ibid. pp. 118-119.

84 Ibid. p. 122.

85 Ibid. p. 120.

86 Ibid. p. 119.

87 *Snus* is taken orally, placed on the gum under the top lip.

5 SWEDISH DRUG POLICY IN PRACTICE

1 Interview with Eva Brännmark, Detective Superintendent, Swedish National Police Board (Stockholm, October 1996).

2 National Criminal Investigation Department (1995), *National Report on the Drug Abuse Situation in Sweden* 1994, p. 2.

3 Based on the rate of April 1997: 100 = US$ 12.66.

4 However, no information is available of the purity.

5 National Criminal Investigation Department (1995), *National Report on the Drug Abuse Situation in Sweden* 1994, p. 3.

6 Ibid. p.4

7 According to interviewed police officer Hans Drontén (Stockholm, October 1996).

8 Esther van Fessem (1996), *Black and White in the Swedish Drug Issue*, p. 64.

9 National Criminal Investigation Department (1995), *National Report on the Drug Abuse Situation in Sweden* 1994, p. 2.

10 Pekka Hakkarainen, Timo Jetsu & Lau Laursen (1996), 'The legal framework and the drug control system' in: Pekka Hakkarainen et. al. (1996), op. cit. p. 29.

11 Interview with Eva Brännmark, Detective Superintendent, Swedish National Police Board (Stockholm, October 1996).

12 Pekka Hakkarainen, Timo Jetsu & Lau Laursen (1996), 'The legal framework and the drug control system' in: Pekka Hakkarainen et. al. (1996), op. cit. p. 27.

13 Arthur Gould (1994), op. cit. p. 86.

14 Interview with Bengt Bager, drug recognition expert (DRE) of Stockholm county (Stockholm, December 1996).

15 Interview with Eva Brännmark, Detective Superintendent, Swedish National Police Board (Stockholm, October 1996).

16 Ibid.

17 Interview with police officer Hans Drontén (Stockholm, October 1996).

18 Esther van Fessem (1996), op. cit. p. 64.

19 100 kronor equals US$ 12.66 (rate April 1997).

20 Interview Eva Brännmark, Detective Superintendent, Swedish National Police Board (Stockholm, October 1996).

21 Interview Anders Stolpe, Detective Chief Inspector of the Gothenburg Police (Gothenburg, October 1996).

22 Interview Anders Stolpe, Detective Chief Inspector of the Gothenburg Police (Gothenburg, October 1996).

23 The information on the urine tests was given by Anders Stolpe, Detective Chief Inspector of the Gothenburg Police (Interviewed in Gothenburg, October 1996).

24 Esther van Fessem (1996), op. cit. p. 65.

25 Börje Olsson (1996), *Drug Trends in Sweden – Spring 1996*.

26 Esther van Fessem (1996), op. cit. p. 66.

27 For a good description of the story of the Docklands' raves and raids, see Esther van Fessem (1996), op. cit. p. 66.

28 Interview Björn Frithiof, The Office of the Prosecutor General (Stockholm, October 1996).

29 Interview Björn Frithiof, The Office of the Prosecutor General (Stockholm, October 1996).

30 Ragnar Hauge (1996),'Nordic data on drug offences: are they comparable?', in: Pekka Hakkarainen et. al. (1996), op. cit. p. 195.

31 Ragnar Hauge (1996),'Nordic data on drug offences: are they comparable?', in: Pekka Hakkarainen et. al. (1996), op. cit. pp. 198-200. This chapter gives a good description of the criminal statistics in the Nordic countries and the problem that arise when comparing them.

32 Ragnar Hauge (1996), 'Nordic data on drug offences: are they comparable?', in: Pekka Hakkarainen et. al. (1996), op. cit. p. 199.

33 Arthur Gould (1994), op. cit. p. 87.

34 National Institute of Public Health (1995a), op. cit. p. 20.

35 See for example: Anders Bergmark & Lars Oscarsson (1988), op. cit., Esther van Fessem, (1996), op. cit., Vera Segraeus, no date, *Compulsory Measures for Treatment and Rehabilitation in Sweden.*, and National Institute of Public Health (1995a), op. cit.

36 Gösta W. Berglund et. al. (1991), 'The SWEDATE Project: Interaction Between Treatment, Client Background, and Outcome in a One-Year follow-up', p. 161.

37 National Institute of Public Health (1995a), op. cit. p. 25.

38 National Board of Institutional Care, no date, *Basic Facts on Sis.*

39 Dolf Tops (1996), op. cit. p. 47.

40 For an overview of the changes in the legislation on compulsory treatment and the debates in Parliament, see Arthur Gould (1989), op. cit.

41 National Institute of Public Health (1995a), op. cit. p. 26.

42 Ibid. p. 10.

43 Birgitta Göransson (1993), *Drug Prevention, Outreach Work and Treatment in Sweden.*

44 National Institute of Public Health (1995a), op. cit. p. 11.

45 Ibid.

46 Henrik Tham (1995b), 'From Treatment to Just Deserts in a Changing Welfare State', p. 108.

47 Interview Riyadh al-Baldawi, psychiatrist at St. Görans Hospital (Stockholm, December 1996).

48 Interview Birgitta Göransson, National Institute of Public Health (Stockholm, December 1996).

49 Interview with Solveig Sandström of the social services of the municipality of Botkyrka (December 1996).

50 It was recently decided to increase the maximum number of methadone clients from 500 to 600.

51 Arthur Gould (1994), op. cit. p. 86.

6 Is the Swedish Drug Policy Effective?

1 CAN & National Institute of Public Health (1997), *Alkohol- och Narkotikautvecklingen i Sverige*, p. 46.

2 Figure taken from National Criminal Investigation Department (1995), *National Report on the Drug Abuse Situation in Sweden* 1994, p. 5.

3 For these data see: CAN & National Institute of Public Health (1993), op. cit. or Börje Olsson (1995), op. cit.

4 National Institute of Public Health (1995a), op. cit. p. 13.

5 CAN & National Institute of Public Health (1993), op. cit. p. 58.

6 See graph 8 in: Henrik Tham (1996a), 'Den svenska narkotikapolitiken – en restrictiv och framgångsrik modell?' ('The Swedish drug policy – a restrictive and successful model?'), p. 186.

7 For American prevalence figures, see the overview of Lana Harrison et. al. (1996), op. cit.

8 K-H Reuband (1995), 'Drug use and drug policy in Western Europe'.

9 School survey show that in 1971 the life time prevalence of cannabis use among 14-21 years was 18%. In 1984 and 1988 the life time prevalence of cannabis among 10-18 years was respectively 5% and 6%. On the basis of these figures a real comparison is difficult to make due to the difference in age groups. If the same age groups are being compared, the decrease cannot be doubted. See:

Dirk J. Korf (1995), *Dutch Treat. Formal control and illicit drug use in the Netherlands*, pp. 76-78.

10 J.P. Sandwijk et. al. (1995), *Licit and illicit drug use in Amsterdam II*, p. 49.

11 Ted Goldberg (1997), *The Swedish Narcotics Control Model - A Critical Assessment*, p. 31.

12 As a comparison: the life time prevalence of solvents among 15-16 year old youngsters in Amsterdam is practically zero. See: J.P. Sandwijk et. al. (1995), op. cit.

13 CAN & National Institute of Public Health (1997), op. cit. p. 49.

14 According to social workers of the youth Treatment Centre *Mini-Maria* in Gothenburg (October 1996).

15 Source: Stockholm Skolförvaltning (1996).

16 National Institute of Public Health (1995a), *Drug Policy*, p. 14.

17 Ibid.

18 Ibid. p. 15.

19 O-J Skog (1993), 'Narkotikamissbrukets utvikling i Sverige 1979 -1992', in: O. Olsson et. al. (1993), *Det tunga narkotikamissbrukets omfattning i Sverige 1992*.

20 National Institute of Public Health (1995a), op. cit. p. 15.

21 The average mortality of heavy drug abusers in Sweden is estimated at 3% a year. This figure is the weighted average of 1.2-2% mortality rate of amphetamine addicts, and 4% for heroin addicts.

22 Cited From Ted Goldberg (1997), op. cit. p. 35. Original source: O-J Skog (1993), 'Narkotikamissbrukets utvikling i Sverige 1979 -1992', in: O. Olsson et. al. (1993), *Det tunga narkotikamissbrukets omfattning i Sverige 1992*.

23 UNO stands for *Utredningen om narkotkamissbrukets omfattning*. Commission on the extent of drug abuse.

24 Ted Goldberg (1997), op. cit. p. 35.

25 Ibid. p. 33.

26 Eckart Kühlhorn et. al. (1996), 'Measures against drug-related offences – a natural experiment in narcotics prevention', Appendix B.

27 National Criminal Investigation Department (1995), op. cit. p. 6.

28 Börje Olsson (1995), op. cit. p. 176.

29 CAN & National Institute of Public Health (1997), op. cit. p. 48.

30 Socialtjänsten (1995), *Socialtjänstens kontakter med missbrukare hösten 1994.*

31 Interview Erik Finne, researcher at Socialtjänsten (Stockholm, December 1996).

32 Interview Riyadh Al-Baldawi, psychiatrist at St. Görans Hospital (Stockholm, December 1996).

33 Ibid.

34 Riyadh al-Baldawi, no date, *Report about Substance Abuse Among Immigrants. A problem with different aspects*, p. 1.

35 The social workers met in Botkyrka (in December 1996) were Jörgen Mouritsen, Hüseyin Yetkin, and Solveig Sandström (head). In 1992 Sandström was working with drug addicts.

36 The areas were visited with the social workers Jörgen Mouritsen and Hüseyin Yetkin, of the social services in the municipality of Botkyrka (December 1996).

37 Cited in: Arthur Gould (1994), op. cit. p. 87.

38 Arthur Gould (1989), 'Cleaning the People's Home', p. 740.

39 Esther van Fessem (1996), op. cit. p. 68.

40 Esther van Fessem (1996), op. cit. p. 68.

41 National Institute of Public Health (1995a), op. cit. p. 11.

42 For a recent overview see: A. van Gageldonk et. al. (1997), *De Nederlandse verslavingszorg. Overzicht van de kennis over aanbod, vraag en effect.*

43 Interview Mia Sundelin, Hassela Solidarity (Stockholm, December 1996).

44 Interview Lars Oscarsson, School of Social Work, Stockholm University (December 1996).

45 See section 2.2 of Anders Bergmark & Lars Oscarsson (1993), 'Behandlings-effekter inom narkomanvården. En diskussion av forsknigläget och dess impli-kationer för den socialtjänstbaserade narkomanvården', pp. 101-117.

46 L. Grönbladh, et. al. (1990), 'Mortality in heroin addiction: impact of methadone treatment'.

47 Gösta W. Berglund et. al. (1991), 'The SWEDATE Project: Interaction Between Treatment, Client Background, and Outcome in a One-Year Follow-Up'.

48 Vera Segraeus, no date, *Compulsory Measures for Treatment and Rehabilitation in Sweden.*

49 L. Grönbladh et. al. (1990), op. cit.

50 Interview Lars Oscarsson, School of Social Work, Stockholm University (December 1996).

51 Anders Bergmark & Lars Oscarsson (1988), *Drug Abuse and Treatment*, pp. 170-171.

52 Interview Bengt Forsman and Gunilla Olofsson, Maria Ungdom Youth Clinic, Stockholm (December 1996).

53 Henrik Tham (1995b), op. cit. pp. 108-109.

54 Anders Bergmark & Lars Oscarsson (1993), op. cit. pp. 101- 117.

55 National Institute of Public Health (1995a), op. cit. p. 26.

56 Interview Lars Oscarsson, School of Social Work, Stockholm University (December 1996). Anna Fugelstad has given a critical overview of compulsory treatment in Stockholm. See Anna Fugelstad (1988), *Gedwongen behandeling van drugsverslaafden in Stockholm* (translation into Dutch).

57 Anders Bergmark & Lars Oscarsson (1993), op. cit.

58 Although not part of the Sauna Club Act, measures were also taken against cruising areas for gays, for example by cutting bushes in parks. See: Jens Rydström (1997), *Panoptikon. Surveillance and Control of Male Homosexuality in Sweden in the 1930s and 1940s.*

59 Anders Bergmark & Lars Oscarsson (1993), op. cit. p. 113.

60 See CAN & National Institute of Public Health (1997), op. cit. p. 154.

61 Jovan Rajs (1994), op. cit. p. 4.

62 See also Anna Fugelstad (1988), op. cit. p. 31.

63 CAN & National Institute of Public Health (1997), op. cit. p. 48.

64 That is the number of deaths from alcohol-related (underlying and multiple) diagnoses (ICD 291, 303, 305.0, 357.5, 425.5, 535.3, 571.0-571.3, E 860, E 980). See CAN & National Institute of Public Health (1997), op. cit. p. 223.

65 National Institute of Public Health (1996), *The Swedish National System Against Narcotics and Drug Addiction. Organisation, Co-operation and Drug Addiction*, p. 18.

66 Kerstin Käll et. al. (1996), *Decreasing Annual Incidence of HIV Among IDUs in Stockholm in Spite of Continued Risk Behaviour.*

67 Gunna Ågren (1993), *The Drug Situation in Stockholm*, p. 6.

68 Interview Magnus Andersson, social worker at the Department of Infectious Diseases, University Hospital, Malmö (December 1996).

69 CAN & National Institute of Public Health (1997), op. cit. p. 281.

70 Henrik Tham (1995a), op. cit. p. 168.

71 Nils Christie & Kettil Bruun (1991), op. cit.

72 Nils Christie (1987), 'Drugs in Dry Societies', p. 20.

73 Arthur Gould (1989), op. cit. p. 740.

74 Arthur Gould (1993), op. cit. p. 89.

75 Ted Goldberg (1997), op. cit. p. 37.

76 Arthur Gould (1993), op. cit. p. 89.

77 Arthur Gould (1993), op. cit. p. 89.

78 See: Henrik Tham (1995b), op. cit. p. 103.

79 Henrik Tham (1995b), op. cit., Nils Christie & Kettil Bruun (1991), op. cit.

80 Norman E. Zinberg (1984), *Drug, Set, and Setting. The basis for controlled intoxicant use.*

81 Thomas Lundqvist (1995), op. cit.

82 Some of the police information material is available in English. See for example: *Narcotic Drugs. Law, Facts, Arguments,* issued by the National Police Board, Carnegie Institute, and the Narcotics Officers' Association (1991).

83 Peter Lindström (1996), *En Utvärdering av våga-programmets korttidseffekter. Delstudie 1.*

84 Henrik Tham (1995a), op. cit. p. 121.

References

AL-BALDAWI, RIYADH (no date), *Report about Substance Abuse Among Immigrants – A problem with different aspects*, Stockholm: Substance Abuse Clinic, Sabbatsbergs Hospital.

ÅGREN, GUNNAR (1993), *The Drug Situation in Stockholm*, Bureau for Research and Development, Social Welfare Administration, City of Stockholm.

BEJEROT, NILS (1975), *Drug Abuse and Drug Policy – An epidemiological and methodological study of drug abuse of intravenous type in the Stockholm police arrest population 1965-1970 in relation to changes in drug policy*, Copenhagen: Munksgaard (Acta Psychiatrica Scandinavica, Supplementum 256).

– (1988), *The Swedish Addiction Epidemic in Global Perspective*, Speech given in France, the Soviet Union and USA, Stockholm: the Carnegie Institute (10 pages).

BERGLUND, GÖSTA W., ANDERS BERGMARK, BAM BJÖRLING, LEIF RÖNBLADH, STAFFAN LINDBERG, LARS OSCARSSON, BÖRJE OLSSON, VERA SEGRAEUS, CHRISTER STENSMO (1991), 'The SWEDATE Project: Interaction Between Treatment, Client Background, and Outcome in a One-Year Follow-Up', *Journal of Substance Abuse Treatment*, Vol. 8, pp. 161-169.

BERGMARK, ANDERS & LARS OSCARSSON (1988), *Drug Abuse and Treatment – A Study of Social Conditions and Contextual Strategies*, Stockholm Studies in Social Work 4, Stockholm: School of Social Work, Stockholm University.

– (1993), 'Behandlingseffekter inom narkomanvården. En diskussion av forskningläget och dess implikationer för den socialtjänstbaserade narkomanvården', Appendix 1 in: Socialstyrelsen (1993), *Effekter av offensiv narkomanvård*, Stockholm.

British Medical Journal, 'The war on drugs. Prohibition isn't working. Some legalisation will help', editorial, Vol. 311, Dec 23-30, 1995.

BRUUN, K. et. al. (1975), *Alcohol Control Policies in a Public Health Perspective*, Helsinki: The Finnish Foundation for Alcohol Studies.

BRUSSEL, G.H.A. van & G.K.T. VAN DER GIESSEN (1996), *Sweden and the*

Drugs Problem Seen Through Dutch Eyes, report of a fact finding mission on February 14 and 15, 1996, Amsterdam: Municipal Health Service (GG&GD).

CAN (Swedish Council for the Information on Alcohol and other Drugs), *Hasch och Marijuana*, Faktablad, Stocholm.

CAN & FÖLKHALSOINSTITUTET (National Institute of Public Health) (1993), *Trends in Alcohol and Drug Use in Sweden*, Nr. 35, Stockholm: CAN & Fölkhalsoinstitutet.

– (1997), *Alkohol – och Narkotikautvecklingen i Sverige*, Rapport 97, Stockholm

CATTACIN, SANDRO, BARBARA LUCAS & SANDRA VETTER (1996),*Modèles de politique en matière de drogue – Une comparaison de six réalités européennes*, Paris: L'Harmattan.

CHRISTIE, NILS (1987), 'Drugs in Dry Societies', in: Per Stangeland (ed.) (1987), *Drugs and Drug Control*, Scandinavian Studies in Criminology Vol. 8, pp. 13-21, Oslo: Norwegian University Press.

CHRISTIE, NILS & Kettil Bruun (1991), *Der nützliche Feind – Die Drogenpolitik und ihre Nutznießer*, Bielefeld: AJZ.

COHEN, PATRICIA & JACOB (1984), 'The Clinician's Illusion', in: *Arch Gen Psychiatry* 41: pp. 1178-1182.

COHEN, PETER (1995), *Cannabis Users in Amsterdam*, Presentation held at the National Conference on the Urban Softdrugs Tolerance Policy, Jaarbeurs Conference Centre, Utrecht, June 7, 1995.

DAUN, ÅKE (1996), *Swedish Mentality*, University Park, Pennsylvania: Pennsylvania University Press.

DURAND, JEAN-PIERRE (1994), 'Vers la normalization du modèle suédois', *Le Monde diplomatique*, novembre 1994.

EDWARDS, GRIFFITH et. al. (1994), *Alcohol and the Public Good*, Oxford: Oxford University Press & World Health Organisation (WHO).

FESSEM, ESTHER VAN (1996), *Black and White in the Swedish Drug Issue – The Opinion Machine at Work*, MA Thesis School of Social Work, Stockholm University/Crisis Research Centre (COT), Erasmus University Rotterdam & Leiden University.

FLETCHER, JACK M., J. BRYAN PAGE, DAVID J. FRANCIS, KIMBERLY COPELAND, MARY J. NAUS, CHESTER M. DAVIS, ROBIN MORRIS, DINA KRAUSKOPF & PAUL SATZ (1996), 'Cognitive Correlates of Long-term Cannabis Use in Costa Rican Men' in: *Arch Gen Psychiatry*, Vol. 53, Nov 1996.

FUGELSTAD, ANNA (1988), *Gedwongen behandeling van drugsverslaafden in Stockholm* (*Compulsory treatment for drug abusers in Stockholm*), Stockholm: Sabbatsberg Hospital.

GAGELDONK, A. VAN, W. DE ZWART, J. VAN DER STEL & M. DONKER (1997), *De Nederlandse verslavingszorg – Overzicht van de kennis over aanbod, vraag en effect*, Utrecht: Trimbos-instituut.

GOLDBERG, LEONARD (1968a), 'Drug abuse in Sweden', *Bulletin on Narcotics* Vol. XX, No. 1, January-March 1968, pp. 1-31.

– (1968b), 'Drug abuse in Sweden (II)', *Bulletin on Narcotics* Vol. XX, No. 2, April-June 1968, pp. 9-36.

GOLDBERG, TED (1997), 'The Swedish Narcotics Control Model – A Critical Assessment', *The International Journal of Drug Policy* Vol. 8, No.2, 1997.

GOULD, ARTHUR (1989), 'Cleaning the People's Home: recent developments in Sweden's addiction policy', *British Journal of Addiction* (1989) 84, pp. 731-741.

– (1984), 'Pollution rituals in Sweden: the pursuit of a drug-free society', *Scandinavian Journal of Social Welfare* (1994), 3, pp. 85-93.

– (1993), *Capitalist Welfare States. A comparison of Japan, Britain & Sweden*, London/New York: Longman.

GRAPENDAAL, MARTIN, ED LEUW & HANS NELEN (1995), *A World of Opportunities – Lifestyle and Economic Behaviour of Heroin Addicts in Amsterdam*, Albany: State University of New York Press.

GRINSPOON, LESTER (1994), *Marihuana Reconsidered – The most thorough evaluation of the benefits and dangers of cannabis*, Oakland: Quick American Archives (Originally published in 1971 by Harvard University Press).

GRÖNBLADH, L, L.S. ÖHLUND & L.M. GUNNE (1990), 'Mortality in heroin addiction: impact of methadone treatment.' *Acta Psychiat Scand* 1990: 82, pp. 223-227.

GÖRANSSON, BIRGITTA (1993), *Drug Prevention, Outreach Work and Treatment in Sweden*, Presentation at the conference *Europe Against Drug Abuse*, May 1993.

HADENIUS, STIG & ANN LINDGREN (1993), *Over Zweden*, Stockholm: The Swedish Institute.

HAKKARAINEN, PEKKA, LAU LAURSEN & CHRISTOFFER TIGERSTEDT (1996), *Discussing Drugs and Control Policy – Comparative studies on four Nordic countries*, Helsinki: Nordic Council for Alcohol and Drug Research (NAD).

HARRISON, LANA D., MICHAEL BACKENHEIMER & JAMES A. INCIARDI (1996), 'Cannabis Use in the United States – Implications for Policy', in: Peter Cohen & Arjan Sas (1996), *Cannabisbeleid in Duitsland, Frankrijk en de Verenigde Staten*, Amsterdam: Centre for Drug Research (CEDRO), University of Amsterdam.

HOLDER, H.D. et. al. (1993), *Assessment of consequences resulting from the elimination of the Swedish alcohol retailing monopoly* (Systembolaget), Stockholm.

Information Department (1996), *Systembolaget and the European Union*, Stockholm.

JOHNSSON, HANS-INGVAR (1995), *Spotlight on Sweden*, Värnamo: Fälths Tryckeri.

KARLSSON, ANNA & MAARTEN SENGERS (1996), *Op weg naar een Europees Drugsbeleid? Een vergelijking tussen de Zweedse en Nederlandse posities in het Nederlandse drugsdebat*, unpublished paper, Stockholm University.

KLEIBER, DIETER, RENATE SOELLNER, CHRISTIANE ROMBUSCH, DIRK ENZMANN & CHRISTIAN WETZEL (1996), *Long-term Effects of Cannabis Use*, Paper presented at the Sixth Annual Conference on Drug Use and Drug Policy: Illicit Drugs in Europe, Amsterdam, September 26-28, 1996 (forthcoming).

KORF, DIRK J. (1995), *Dutch Treat. Formal control and illicit drug use in the Netherlands*, Amsterdam: Thesis.

KORTTEINEN, TIMO (ed.) (1989), *State Monopolies and Alcohol Prevention*, Report and Working Papers of a Collaborative International Study, Report No. 181, Helsinki: Social Research Institute of Alcohol Studies.

KÄLL, KERSTIN, I. JULANDER, A. KROOK, R. OLIN & P. STENDAHL (1996), *Decreasing Annual Incidence of HIV Among IDU's in Stockholm in Spite of Continued Risk Behaviour*, Presentation at the XI International Conference on Aids in Vancouver July 7-12, 1996, Stockholm: European Cities Against Drugs, Vol. III, No. 26, August 29, 1996.

KÜHLHORN, ECKART, ANDERS KASSMAN & MATS RAMSTEDT (1996), 'Measures against drug-related offences – a natural experiment in narcotics prevention', Appendix B, draft. Originally published in Swedish: 'Åtgärder mot drogbrottslighet – ett naturligt experiment inom narkotikapreventionen', Stockholm: BRÅ-rapport 1996:4.

LACHMAN, DENNIS, ADAM BENETT, JOHN H. GREEN, ROBERT HAGEMANN &

RAMANA RAMASWAMY (1995), *Challenges to the Swedish Welfare State*, Washington DC: International Monetary Fund.

The Lancet, 'Deglamorising cannabis', editorial, Vol. 346, November 11, 1995.

LENKE, LEIF (1991), *The Significance of Distilled Beverages. Reflections on the Formation of Drinking Cultures and Anti-Drug Movements*, paper presented at the meeting of the Kettil Bruun Society for Social and Epidemiological Research on Alcohol, Sigtuna, Sweden, June 1991.

LENKE, LEIF & BÖRJE OLSSON (1995), *Constructing a Drug-Free Society – Swedish Drug Policy in Perspective*, unpublished draft.

LENKE, LEIF & BÖRJE OLSSON (1996a), 'Sweden: Zero Tolerance Wins the Argument?' in Nicholas Dorn, Jørgen Jepsen and Ernesto Savona (1996), *European Drug Policies and Enforcement* (Eds.), Wiltshire: Macmillan.

– (1996b), *Legal Drugs – The Swedish Legalizing Experiment of 1965-1967 in Retrospect*, Paper presented at the Conference on Drug Use and Drug Policy, Amsterdam, September 26-28, 1996.

LEUW, ED. & I. HAEN MARSHALL (1994), *Between Prohibition and Legalisation – The Dutch Experiment in Drug Policy*, Amsterdam/New York: Kugler.

LEVINE, HARRY G. (1992), 'Temperance cultures: concern about alcohol problems in Nordic and English-Speaking cultures' in: M. Lader, G. Edwards and D.C. Drummond (eds) (1992), *The Nature of Drug Related Problems*. New York: Oxford University Press, pp.15-36.

LINDSTRÖM, PETER (1996), *En Utvärdering av våga-programmets korttidseffekter. Delstudie 1*, Stockholm: Polishögskolan.

LUNDQVIST, THOMAS (1995), *Cognitive Dysfunctions in Chronic Cannabis Users Observed During Treatment – An Integrative Approach*, Stockholm: Almquist & Wiksell International.

Ministry of Health and Social Affairs (1993), *The Swedish Alcohol Policy. Caring About People's Health*, Stockholm.

NAHAS, GABRIEL (1990), *Keep off the Grass*, Middelbury: Eriksson.

National Board of Institutional Care (no date), *Basic Facts on SiS*, Stockholm.

National Criminal Investigation Department (1995), *National Report on the Drug Abuse Situation in Sweden 1994*, Stockholm: Intelligence Service, National Criminal Investigation Department.

National Institute of Public Health (1994), *Hasch boken*, Stockholm: National Institute of Public Health.

– (1995a), *Drug Policy – The Swedish Experience*, Stockholm.

– (1995b), *Swedish Alcohol Policy – Background and Present Situation*, Stockholm.

– (1996), *The Swedish National System Against Narcotics and Drug Addiction – Organisation, Co-operation and Drug Addiction*, Report to EMCDDA, Stockholm: Alcohol and Drug Department, National Institute of Public Health.

– (1996), *The Drug Situation in Sweden – Report on the Situation Today and Developments Leading up to Today's Situation*, Report to EMCDDA, Stockholm: Alcohol and Drug Department, National Institute of Public Health.

National Police Board, Carnegie Institute, & Swedish Narcotics Police Association (1990), *Narkotika – Illustrerad information*, Stockholm.

– (1991), *Narcotic Drugs – Law, Facts, Arguments*, Stockholm.

NILSSON, MIKALEL (1995), 'La législation suédoise relative à la drogue' in: Bulletin de liaison du CNDT, No.21, *Pays nordiques – Etats de lieux sur les toxicomanies*, Lyon: Pierre Guette.

OLSSON, BÖRJE (1994), *Narkotikaproblemets bakgrund – Användning av och uppfattningar om narkotika inom svensk medecin 1839-1965* (*The Background of the Drug Problem – Use of and conceptions about narcotic drugs in Swedish medicine 1939-1965*), Stockholm: CAN.

OLSSON, BÖRJE (1995), 'Utilization et abus de narcotiques et de drogues illégales en Suède' in: Bulletin de liaison du CNDT, No.21, *Pays nordiques – Etats de lieux sur les toxicomanies*, Lyon: Pierre Guette.

– (1996), *Drug Trends in Sweden – Spring 1996*, Report to the Pompidou Group, April 1996.

OLSSON, O., S. BYQVIST, & G. GOMÉR (1993), *Det tunga narkotikamissbrukets omfattning i Sverige 1992*, Stockholm: CAN.

PETERSON, TORGNY (1993), Brochure *Hassela Solidarity Sweden*.

RAINERMAN, CRAIG (1994), 'The Social Construction of Drug Scares' in: Patricia and Peter Adler (eds.) (1994), *Constructions of Deviance – Social Power, Context, and Interaction*, Belmont, CA: Wadsworth Publishing, pp. 92-105.

RAJS, JOVAN (1994), *Narcotic-Related Deaths in Stockholm 1986-1993*, Stockholm: Ministry of Health and Social Affairs.

REUBAND, KARL-HEINZ (1995), 'Drug use and drug policy in Western Europe', *Eur Addict Res*, 1 (1-2): pp. 32-41.

RUBIN, VERA & LAMBROS COMITAS (1975), *Ganja in Jamaica – A medical anthropological study of chronic marihuana use*, The Hague: Mouton.

RYDSTRÖM, JENS (1997), *Panoptikon. Surveillance and Control of Male Homosexuality in Sweden in the 1930s and 1940s*, (to be published).

SANDWIJK, J.P., P.D.A. COHEN, S. MUSTERD & M.P.S. LANGEMEIJER (1995), *Licit and Illicit Drug Use in Amsterdam II – Report of a household survey in 1994 on the prevalence of drug use among the population of 12 years and over*, Amsterdam: Department of Human Geography.

SEGRAEUS, VERA (no date), *Compulsory Measures for Treatment and Rehabilitation in Sweden*.

SKOG, O-J (1993), 'Narkotikamissbrukets utvikling i Sverige 1979 – 1992', in: O. Olsson et. al (1993), *Det tunga narkotikamissbrukets omfattning i Sverige 1992*, Stockholm: CAN.

SKRETTING, ASTRID (1996), *Ungdom og rusmidler*, Oslo: Rusmiddeldirektoratet.

SOCIALTJÄNSTEN (1995), *Socialtjänstens kontakter med missbrukare hösten 1994*, FoU-rapport 1995: 28, Stockholm.

STANGELAND, PER (ed.) (1987), *Drugs and Drug Control*, Scandinavian Studies in Criminology Vol. 8, Oslo: Norwegian University Press.

STEFANIS, COSTAS, RHEA DORNBUSH & MAX FINK (eds.) (1977), *Hashish – Studies on Long-Term Use*, New York: Raven.

STENGERS, ISABELLE & OLIVIER RALET (1991), *Drogues, le defi hollandais*, Paris: Les empêcheurs de penser en rond.

Swedish Institute, Fact Sheets on Sweden, *Alcohol and Narcotics in Sweden*, September 1995.

–, *General Facts on Sweden*, April 1996.

–, Fact Sheets on Sweden, *Immigrants in Sweden*, October 1994.

–, *Mass Media in Sweden*, September 1994.

–, *The Swedish Economy*, March 1996.

–, *Swedish Labor Market Policy*. December 1995.

–, *The Swedish Political Parties*, January 1995.

TILTON, TIM (1991), *The Political Theory of Swedish Social Democracy – Through the Welfare State to Socialism*, New York: Oxford University Press.

THAM, HENRIK (1995a), 'Drug Control as a National Project: The Case of Sweden', *The Journal of Drug Issues*, 25 (1), pp. 113-128, 1995.

– (1995b), 'From Treatment to Just Deserts in a Changing Welfare State' in: A. Snare (ed.) (1995), *Beware of Punishment*, Scandinavian Studies in Criminology Vol. 14, pp. 89-122, Oslo: Pax Forlag.

– (1996a), 'Den svenska narkotikapolitiken – en restrictiv och framgångsrik modell?' ('The Swedish drug policy – a restrictive and successful model?'), *Nordisk Alkoholtidskrift* Vol. 13, 1996: 4, pp. 179-193.

– (1996b), *Sweden: the Case for a Restrictive Drug Policy*, December 1996, unpublished (draft).

TOPS, DOLF (1996), *Zweden en het Nederlandse drugsbeleid*, (unpublished) report for the Dutch Ministry of Health, Welfare and Sport, Malmö.

WESTERBERG, B. (1994), 'Reply to Arthur Gould: "Pollution rituals in Sweden: the pursuit of a drug-free society"', *Scandinavian Journal of Social Welfare* (1994), 3, pp. 94-96.

WIJKSTRÖM, FILIP (1996), *Movements, Members and Volunteers in Sweden*, Paper presented at the Third Research Conference on the Nordic Nonprofit Sector, Oslo 22-23 November 1996.

ZINBERG, NORMAN E. (1984), *Drug, Set, and Setting – The basis for controlled intoxicant use.* New Haven: Yale University Press.

People Consulted

Gunnar Ågren, MD, Research Director, Social Welfare Administration, Stockholm;

Riyad Al-Baldawi, MD, psychiatrist, St Görans Hospital, Stockholm,

Bengt Andersson, Department of Health and Addiction, National Institute of Public Health, Stockholm;

Magnus Andersson, social worker at the needle exchange programme, Department of Infectious Diseases, University Hospital, Malmö;

Ylva Arnhof, Head of the Department of Health and Addiction, National Institute of Public Health, Stockholm;

Ola Arvidsson, Department of Health and Addiction, Department of Health and Addiction, National Institute of Public Health, Stockholm;

Eva Asplund, immigrant project, municipality of Gothenburg;

Bengt Bager, drug co-ordinator, Stockholm police;

Stefan Borg, Head methadone clinic, St Görans Hospital, Stockholm;

Eva Brännmark, Detective Superintendent, Swedish National Police Board;

Alec Carlberg, Chairman Swedish Organisation of Help and Assistance to Drug Abusers (RFHL);

Hans Drontén, police officer of 'Plattan police', Stockholm;

Kristina Engholm, Legal Adviser, Division for Criminal Law, Ministry of Justice.

Erik Finne, researcher at the Social Services (*Socialtjänsten*), Stockholm;

Bengt Forsman, Maria Ungdom Youth Clinic, Stockholm;

Björn Frithiof, Senior Administrative Officer, Prosecutor General's Office, Stockholm;

Ted Goldberg, Assistant Professor, School of Social Work, Stockholm University;

Gunnel Gomér, Parents Against Drugs (FMN), and Department of Health and Addiction, National Institute of Public Health, Stockholm;

Birgitta Göransson, Alcohol and Drug Programme, National Institute of Public Health, Stockholm;

Ulf Guttormsson, the Swedish Council for Information on Alcohol and other Drugs (CAN);

Sten Heckscher, National Police Commissioner, Swedish National Police Board;

Kristina Hillgren, psychologist, methadone clinic, St Görans Hospital, Stockholm;

Lisa Jonsson, social worker in Skärholmen, municipality of Stockholm;

Per Johansson, Association for a Drug-Free Society (RNS), Stockholm;

Kristina Jung, Coordinator of Municipal Care and Rehabilitation, Department of Public Health, Gothenburg;

Elisabeth Karlsson, fieldworker in Angered, suburb of Gothenburg;

Eckart Kühlhorn, Professor of Sociology, Stockholm University;

Leif Lenke, Associate Professor, Department of Criminology, Stockholm University;

Ralf Löfstedt, First Secretary, Ministry of Health and Social Affairs;

Ove Lundgren, Department of Public Health, Gothenburg;

Several staff member of the Mini-Maria Youth Clinic in Gothenburg;

Jörgen Mouritsen and Hüseyin Yetkin, social workers in the municipality of Botkyrka;

Bengt Forsman and Gunilla Olofsson, Maria Ungdom Youth Clinic, Stockholm;

Börje Olsson, Swedish Council for the Information and other Drugs (CAN) and Department of Criminology, Stockholm University;

Lars Oscarsson, Associate Professor in Alcohol Research, Department of Social Work, Stockholm University;

Anders Romelsjö, Head Alcohol and Drug Prevention Centre, Huddinge Hospital;

Birgitta Rosén, Education Group, treatment programme in Gothenborg;

Ulf Rydberg, MD, Professor, Section of Clinical Alcohol and Drug Addiction, Karolinska Hospital;

Solveig Sandström, Head of Social Services in the municipality of Botkyrka;

Åke Setréus, European Cities Against Drugs (ECAD) and National Board of Health and Welfare, Stockholm;

Ola Sigvardsson, reporter on the daily newspaper *Dagens Nyheter*;

Anders Stolpe, Detective Chief Inspector, County Criminal Investigation Division, Göteborg and Bohus County Police, Gothenburg;

Mia Sundelin, Hassela Solidarity, Stockholm;

Daniel Svensson, Department of Health and Addiction, National Institute of Public Health, Stockholm;

Henrik Tham, Professor in Criminology, Stockholm University;

Dolf Tops, researcher at the Institute of Social Work, University of Lund.

LIST OF CEDRO PUBLICATIONS

1 D.J. KORF, m.m.v. P.W.J. VAN POPPEL, *Heroïnetoerisme – Een veldonderzoek naar het gebruik van harddrugs onder buitenlanders in Amsterdam.* Amsterdam 1986: Stadsdrukkerij.

2 J.M. KERSLOOT en S. MUSTERD, *Leefbaarheid en drugs in Amsterdam – De spreiding van drugsscenes óver en de relatie met de leefbaarheid in de stad.* Amsterdam 1987, ISBN 90-6993-011-0, NLG 29,50.

3 D.J. KORF, *Heroïnetoerisme II – Resultaten van een veldonderzoek onder 382 buitenlandse dagelijkse opiaatgebruikers.* Amsterdam 1987, ISBN 90-6993-016-1, NLG 25,00.

4 H.T. VERBRAECK, *De staart van de Zeedijk – Een bliksemonderzoek naar enkele effecten van het Zomerplan 1987 in het Wallengebied.* Amsterdam 1988, ISBN 90-6993-022-6, NLG 24,00.

5 J.M. KERSLOOT en S. MUSTERD, *Leefbaarheid en drugs in Amsterdam II – Een analyse van enkele ontwikkelingen in de periode 1986-1987.* Amsterdam 1988, ISBN-6993-027-7, NLG 27,50.

6 F. VAN GEMERT, *Mazen en netwerken – De invloed van beleid op de drugshandel in twee straten in de Amsterdamse Binnenstad.* Amsterdam 1988, ISBN 90-6993-030-7, NLG 32,50.

7 P. VAN GELDER & J. SIJTSMA, *Horse, coke en kansen I – Sociale risico's en kansen onder Surinaamse en Marokkaanse harddruggebruikers in Amsterdam. Deel I: Surinaamse harddruggebruikers.* Amsterdam 1988, ISBN 90-6993-035-8, NLG 35,00.

8 P. VAN GELDER & J. SIJTSMA, *Horse, coke en kansen II – Sociale risico's en kansen onder Surinaamse en Marokkaanse harddruggebruikers in Amsterdam. Deel II: Marokkaanse harddruggebruikers,* ISBN 90-6993-038-2 (sold out).

9 J.P. SANDWIJK, I. WESTERTERP & S. MUSTERD, *Het gebruik van legale en illegale drugs in Amsterdam – Verslag van een prevalentie-onderzoek onder de bevolking van 12 jaar en ouder,* 130 p. ISBN 90-6993-039-0 (sold out).

10 P. COHEN, *Cocaine Use in Amsterdam in Non Deviant Subcultures*, with two addenda (Biomedical and NeuroPsychoPharmacological Issues by E. Ch. Wolters; and Physical and Psychological Items in Chronic Recreational Cocaine Use by E.H. Collette, Ph. Scheltens & E. Ch. Wolters) 1989, ISBN 90-6993-045-5 NLG 29,00.

11 D. KORF & H. HOOGENHOUT, *Zoden aan de dijk – Heroïnegebruikers en hun ervaringen met en waardering van de Amsterdamse drugshulpverlening*, ISBN 90-6993-053-6, NLG 37,00.

12 J.P. SANDWIJK, P.D.A. COHEN, S. MUSTERD, *Licit and illicit drug use in Amsterdam – Report of a household survey in 1990 on the prevalence of drug use among the population of 12 years and over*, ISBN 90-6993-063-3 NLG 28,00.

13 PETER COHEN, ARJAN SAS, *Ten years of cocaine – A follow-up study of 64 cocaine users in Amsterdam*, ISBN 90-6993-081-1, NLG 32,50.

14 PETER COHEN, ARJAN SAS, *Cocaine use in Amsterdam II – Initiation and patterns of use after 1986*, ISBN 90-6993-099-4, NLG 35,00.

15 J.P. SANDWIJK, P.D.A. COHEN, S. MUSTERD, M.P.S. LANGEMEIJER, *Licit and illicit drug use in Amsterdam II – Report of a household survey in 1994 on the prevalence of drug use among the population of 12 years and over*, ISBN 90-6993-101-X NLG 35,00.

16 PETER COHEN & ARJAN SAS (eds), *Cannabisbeleid in Duitsland, Frankrijk en de Verenigde Staten* (in Dutch, English, French and German), Amsterdam, 1996, ISBN 90-6993-105-2, NLG 45,00.

17 TIM BOEKHOUT VAN SOLINGE, *Heroïne, cocaïne en crack in Frankrijk – Handel, gebruik en beleid / L'héroïne, la cocaïne et le crack en France – Trafic, usage et politique*, Amsterdam, 1996, ISBN 90-6993-106-0, NLG 41,50.

Publications 1 to 15 can be ordered at the Department of Human Geography, University of Amsterdam, Nieuwe Prinsengracht 130, NL-1018 VZ Amsterdam. Prices exclude postage costs by surface mail. Excluded olso are banking charges (NLG 15,00 per banking operation).

Ordering by creditcard

The publications 16 en 17, as well as this book can be ordered by creditcard (Mastercard, Visa, American Express or Diners Club). Send a fax to V.O.F. Uitgeverij Jan Mets (+31 20 6270242) with your name, adres, creditcardnumber, expiration date and your signature. Please make clear which titles you want and how many copies. We will send you the books as soon as authorisation for the total amount plus postage costs is given by the creditcard company.

Orderform on internet

http://www.frw.uva.nl/cedro/order

ISBN 90 5330 211 5
NUGI 651/654/691

TEXT CORRECTION
Louise Millar, London

COVER DESIGN
Victor Levie and Christine Alberts, Amsterdam

CEDRO (Centre for Drug Research)
University of Amsterdam
Nieuwe Prinsengracht 130
NL-1018 VZ Amsterdam
Fax. +31 20 5254051
http://www.frw.uva.nl/cedro

v.o.f. Uitgeverij Jan Mets
Westeinde 16
NL-1017 ZP Amsterdam
Fax. +31 20 6270242

Orderform on internet:
http://www.frw.uva.nl/cedro/order